Transforming Primary QTS

Primary ICT across the Curriculum

Transforming Primary QTS

Primary ICT across the Curriculum

Edited by Debbie Simpson and Mike Toyn

LearningMatters

UNIVERSITY OF CHICHESTER

First published in 2011 by Learning Matters Ltd

British Library Cataloguing in Publication Data
A CIP record for this book is available from the British Library

ISBN: 978 0 85725 393 4
Adobe ebook ISBN: 978 0 85725 395 8
EPUB book ISBN: 978 0 85725 394 1
Kindle ISBN: 978 0 85725 396 5

Cover and text design by Toucan Design
Project management by Deer Park Productions, Tavistock
Typeset by PDQ Typesetting Ltd, Newcastle under Lyme
Printed and bound by Bell & Bain Ltd, Glasgow

Learning Matters Ltd
20 Cathedral Yard
Exeter EX1 1HB
Tel: 01392 215560
info@learningmatters.co.uk
www.learningmatters.co.uk

Mixed Sources
Product group from well-managed forests and other controlled sources
www.fsc.org Cert no. TT-COC-002769
© 1996 Forest Stewardship Council

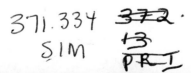

what skills are used in Scratched that can be replicated in other disciplina?
ie. mathematics - flow diagram
g — then —

Contents

Introduction

This book is one of the first in the new *Transforming Primary QTS* series, which has been established to reflect current best practice and a more creative and integrated approach to the primary school curriculum. Technology is developing rapidly and new innovations are being made available to children and schools daily. This book encourages you, as a trainee teacher, to take a critical and creative look at how you can make best use of ICT to support learning in a safe and secure environment across the curriculum.

The status of Information and Communications Technology (ICT) should not be underestimated. Not only is ICT a National Curriculum subject in its own right, it is also unique in that it provides virtual tools that have huge potential to shift the way that children think and learn across the curriculum. At this time, teachers and student teachers face challenges in using ICT effectively to enhance learning. This book offers a number of opportunities to address many of the challenges, including covering discrete teaching of ICT, strategies for embedding ICT across the curriculum and suggestions for tackling progression and assessment. Furthermore it incorporates using ICT to develop creativity and pupils' thinking skills.

About the book

The book is presented in two parts. Part 1 focuses on the role of ICT in the National Curriculum and discusses what is meant by ICT capability. It takes a practical look at how teachers and trainees can develop children's ICT knowledge, skills and understanding across the four strands of the statutory programme of study for ICT, consisting of:

- finding things out;
- developing ideas and making things happen;
- exchanging and sharing information;
- reviewing, modifying and evaluating work as it progresses.

You are encouraged to take a wide-ranging approach to identify opportunities for developing children's ICT capability, both within discrete ICT lessons and embedded into the teaching of other subjects. However, whilst ICT offers great potential in the support of learning, it is not the answer to everything, and you are also encouraged to take a critically reflective approach to its application. You will learn how applying evaluative frameworks can help you decide when the use of ICT will deliver real learning benefits, and when it may be less effective than other methods.

Part 2 takes a look at some of the wider issues of ICT in primary education, including essential guidance on current debates and practice surrounding social networking and e-safety. The role of ICT tools and resources in enabling and enhancing learning across the curriculum is also discussed illustrating, through a series of case studies, how ICT can help to motivate and enthuse children, provide new approaches to learning and raise achievement across all subjects. You will discover how to plan for appropriate use of ICT, manage lessons and resources, and assess children's achievements: all key steps on your journey to becoming an independent and discerning teacher of (and with) ICT.

Your role as a reflective practitioner is developed in this section, providing advice on how to locate and evaluate current research, apply its findings in your teaching and conduct your own research project that will add your voice to the wider debate. Finally, you are invited to explore ways in which schools can use ICT to create opportunities to extend learning beyond the classroom, through developing links with a range of educational and cultural settings and participating in national and international school-linking projects.

Learning Matters have published a number of other ICT-related titles. This book is complementary to these because it moves on from the core knowledge and understanding required to teach ICT effectively.

Using the book

Throughout this book the authors have drawn upon their extensive experience of teaching and mentoring trainee teachers to present a wide range of case studies that you can adapt and use in your own classroom. The book contains a number of features that will help you to strengthen your subject knowledge and develop your skills in teaching ICT.

Features

At the start of each chapter you will find a list of **learning outcomes**. These provide the intended focus of each chapter. You can skim these to see the structure and content of each chapter.

Following these are the relevant **professional standards for qualified teacher status** that the particular chapter will help you to understand and demonstrate. You may wish to search for individual standards that you have identified as areas for development, or alternatively to make a note of your reading and associated activities in your teacher training notes or portfolio.

Each chapter contains a number of **activities** that help you to become actively engaged with the content of the chapter. Sometimes these will ask you to reflect on your reading or placement experiences, or they may be tasks that you will need to undertake using ICT. You may find it helpful to undertake the activities with a friend, or discuss the outcomes with your tutors or school mentors.

Case studies are provided to illustrate how the ideas presented in each chapter can be achieved in a real context.

In order to reflect the cross-curricular nature of this book, **links to the National Curriculum** are provided in order to help you examine how ICT can be used to support learning in other curriculum subjects, or how ICT capacity can be developed through other curriculum subjects. In every case, the links are not exclusive and you should think about other opportunities beyond those presented to you.

Research underpins high-quality teaching. Each chapter contains **research focus** features that highlight key literature sources related to the topic under discussion. The features provide an overview of current research in that area.

Each chapter concludes with a **learning outcomes review** which summarises the main points raised.

Finally, **self-assessment questions** are provided for you to reflect upon the key components of the chapter. Suggested responses to these self-assessment questions are included at the end of the book.

ICT across the curriculum

To help you find your way around this book, you can use the following tables to locate where particular subjects and themes are discussed.

Table 1 on p. 4 shows where National Curriculum subjects are addressed specifically throughout the book.

ICT-specific issues and themes are also dealt with, and these are shown in Table 2 on p. 5.

Primary ICT across the Curriculum is an essential book for trainee teachers who are eager to contribute to the transformation of the primary curriculum. We hope that you will enjoy exploring how you can use ICT in your classroom to enhance both children's learning and your own teaching.

Subject	Chapter	Brief description
English	1	Suggested methods for enhancing instructional writing with presentational software; developing journalistic writing using audio podcasts
	3	Considering procedural and instructional language using flow charts
	4	Using a range of sources to locate information. Evaluating and presenting information; developing collaborative texts and presentations; writing for different audiences
	5	Word processors to develop writing; structuring writing and developing a sense of audience; using multimedia as a stimulus for writing
	6	Critical evaluation of information; developing speaking and listening skills through multimedia
	6, 7, 8	Considering research evidence for ICT promoting literacy skills
	7	Using video and e-mail to enhance story-writing
	9	Persuasive writing
Mathematics	1, 3, 7	Developing understanding of *Space, Shape and Measure* using floor robots
	2, 3	Developing problem-solving and calculation skills using spreadsheets
	3, 9	Handling data
Science	2, 3	Using information-handling software to enrich activities linked to *Life Processes and Living Things*
	3	Using sensors and data-loggers to support investigative science and the study of *Life Processes and Living Things*
	4	Healthy living
	7	ICT to support fieldwork
Design and technology	3	Developing, planning and communicating ideas; designing and creating computer-controlled models
History	2	Information-handling software supporting study of the local area; computer databases used to enrich understanding of 'The Victorians' topic
	5	Presenting historical findings using multimedia
	7	Creating 'Tudor blogs'
	9	Accessing museums, artefacts and cultural settings online
Geography	2	Information-handling software, supporting study of the local area
	3	Recording and analysing weather data
	4	Conducting investigations outside the classroom
	6, 7, 9	Comparing and contrasting localities
Art and design	5, 9	Evaluating work and collaborating on presentations; investigating different kinds of art, craft and design [for example during visits to museums, galleries and sites, on the internet].
	9	
Music	3	Exploring musical pitch and duration using Roamer
	4	Researching the lives and music of famous composers; potential of podcasts for recording and presenting musical performances
Physical education	1, 5	Using video to analyse athletic performance
Personal, social and health education and citizenship	2	Investigating a charity website
	4, 9	Caring for the environment; healthy eating, exercise and staying healthy
	6	Social aspects of behaviours, identifying risky situations and seeking and locating appropriate advice; exploring issues of identity and self-image
	9	Recognising membership of community and playing an active role as citizens; recognising and respecting diversity and difference

Modern foreign languages	4, 9 9	Using automatic translators to investigate languages. Potential of school-linking for developing awareness of other languages
Religious Education	6, 9	Awareness of and developing respect of religious and cultural differences
Other	2	'Thinking Skills' as a statutory cross-curricular requirement

Table 1 Cross-curricular links

Issue	*Chapter*	*Brief description*
Thematic planning incorporating ICT	1, 3, 9	Medium-term planning around topics and themes
Learning in settings outside the classroom	3 4 7 9 6, 9	Potential of data-loggers on field trips; identifying control and monitoring technology Conducting geographical fieldwork Conducting scientific fieldwork Alternatives and supplements to visiting out-of-school settings School-linking across national and global boundaries
Promoting home–school links	4, 6 6 7	Sharing children's work with parents and the wider community Partnerships with parents for raising awareness of e-safety issues Open evenings as a showcase for children's work
Health and safety using ICT	4 6 6 6	Safeguarding children using collaborative web tools E-safety policy and practice; cyberbullying Children's emotional and social development in online and offline relationships ICT Acceptable Use Policies in school
Ethics and ICT	5, 6 9	Copyright and intellectual property Challenging stereotypes
Classroom management	7, 9	Strategies for managing ICT resources

Table 2 ICT-specific issues

PART 1
ICT IN THE NATIONAL CURRICULUM

1. ICT as a core skill
Debbie Simpson, Ian Todd and Mike Toyn

Learning Outcomes

By the end of this chapter you should:
- understand the difference between ICT skills and ICT capability;
- understand your own use of ICT and your development of ICT capability;
- understand the historical context behind the use of ICT in schools;
- develop your understanding of the importance of supporting children to develop their ICT capability.

Professional standards for QTS

Q8 Have a creative and constructively critical approach towards innovation, being prepared to adapt their practice where benefits and improvements are identified;

Q14 Have a secure knowledge and understanding of their subjects/curriculum areas and related pedagogy to enable them to teach effectively across the age and ability range for which they are trained;

Q15 Know and understand the relevant statutory and non-statutory curricula and frameworks, including those provided through the National Strategies, for their subjects/curriculum areas, and other relevant initiatives applicable to the age and ability range for which they are trained;

Q22 Plan for progression across the age and ability range for which they are trained, designing effective learning sequences within lessons and across series of lessons and demonstrating secure subject/curriculum knowledge;

Q23 Design opportunities for learners to develop their literacy, numeracy and ICT skills;

Q25a Use a range of teaching strategies and resources, including e-learning, taking practical account of diversity and promoting equality and inclusion.

Introduction

This chapter aims to set the scene for the rest of the book by discussing some key areas. As such it does not focus on developing your understanding of how to teach ICT effectively or use ICT in your teaching; rather it aims to support your learning about the way ICT should be used. It does this by making distinctions between different approaches to teaching ICT and by considering the impact that the history of ICT use in schools has had on the way it is taught. It also asks you to consider why and how you use ICT. This will provide opportunities for you to apply your own experiences to the way you teach ICT, and teach with ICT.

This chapter will underpin Part 1 and Part 2 of this book. You will see the importance of the need to develop children's ICT capability and this will guide your learning when you read the chapters in Part 1 about teaching the ICT National Curriculum. By reflecting on the way you have learned to use ICT you will begin to realise the importance of context when using ICT to support learning across the curriculum. This will be helpful to you as you read the chapters in Part 2.

As an aid to developing your understanding, case studies are used to exemplify the key ideas presented in this chapter.

A brief history of ICT in primary classrooms

Even though every child at school in the UK today has been brought up in a world where computers are very commonplace, this has not always been the case. The significance of this is that even though it is easy to take ICT for granted, it is a very new phenomenon in education compared to the teaching of English and literacy, for example.

Within the short time that computers have been in classrooms there have been a number of different approaches to the way they should be used. Interestingly, the first computers that appeared in classrooms were not funded by the (then) Department for Education and Science (DES) but the (then Department for Trade and Industry (DTI). This underlined the perception that computers were a part of the world of work and that children needed to learn about them to prepare themselves for leaving school. The impact of this was that the curriculum was focused on learning how to operate computers and was known at the time as Computer Studies.

However, there were competing theoretical perspectives. Others, particularly influenced by 'learning machines' which had been developed in America, believed that computers would eventually become curriculum deliverers and that their role should be to deliver Computer Assisted Learning (CAL). Consequently, the development of a *drill and practice* curriculum for computers was advocated. An example of this would be the use of computers to test children's recall of number bonds to ten, or common spelling patterns.

Around the same time a professor at the Massachusetts Institute of Technology (MIT), Seymour Papert, was advocating a radically different standpoint. Papert developed the LOGO programming language and argued that there was far more educational value in children *teaching* computers through developing programming skills, than in children being taught by computers through drill and practice techniques. Consequently, a discovery-based approach was advocated, with children working on problems and developing their understanding of mathematics, communication, problem solving and logic, etc. along the way.

Alongside these perspectives, which have influenced the ways in which ICT has been used in UK schools, is the issue of funding and its impact on provision. At present, many schools have impressive quantities of ICT resources and teachers are often challenged to ensure they are used to their optimum effect. However, this has not always been the case. In the 1980s the Microelectronics Education Programme (MEP) was one of the first to fund computer provision in schools and £32 million was made available, with the result that by the end of the 1980s most schools owned at least one computer (in total, not per class). This presented a dilemma as, whilst teachers recognised that using this precious resource for activities such as number bond practice seemed rather wasteful, the extended use of LOGO as advocated by Papert could not be accommodated with only one computer in a school. This tension resulted in teachers making pragmatic and practical choices about ICT teaching.

The limited provision of ICT resources continued to have an impact on the way ICT skills were taught until the late 1990s when the National Grid for Learning (NGfL) provided significant funding (£100 million in 1998/1999 for example) allowing schools to vastly increase their ICT provision, and school leaders and teachers made strategic decisions about the way that resources should be allocated. Many schools initially tried to place one computer in each class then, as NGfL money became available, began to put a second computer into classrooms. Often they found that classrooms were not large enough to accommodate any further computers and that there were still problems ensuring that each child in the class had adequate access to the resources. This led to the development of computer suites, which had an impact on the way that ICT was managed, as now a whole class of children could be taught at once. However, having all the computer resources in one room required the relocation of the class to the computer suite, and there could be difficulties in scheduling access to the room. Many schools are now adopting a more flexible approach through the use of portable computing combined with classroom computing and some centralised provision.

It is sometimes easy to assume that the way things are now is the way they have always been, but this has not been the case for ICT within primary education. Indeed the current situation where ICT is a curriculum subject and children have to learn about ICT as well as using it to support learning in other subjects had been scheduled to change under the implementation of the *Primary Curriculum Review* (Rose, 2008). Indeed, had it not been for a change of government in 2010, this change would already be being implemented in schools.

Theoretical perspectives, ICT provision and political decisions have all influenced the way that ICT has been taught and used in primary schools and will continue to do so. Your developing understanding of what ICT capability is will stand you in good stead as you make significant and effective use of ICT to support children's learning.

Activity

By considering your own experience you will be able to place this within a framework of time/provision/and theoretical perspective. What was your experience of ICT at school? Were there computers, and were they PCs or some other form of computer? Did you use LOGO or did you spend time using the computer for practising spellings or times tables?

How do you foresee the use of ICT in the next five or ten years?

What is ICT capability?

The previous section outlined briefly the history of ICT provision in UK schools and some of the competing theories about the purpose of ICT, its pedagogy and curriculum structure. This section will explore these issues in more detail by considering what is meant by *ICT capability*.

Fox (2003, page 57) distinguishes between ICT techniques, such as recognising and using the font tool to change the appearance of word-processed text, and ICT skills by noting that *a skill is something that you can get better at*. Using ICT to change fonts to suit a specific purpose and intended audience however, is a *skill*, as children can improve their decision-making based on experience and feedback. It is possible to make a similar distinction between ICT skills and ICT capability. In theory, it would be perfectly possible to plan an ICT curriculum that was entirely skills-based and that allowed learners to get better at *skills* but did not develop their *capability* in any way. This curriculum might be characterised by a focus on learning how to operate specific software titles using examples that were not related to other areas of the children's learning.

The South West Grid for Learning (SWGfL) website represents ICT capability using a Venn diagram (Figure 1.1). Techniques are the 'nuts and bolts' of ICT, for example, the ability to cut and paste text in a word processed document. Process skills relate to the purposeful application

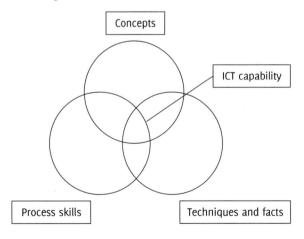

Figure 1.1 ICT capability

of techniques, for example choosing and using an appropriate font for a specific purpose. It is to these two elements of the diagram that Fox's distinction applies. However, the SWGfL diagram also includes a third aspect of ICT: *concepts*. Conceptual understanding implies an awareness of the contribution that ICT tools and resources can make to learning, and the ability to make informed choices about which technology to use, when and where to use it and, indeed, whether it is appropriate to use ICT for a task at all. It can be seen therefore that the distinction between techniques and skills is only part of the picture of ICT capability, and that higher order conceptual understanding must also be taken into account.

> ## Activity
> Have you gained an ICT qualification? Perhaps a GCSE or O level in ICT or a European Computer Driving Licence (ECDL)? If so, consider how much of your learning was spent on each of the segments in Figure 1.1. Would you describe the syllabus as having been focused on skills and techniques or was it aimed at developing your ICT capability?

Ofsted ICT inspections (which include a focus on the extent to which schools develop children's ICT capability) have found recently that the number of schools which are doing this is rising but that it is still erratic and *opportunities for [children] to build on their knowledge and skills were insufficient* (Ofsted, 2008, page 2). This is in a context where one out of five schools inspected (across both primary and secondary phases) was deemed inadequate in this respect. Ofsted (2005) found that in a sample of schools, although there was some balance between teaching of ICT and using ICT in other subjects, this was not embedded to the extent that it was a daily occurrence. Ofsted (2005) also researched the effect of teacher monitoring of ICT and found that the most effective implementation of ICT use occurred when children's use of ICT opportunities was monitored rather than the way teachers used ICT. This provides further evidence that the development of ICT capability plays a role in child development.

Teaching skills and techniques to children is straightforward and if a lesson learning objective is *that children should be able to cut and paste text* then it is easy to assess as children can either do it or they can't, using a straightforward 'ticklist' approach. What is more challenging is developing children's ICT capability beyond working with skills and techniques. Another way to view the elements of ICT capability in Figure 1.1 (on p. 9) is as a series of rings, as in Figure 1.2. This approach shows how techniques and facts are the starting point and these can then be built on to become process skills and finally children can begin to apply these skills along with higher order skills to develop ICT capability.

It is important not to neglect the development of skills and concepts by focusing solely on techniques and facts, otherwise an important aspect of children's learning will not be advanced. An analogy might be drawn with teaching children how to use a protractor. There are a certain number of techniques that must be mastered if it is to be used correctly (how to position it, how to read the scale etc.). Once these have been learned it can be used in a purposeful manner in order to solve some mathematical problem (e.g. the size of a particular angle). However, a protractor comes into its own when it is used to develop conceptual understanding, for example about whether the sum of internal angles in a pentagon is always the same. It would be unthinkable to consider simply teaching children how to use a protractor for the sake of it. It should also be unthinkable to teach children the techniques and facts necessary to simply operate ICT hardware and software without developing their conceptual understanding at the same time.

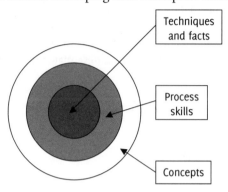

Techniques and facts

Process skills

Concepts

Figure 1.2 ICT capability as a hierarchy

Case Study: Moving from skills to capability

John is a third year undergraduate trainee teacher on a five-week block practice in a Year 3 class. There are 24 children, evenly split between boys and girls, a teaching assistant and a one-to-one support assistant. John is introducing the *Photostory* (Microsoft) program to them (simple, user-friendly software which allows children to combine text and photographs and add music and record voice-overs as required). The children have no prior experience of the program but have been introduced to *Word* (Microsoft).

In his planning John identifies the following strands of the National Curriculum for ICT as being covered previously:

3a. Exchanging and Sharing Information: *how to share ... information in a variety of forms*

4c. Reviewing, modifying and evaluating work: *talk about how they could improve future work*

The lesson takes place in the ICT suite, where the children are working in mixed ability pairs. John introduces the software to the whole class on the interactive whiteboard and takes them through its features step by step, using prepared photos in a shared folder. He adds text, music (again from a shared folder) and points out the narration function, though says they will explore that another time. He also indicates that any pictures/sound can be used, from the internet or uploaded from a camera. The children are attentive and motivated as they observe

$\rightarrow$

John creating a story with words, music and pictures. John has also prepared a prompt sheet for the children, a copy of which is placed by each computer workstation, outlining the steps he has just shown them. He then divides the class into three groups, with each adult being responsible for four pairs of children. The adults have used *Photostory* before and are well briefed.

The children are challenged to use any of the pictures from the shared folder (a variety of photos taken at random) and any music to create a simple story, perhaps one that would be suitable for infants. Each pair of children spends 30 minutes completing their story and some are shown in the plenary. The children are pleased with their efforts. John differentiates by outcome, though early finishers could 'have a go at another one'.

Below is an extract from the feedback given to John by Rachel, the regular Year 3 teacher and John's school mentor:

Rachel: How did you think it went?

John: OK, really. I thought I was well organised, the children were on-task and they really enjoyed it, and by the end nearly all of them had got a story with words and music. I didn't feel any were struggling.

Rachel: Yes, they seemed to pick it up very well. Why did you use Photostory? *It's a nice piece of software, but why now for this Year 3 class?*

*John: Well, it fits in with our **'Combining Text and Graphics' unit of work, and with the Exchanging and Sharing Information** strand of the ICT National Curriculum.*

Rachel: So is this part of a longer topic on Combining Text and Graphics?

John: Well, if Photostory *has a downside it's that it is limited in scope. We'll probably do another session, so they can have a go at the sound function and maybe use some pictures from the internet but I think then we might have to move on, perhaps using* Word *or* PowerPoint.

Rachel: You might want to reconsider this. Yes, Photostory *is simple to use in terms of pure ICT skills but have you thought about broadening its use? Rather than using it as a one-off to see if the children can master its basic functions then moving on, what about giving them a real purpose or context for its use? For instance, you've just finished a super English unit of work on instructions. Could you have combined* Photostory *with that and used it to write some clear instructions? I know that Year 2 children are making pizzas this half term as part of our **European Week**. If you had used* Photostory *to write instructions on how to make pizzas, you could have shared it with them. Not only would you have a context, you would have a real audience, too. The children would be using ICT to serve a purpose, not just as an end in itself.*

In the case study above, Rachel (who is not a subject leader for ICT but is passionate about using it to support other subjects) was keen to point out that, while it was a good lesson in terms of organisation and structure, it was essentially a stand-alone lesson. It was not placed in the context of children's prior learning and experience nor was John really clear about where it was going next. Crucially, he had missed several opportunities to place it in a meaningful context. Therefore, while the children would have enjoyed the lesson and mastered the skills of that program, they would not apply them elsewhere in the curriculum. An analogy might be that they learned to drive, and then parked the car in the garage while moving on to another skill.

Activity

Consider which of the following are techniques, skills or concepts. Then add an activity or idea of your own to each list.

- Learning how to save documents to the school's network.
- Selecting an onscreen paint package to create a design for some wrapping paper in order to try out several different designs.
- Compiling photographs and video from a visit into a presentation to show to parents.
- Finding information on the internet about the climate in Nairobi.
- Learning how to add a record to a database.
- Presenting a story as an audiobook (rather than a piece of writing) to be shared with younger children.

Children developing ICT capability

Consider the contexts and purposes for which you and your friends use ICT tools in everyday life, such as a mobile phone, the internet, and computer software. It is likely that you learned to use these tools because they help you to achieve something that you want to do; talk to friends, book a holiday or concert tickets, or research and present an assignment.

Try to remember the first time you used an automatic telling machine (ATM) or mobile phone, and think about *why* and *how* you learned these techniques. Most likely you were very clear about your purpose and your motivation was high. Learning to use the technology in the first place demanded some investment of time and effort but you were carried along by your enthusiasm and sense of purpose. You watched someone else or asked for advice, or even read the instructions; and then you practised until the techniques became automatic. Alternative methods exist for withdrawing cash and communicating with friends; however, you chose to use technology when it was the most convenient or efficient tool. You also developed transferable skills. When you changed your mobile phone model you learned how to use it much more quickly for three reasons. You were already aware of the benefits of using technology; some of the features were similar so you already had a head start; and your confidence was high: you mastered one system so you knew you could master another.

With someone who was new to the technology, you became a *teacher*, helping your grandfather to use the ATM or showing off phone features to someone with the same model as you. Without deliberately setting out with the intention, you nevertheless attained expert status.

Now you are in the classroom and you are expected to teach Year 5 children how to use technology that is new to them – spreadsheet software, for example. How might your experience of learning and teaching technical skills informally help you to plan your approach? Before answering the question, read the research below describing how a group of children tackled the process of learning to use technology without any adult intervention.

Research Focus: The 'Hole in the Wall' computer

A computer is placed in an area where a large group of children play. The children are not shown how to use the computer nor does anyone suggest any reason why they might wish to do so. None of the children has ever seen or used a computer before; many of the children do not even attend school.

This was the basis for a research project carried out during the first decade of this century, beginning in the slums of New Delhi, but since replicated in other less economically developed countries (LEDC). Researchers installed a computer into a *hole in the wall* in a safe space where children gather to play, and then leave it for children to discover. The findings of the studies are remarkably consistent.

The children explore what the computer can do using trial and error methods at first. Soon one child will make a discovery, for example that moving the cursor over an icon and clicking will open a new screen. The technique is shown off to friends who mimic the action and make new discoveries of their own. Children quickly create their own vocabulary so that they can talk about the computer and what it does: for example the children in the New Delhi study called the *hourglass* icon a *damaru*, because it reminded them of a double-sided drum. This spiral of discovery and self-instruction continues and children's activities gradually become more purposeful as they combine new techniques into meaningful processes to achieve particular outcomes, such as creating and editing images. Children gain group status through sharing these skills.

The findings of the hole in the wall studies led one of the researchers to suggest the following hypothesis:

> *The acquisition of basic computing skills by any set of children can be achieved through incidental learning provided the learners are given access to a suitable computing facility, with entertaining and motivating content and some minimal (human) guidance.*

(Mitra 2000, page 3)

Activity

Consider what your own experiences of learning to use technology in everyday life and the experiences of the children in the case study tell us about how people learn to use technology. You can read more about the project online at **www.hole-in-the-wall.com**. Are there any similarities between your own learning strategies and those of the children in the study?

The initial motivator for the children using the *hole in the wall* computer is likely to have been its novelty and a lack of competing attractions; the children in your class will already be much more familiar with technology. It is not suggested that access to technology alone is sufficient for children to learn how to use it (although sometimes this will happen). It is however possible to draw some inspiration from the way children independently developed ICT capability in the case study.

A precondition for all learning is motivation. Sometimes a technology tool may in itself be novel and interesting, and relatively easy to use; graphics programs, adventure games and digital video cameras are good examples. If this is the case then allowing children some time for free exploration and discovery can be a good teaching strategy. Children are naturally curious and may surprise you by what they find out. This also relieves you as the teacher from feeling that you must be an expert in every aspect of ICT. You can learn and share new techniques alongside the children. Once children are familiar with basic techniques then, with your guidance, they can begin to build ICT skills by combining and applying techniques purposefully and independently.

As outlined in the preceding section, children's developing ICT capability reaches beyond techniques and skills into understanding how and why technology is used in everyday life. It involves making informed choices about appropriate use of ICT and recognising that ICT can help us to accomplish tasks more efficiently or effectively, and achieve new outcomes that would not be otherwise possible.

Research Focus: Theories of learning

The progress of the children in the *'hole in the wall'* research study illustrates some well-established theories of learning. Bruner (1978) emphasised the social nature of learning and used the metaphor of *scaffolding* to describe the support provided to a learner by more knowledgeable others. In the *'hole in the wall'* case study children observed each other and absorbed just enough information at a time to learn a new technique or skill. They practised and advised each other as necessary, maintaining a constant dialogue about what they were doing.

The number of times an individual child will need to see an ICT technique demonstrated and the amount of practice they will need to become competent will

$\rightarrow$

depend upon the age and experience of the child, but demonstrations do not always have to be teacher-led. The children in the *hole in the wall* research managed well without adult intervention through collaboration with more capable peers, usually followed by intervals of independent practice of new skills. Discussing the research, Dangwal and Kapur (2009) point to the role of group support and approval as a prime means and motivator for these children. Individuals learn from the group, by asking each other how things are done, and the whole group benefits from the individual learning of each child.

Vygotsky (1978) predicted that children would learn most effectively the skills that fell within their zone of proximal development (ZPD), which he described as the difference between what they could achieve alone and what they could achieve with help. In your classroom your judgement as a teacher will be crucial. When designing realistic but challenging activities to develop ICT capability, take into account the children's existing experience and abilities and consider the '*Goldilocks factor*': not too difficult, not too easy, but just right.

The contribution of ICT to other subjects

ICT maintains a key place in the curriculum because it is recognised that children need time and focused opportunities to develop ICT capability. However the National Curriculum requires teachers to:

> *provide pupils with opportunities to apply and develop their ICT capability in all subjects (except physical education and the non-core foundation subjects at key stage 1).*

> (DfEE/QCA 1999, page 39)

A current, statutory requirement to use ICT across subjects, however, is only part of the reason we should consider using technology outside ICT lessons. The power of technology, when used appropriately, to transform, enrich and inspire learning is embraced by an increasing number of teachers not just in the areas outlined above, but throughout the entire curriculum at Key Stages 1 and 2. Research has found that where primary teachers plan for the use of ICT in subject teaching they report a positive impact on children's learning. ICT can promote interest, engagement and motivation, and consequently lead to improvements in children's attitudes and behaviour (Passey *et al.*, 2004).

Activity
Take a few minutes to consider an occasion when you observed ICT being used within the teaching of another subject. How was the technology used, in relation to the learning objectives for the lesson?

Did it:

Enable children to experience or achieve outcomes that would otherwise not be possible, for example watching the process of seed germination using time-lapse photography;

Enrich subject learning, for example using control software to animate models made during D&T lessons;

Enhance children's work, for example through using publishing or presentation software to create and refine publications for sharing with a wider audience?

If the use of ICT did not enrich or enhance the lesson, or enable children to learn more effectively, then consider what purpose was served. In your opinion did the use of technology support children's subject learning or impede it?

It can be challenging to plan integration of ICT into the teaching of other subjects when on placement. There is a wide variation across schools in the range of ICT resources, and of children's prior experience with it. The classroom management implications of technology use can also prove daunting. However, thematic planning (see Chapter 3), where a whole-school theme or topic provides a context for ICT and other subject lessons, is a good starting point. This approach can transform subject teaching by considering at the planning stage how ICT tools and resources might provide access to deeper and broader learning experiences than would otherwise be possible.

Case Study: Medium Term Planning for ICT

Tasneem is planning for her forthcoming block placement with a Year 3 class. The Year 3 cross-curricular theme is *It's Not Easy Being Green* (Improving the Environment) and the history topic is The *Victorians*. Tasneem uses a Medium Term Planning document for ICT provided by her placement school. This subdivides three of the National Curriculum ICT strands into elements as follows, to ensure a balanced coverage of aspects of ICT over the year.

Exchanging and Sharing Information
Text & Multimedia
Images, Video & Animation
Sound
Electronic Communication

Finding Things Out
Digital Research
Data Handling

$\rightarrow$

Developing ideas and making things happen
Data-logging
Logo & Control
Simulations & Spreadsheet Modelling

The fourth strand, of *reviewing, modifying and evaluating work as it progresses* is developed throughout the curriculum. For further information about progression and planning for ICT using this system, see: **www.lancsngfl.ac.uk/ictprogression**

Tasneem considers the following questions:

- Which elements of ICT learning will I cover, and which other subjects have links to these areas?
- Where might ICT be embedded in subject teaching?
- Where will I need to focus upon ICT as the main subject?
- What concepts do children need to understand?
- What skills and techniques do children need to learn – should these be taught, or can children discover them through exploration and sharing?
- What ICT resources do I need?

Tasneem begins to complete the Medium Term Planning sheet identifying how children's ICT capability and skills development can be embedded within a thematic plan and linked with other subjects. Her initial plan can be seen in Table 1.1.

Activity

A Medium Term Planning sheet for ICT is shown in Table 1.1. The next planning stage is to consider which ICT skills and concepts should be taught during discrete ICT lessons and which can be embedded into the teaching of other subjects. Basing your ideas on this plan, identify how you would manage this process. Remember that if you are teaching English or mathematics lessons the subject objectives must have priority; children should only practise and consolidate their existing ICT skills during these lessons. Within other subject lessons either ICT or subject objectives may be foregrounded.

Think about how you might differentiate tasks. How might you ensure that all children are included in lessons, including those with Special Educational Needs (SEN), children with English as an Additional Language (EAL), and more able children?

ICT Element	Concepts	Skills	Subject links	ICT resources
Text & Multimedia	Recognise features of good page design. Consider how these meet the needs of the audience. Understand that ICT allows changes to be made quickly and efficiently. Compare and contrast the impact of using different words and images from a variety of electronic sources. Use different font sizes, colours and effects to communicate meaning for a given audience.	Use various layouts, formatting, graphics and illustrations for different purposes or audiences. Use cut, copy and paste to refine and reorder content. Select and import graphics from digital cameras and prepare for use, e.g., cropping, resizing. Recognise and use key layout and design features, e.g., text boxes, columns and borders.	Science – properties of materials, recycling poster. Literacy – litter calligrams and shape poems. Literacy – Work collaboratively on an ICT-based presentation (cross-curricular link to science topic) which includes different text types.	Publishing/word-processing software.
Images, Video & Animation	Understand that a digital image can be captured from different devices and stored, developed and enhanced. Begin to understand how images from different sources are used to enhance a presentation or communicate an idea.	Acquire, store and retrieve images for a purpose. Use ICT to edit/change an image. Explore the use of graphics and paint packages to design and plan an idea. Use digital camera to capture still and moving images for a purpose. Discuss and evaluate images and make decisions whether to keep, delete or change them. Arrange, trim and cut video clips to create a short film that conveys meaning. Add simple titles, credits and special effects	Science – recycling poster. History/Design technology – Victorian Christmas cards. History – video diary of a Victorian child.	Publishing/word-processing software. Graphics software. Digital cameras. Video software, e.g. Microsoft Photostory/Moviemaker or i-movie.
Sound	Not covered in this half term			
Electronic Communication	Respect the ideas and communications of others they encounter online. Understand the need to keep personal information and passwords private in order to protect themselves when communicating online.	Know the school's rules for keeping safe online and be able to apply these beyond school. Log on to a Learning Platform account and create and send messages Use a range of digital tools to communicate, e.g., school's Learning Platform Begin to publish their work to a wider audience.	Use school Learning Platform to share posters and video work with parents and exchange e-mails between classes	Use school's own Learning Platform

Digital Research	Talk about and describe the process of finding specific information, noting any difficulties during the process and how these were overcome. Begin to understand that information found as a result of a search can vary in relevance and accuracy.	Use a range of child-friendly search engines to locate different media, e.g., text, images, sounds or videos. Develop key questions and key words to search for specific information. Use appropriate tools to save and retrieve accessed information, e.g., through the use of copy/paste.	Science – find out about recycling and properties of materials. History – researching lives of Victorian children and Literacy – research using ICT; locate, read and note relevant information.	Internet access and child-friendly safe search engine.
Data Handling	Recognise similarities and differences between ICT and paper-based systems. Know that ICT can create a variety of tables and graphs that are used for different purposes. Understand some graphs and charts are more appropriate and easier to read than others.	Create frequency diagrams and graphs to answer questions. Begin to identify what data should be collected to answer a specific question. Compare different charts and graphs, and understand that different ones are used for different purposes.	Mathematics – litter survey (organise and interpret data in pictograms, tally charts and frequency tables).	Graphing software.
Data-logging	Not covered in this half term			
Logo & Control	Be aware that Logo is a computer programming language.	Plan, create, test and modify sequences of commands to solve open-ended problems using a floor robot, screen turtle or other programmable devices.	Mathematics/ICT – use floor turtle to deliver sorted recycling to 'depots' on large floor map. Use logo to create repeating patterns onscreen.	Roamers. Logo software.
Simulations & Spreadsheet Modelling	Understand how computer simulations can represent real or imaginary situations and how these can help in the wider world.	Explore the effects of changing variables in models and simulations, asking 'What if?' questions. Use a pre-prepared spreadsheet to explore simple number patterns.	Geography – use online simulations to explore recycling. Mathematics – addition and subtraction number patterns.	Online recycling simulation. Spreadsheet software.

Table 1.1 ICT cross-curricular planning

Case Study: Using ICT to support other subjects

Helen is a Year 6 teacher in her NQT year. She is teaching in a large urban primary school serving a socio-economically disadvantaged area. She has a class of 34 lively children, 25 of whom are boys. She is committed to using ICT wherever possible to support her teaching, not least because of the motivational value it brings to her children. Below are some of the thoughts she has recorded prior to a typical day's teaching, in which she aims to incorporate ICT into three of her four sessions. She looks realistically at some of the issues she will face, always aiming to find practical solutions to any barriers.

Subject 1: Mathematics

Context

We are in the middle of a one-week revision unit on *angles*. I am happy that the basics of measuring, drawing and calculating angles are covered and embedded, and I want to use Roamer to help me to stretch my most able group with a view to calculating angles in regular polygons (beyond triangles and quadrilaterals) and calculating exterior angles.

Prior learning

Angles – they have had an introduction to measuring/calculating exterior angles and have looked at angles in larger polygons

Roamer – used in Year 2 at a very basic level with right angles. The children have vague memories of *doing an obstacle course* with it.

Potential barriers to learning

Motivation – will it be seen as an infant *toy?*

Organisation – will it be a teacher-led activity? If so, what will the other children do? Where will the activity take place? Will all the class get to use the Roamer? If so, what will the less able children do? The children haven't used Roamer for four years. How much of the lesson will be spent teaching the Roamer and how much actually supporting the mathematics work?

Assessment

How will I tell from a group activity what the children can actually do?

Possible solutions

In our ICT session the day before I need to use the Roamer, I will start by reminding

→

the children of how to operate it, in the ICT suite. Then, while the rest of the class continues with our ongoing ICT work, each group will have 15 minutes to familiarise themselves with the Roamer.

In the mathematics lesson the following day, I will target the most able group to use Roamer first. This should raise its status as a *learning tool* rather than just a toy.

Organisationally, we will clear a floor space by moving a group's tables. I will work with the *Roamer* group for the input, with the Teaching Assistant (TA) 'floating', to sort out any initial problems with the other groups. I will gradually withdraw from the focus group, once I have given them their challenge, which will be to use the Roamer to draw a pentagon, then hexagon and so on (harder than it seems as they will have to calculate exterior angles of turn to do this).

I will then work with the middle group, while the TA works with the less able group.

I will use the Roamer on a rolling programme basis, one group per day. My middle ability groups will be set challenges involving acute/obtuse angles, lower ability acute only.

Assessment can be by observation as I am working with each group.

Does the ICT enhance my teaching?

Once we have established Roamer as a tool 'worthy' of Year 6, it will provide motivation. It gives a practical context for angles work and, as everything will be presented in a problem-solving context, it will develop aspects of the Using and Applying Mathematics strand as well.

Subject 2: English

Context

We are about to start Week 2 of a three-week unit on journalistic writing. I want to record some radio news broadcasts that the children will be writing.

Prior learning

Journalistic writing – unit of work in Year 4 on newspaper/magazine articles. In Year 6, we spent the first week of this unit looking at radio/TV scripts and listening to samples of news reports. Children are familiar with the *Audacity* (sourceforge. net) software we will use to record the broadcasts.

Potential barriers to learning

Organisation – where and when will the children record the broadcasts?

→

Differentiation/assessment — will it be group or individual work? How can I differentiate/assess?

ICT — is it helping or is it just an *'add-on'* after the learning has taken place?

Possible solutions

I am going to attempt to get the children to do this individually. While it will be more fiddly to get them to record it individually, it is possible, with the help of the TA. The advantage is that differentiation can be largely by outcome, though I can set challenges for the more able, for example to write it in a specific style, such as World Service, Radio 4 or commercial radio. It will also make assessment more robust and I can have evidence of what the children have produced.

Does the ICT enhance teaching/learning?

It provides a real context and audience for the work — it is leading to an actual broadcast. Also, the use of internet/radio/TV clips in the first week has helped the children to be immersed in the genre. The use of ICT is not so intrusive as to take over what is a series of English lessons. Finally, while this is a unit of writing, there are obvious benefits to speaking and listening.

Subject 3: PE – Dance

Context

We are coming to the end of a gymnastics unit of work. I want to use a digital camcorder to record each group's sequence of movements (partly for my own assessment purposes, partly to allow the children to evaluate their own work).

Prior learning

This has been a six-week gymnastics topic, culminating in sequences of moves using large and small apparatus.

Potential barriers

Organisation — how will it be recorded? Will this interrupt the flow of the lesson? Will the children 'clam up' or become silly if recorded? When will the evaluation take place? Can I build in time for improvements to then be made?

Possible solutions

We will devote a whole session (following the warm-up) to watching/recording the performances. This will be 'artificial' in the sense of omitting the usual sequence of floor or apparatus work, but will be invaluable in terms of the children being able to evaluate their own work. They have experience of peer-assessing work, though

$\rightarrow$

only on a superficial basis, but not of self-assessment. The children will use the camcorder to record each other's work.

We will start the next PE lesson in the ICT suite. Each group will have their own performance to watch and they will have the task of each making three improvements or refinements. We will then go to the hall where the changes can be made. If time permits and enthusiasm persists we will record the improved versions and the children can compare the two. Recording it a second time should help to improve behaviour and focus.

Does the ICT help?

Although it will lead to an unusual two or three lessons, it should improve the quality of children's movements and sequences by allowing them to actually see themselves and it will provide a useful assessment base. It could also lead to a presentation for other children or parents.

For a related case study, using video to analyse the performances of professional athletes, and those of the children, see Chapter 5, Case Study, pages 96–7.

You will have realised that many of the strategies for developing ICT capability discussed in this chapter – demonstration of techniques and skills, the use of peer tutors, opportunity for free exploration of resources, time to practise and consolidate skills etc. – do not need to be conducted during a whole-class lesson in an ICT suite, but can be planned into your daily classroom routine using one or two computers or laptops (or a single floor robot or camera) for a small group of children. It is useful to think of an ICT suite as a potential setting for any curriculum subject, and ICT lessons taking place during any part of the normal school day in your own classroom. Try to be flexible and plan ahead to identify the most appropriate setting for a task.

Learning Outcomes Review

This chapter was introduced with a section which provided some background to the development of ICT in UK primary schools. It then explored the differences between ICT skills and ICT capability; which drew your attention to the importance of ensuring that you develop children's ICT capability in order to avoid restricting their learning to the narrow area of ICT skills. It also provided an opportunity for you to consider the way in which you have learned to use everyday ICT resources, and provided opportunities for you to reflect on your own learning and to apply this to classroom situations. Focusing on the practice of trainee and newly qualified teachers, several perspectives on planning for ICT both as a discrete subject and as a cross-curricular support were explored.

Self-assessment questions

1. What three elements make up ICT capability? Provide an example of each.
2. How might mobile hand-held computing have an impact on the way ICT is taught?
3. Many children arrive in school as confident users of technology. Why is it important to develop their capability?
4. In what circumstances would you decide not to use ICT to support learning?

References

Bruner, J. (1978) The role of dialogue in language acquisition, in Sinclair, A., Jarvelle, R.J. and Levelt, W.J.M. (eds) *The Child's Concept of Language*. New York: Springer-Verlag.

Dangwal, R. and Kapur, P. (2009) Learning through teaching: Peer-mediated instruction in minimally invasive education. *British Journal of Educational Technology*, 40(1): 5–22.

DfEE/QCA (1999) *The National Curriculum: Handbook for Primary Teachers in England*. London: DfEE/QCA.

Fox, B. (2003) *Successful ICT leadership in primary schools*. Exeter: Learning Matters.

Lancashire Schools' ICT Centre (2010) *Lancashire Schools' ICT Skills Progression*. Available at **www.lancsngfl.ac.uk/ictprogression**

Mitra, S. (2000) Minimally invasive education for mass computer literacy. *Conference on Research in Distance and Adult Education*, pp. 21–25. Available at **http://citeseerx.ist.psu.edu/viewdoc/download?doi=10.1.1.112.9984&rep=rep1&type=pdf**

Ofsted (2005) Embedding ICT in schools – a dual evaluation exercise. Available at **www.ofsted.gov.uk**

Ofsted (2008) *ICT in primary and secondary schools*. Available at **www.ofsted.gov.uk**

Passey, D., Rogers, C., Machell, J. and G. (2004) The motivational effect of ICT on pupils. UK: *Becta* (retrieved, December 2003).

Rose, J. (2008) *Primary curriculum review*. UK: QCDA. Available at **publications.education.gov.uk/default.aspx?PageFunction=productdetails&PageMode=publications&ProductId=QCDA/09/4355**

SWGfL (no date) *What is ICT capability?* UK: SWGfL. Available at **http://www.plymouthcurriculum.swgfl.org.uk/resources/ict/spreadsheetsks2/WhatisICTCapability.doc**

Vygotsky, L.S. (1978). *Mind and society: The development of higher psychological processes*. Cambridge, MA: Harvard University Press.

2. Finding and selecting information
Ray Potter and Deborah Roberts

Learning Outcomes

By the end of the chapter you should have an understanding of:
- 'Higher Order Information Handling Skills' and 'Thinking Skills';
- key issues in finding and selecting information;
- the 'Finding Things Out' strand of the English ICT National Curriculum;
- appropriate activities and applications to develop the skills and capabilities of the 'Finding Things Out' strand of the English ICT National Curriculum.

Professional standards for QTS

Q14 Have a secure knowledge and understanding of their subjects/curriculum areas and related pedagogy to enable them to teach effectively across the age and ability range for which they are trained;

Q15 Know and understand the relevant statutory and non-statutory curricula and frameworks, including those provided through the National Strategies, for their subjects/curriculum areas, and other relevant initiatives applicable to the age and ability range for which they are trained;

Q22 Plan for progression across the age and ability range for which they are trained, designing effective learning sequences within lessons and across series of lessons and demonstrating secure subject/curriculum knowledge;

Q23 Design opportunities for learners to develop their literacy, numeracy and ICT skills.

Introduction

It is often said that we live in an information age, an economy based on the storage and manipulation of colossal quantities of information which are now more accessible than ever before. Although much of this explosion has been driven by the digital age it is worth considering the various ways that humans have stored information over the years.

Activity
Pause for a moment and try to record some of the ways that we hold information.

Perhaps your list includes some of the following; filing cabinets, people's minds, pictures, graphs, songs, videos, poems, photographs, books, CDs, computers, MP3 players, etc. Some are more reliable than others of course and the human mind is especially fallible in this respect, with its tendency to both forget and distort simple facts after time, while information stored in electronic media is claimed to remain stable for decades, if not longer. It is not only technology's ability for long-term storage, but also the ease with which it allows us to search and generally exploit the information available, that has led to the greater use of electronic means and to the massive proliferation of information. A simple query in the Google search engine for '*the Tudors*' generates over 42 million websites: an unfathomable quantity of information that few would hope to explore in a lifetime.

Learners of any age need strategies to manage this abundance of information and that is the purpose of this chapter. We explore how children can be taught to translate information into understanding and the 'Higher Order Information Handling Skills' of analysis, synthesis and evaluation.

The concept of higher order thinking stems from Bloom et al.'s (1956) *Taxonomy of Educational Objectives* which represents a classification scheme of cognitive learning objectives and is hierarchically organised into six major classes. Intellectual skills are seen as developing in the following order, from lowest to highest:

- knowledge – the ability to identify, define, recall and recognise;
- comprehension – the ability to explain, restate, demonstrate;
- application – the ability to apply, generalise, organise, and restructure knowledge;
- analysis – the ability to categorise, distinguish, deduce, compare;
- synthesis – the ability to produce, develop, write or tell;
- evaluation – the ability to justify, judge, argue and assess.

You will see that 'knowledge', although often prized and rewarded in popular culture through television programmes such as *Mastermind* and *The Weakest Link* is in fact regarded as less vital than the higher order 'Thinking Skills': analysis, synthesis and evaluation.

The National Council for Education Technology (NCET, 1995) adapted Bloom's Taxonomy to make it more relevant to the information age, and produced a list of 'Higher Order Information Handling Skills'. These are:

- decision making;
- classifying;
- questioning;
- analysing;
- explaining;
- presenting.

In a digital age these 'Higher Order Information Handling Skills' are a component of digital literacy. Becta (2010, page 4) defines digital literacy as:

> *The combination of skills, knowledge and understanding that young people need to learn in order to participate fully and safely in an increasingly digital world. It involves:*
>
> - *the functional skills of knowing about and using digital technology effectively,*
> - *the ability to analyse, evaluate and present digital information,*
> - *knowing how to act sensibly, safely and appropriately online,*
> - *and understanding how, when, why and with whom to use technology.*

The second of these, *the ability to analyse, evaluate and present digital information*, mirrors some of the higher order skills listed above.

Links to the National Curriculum

There is a huge overlap between the 'Higher Order Information Skills' listed earlier and the National Curriculum 'Thinking Skills' (DfEE/QCA, 1999, page 22) and these terms are used interchangeably in this chapter. As part of the National Curriculum, 'Thinking Skills' are a statutory requirement to be embedded across the curriculum. They are listed as:

- *Information-processing skills:* locating and collecting relevant information, sorting, classifying, sequencing, comparing and contrasting, and analysing part/whole relationships;
- *Reasoning skills:* giving reasons for opinions and actions, drawing inferences and making deductions, using precise language to explain thoughts, and making judgements and decisions informed by reasons or evidence;
- *Enquiry skills:* asking relevant questions, posing and defining problems, planning what to do and how to research, predicting outcomes and anticipating consequences, testing conclusions and improving ideas;
- *Creative thinking skills:* generating and extending ideas, suggesting hypotheses, applying imagination, and looking for alternative innovative outcomes;
- *Evaluation skills:* evaluating information, judging the value of what they read, hear and do, developing criteria for judging the value of their own and others' work or ideas, and having confidence in their judgements.

Govier (2010) introduces a cautionary point; she describes a number of scenarios with increasingly advanced ICT applications, pointing out that the example featuring the most sophisticated ICT (hand-held computers, powerful search engines and multimedia software) exacts the lowest cognitive demand; while the example using less complex ICT (basic computers and branching database software) promotes the most sophisticated thinking. You cannot assume that using ICT will lead to the automatic development of 'Thinking Skills'. A key issue, therefore, is that ICT can facilitate the development of 'Thinking Skills' – but does not guarantee it. Good planning and teaching is a prerequisite for their effective development. This point is consistent with Becta's contribution to the Rose Review of the National Curriculum where they suggest that:

> *Currently only one in four primary schools is taking full advantage of the (ICT) curriculum, in a way that directly impacts upon quality and pupils' achievement. We now need a step change to ensure that all schools use and apply technology to maximum effect.*

> *(Becta, cited in Rose, 2009, page 70)*

While recognising the potential of ICT, Rose also acknowledges the important role played by teachers, stating that:

> *...embedding ICT throughout the primary curriculum will yield a number of benefits, such as the use of technology to develop deeper cognitive skills.*

> *(Rose, 2009, page 70)*

However,

> *Good teaching will be needed to take these requirements forward and to ensure that technology is not used superficially – for instance, that it is not used only to assist with the presentation of work, rather than for researching, analysing and problem solving.*

> *(Rose, 2009, page 71)*

Potter and Darbyshire (2005) identify a related issue, that using well-designed database software is technically simple, in the way that typing a word into a search engine and selecting the 'Go' button requires a low level of ICT skill. However, using a datafile well is cognitively challenging. This is because effective use of a datafile requires children to translate data into understanding.

Therefore, a key issue in the effective use of ICT to find things out is the need to develop information handling skills which promote the transformation of data into understanding. It can be helpful to make a distinction between:

- *data* – facts which may be meaningless;
- *information* – which begins to tell us something, or inform us; and
- *understanding* – which ensures that children *learn* something new.

Understanding is facilitated by the *practical application* of information, for example to answer a question or hypothesis. Understanding is also promoted by the use of contexts which are meaningful and relevant to children; for example see *Case Study: The interactive estate agency* later in this chapter.

Links to the National Curriculum

The Primary National Curriculum for England (DFEE/QCA, 1999) refers to the Handling Information aspect of ICT capability as 'Finding Things Out'. Table 2.1 summarises progression for this ICT strand.

Activity

Review the National Curriculum programmes of study listed in Table 2 against your experiences in schools to date. What sort of information-handling activities have you observed? Have you seen children gathering information, talking about what information they need and how they can find and use it, preparing information for development using ICT etc.?

Review the National Curriculum 'Thinking Skills' listed above. Have you observed the explicit development of 'Thinking Skills'? Have these been articulated as lesson objectives?

The introduction to this chapter emphasised the importance of information-handling skills and the distinction between data, information and understanding. When 'Finding Things Out' your focus should be on developing information-handling skills, rather than using a particular form of ICT; and you might begin by reviewing your own or your school's medium-term planning to identify appropriate cross-curricular opportunities for information handling. If a high level of technical competence is required then some discrete teaching of ICT skills may be needed.

The following sections discuss a number of ICT applications that are typically used to handle information, including databases, graphing software, and 'Rich Information Sources' such as CD-ROMs and the World Wide Web.

Finding things out with databases

This section focuses upon databases and indicates ways in which they can be used to develop information handling skills. The term *database* refers to a range of software which organises, stores and manipulates large quantities of information, with tools for its effective retrieval and display. Several types of databases are available to primary schools and these include branching databases, flatfile databases and relational databases.

- Branching databases allow the user to ask/answer 'yes' and 'no' type questions in order to classify/identify an object (see example in Chapter 7, Figure 7.3, on page 150). Examples include *Flexitree* (Flexible Software Ltd) and *Textease Branch* (Softease).

- Flatfile databases are usually arranged as tabular rows and columns, where each individual record features a consistent set of fields or headings. All the records together constitute the datafile. *Junior Viewpoint* (Logotron Educational Software) is one example of a flatfile

The National Curriculum: ICT: 'Finding Things Out' strand (DfEE/QCA, 1999)

	National Curriculum Programme of Study		National Curriculum level descriptions	Use of ICT is characterised by:(QCDA, 2010)
KEY STAGE 1	1. Pupils should be taught how to: a. Gather information from a variety of sources [for example, people, books, databases, CD-ROMs, videos and TV] **(NC, KS1, 1a)** b. Enter and store information in a variety of forms [for example, storing information in a prepared database, saving work] **(NC, KS1, 1b)** c. Retrieve information that has been stored [for example, using a CD-ROM, loading saved work]. **(NC, KS1, 1c)**	1	Pupils explore information from various sources, showing they know that information exists in different forms.	**exploring options** and **making choices** to **communicate meaning.** Pupils develop **familiarity** with simple ICT tools.
		2	Pupils use ICT to organise and classify information and to present their findings.	**purposeful** use of ICT to achieve **specific outcomes.**
		3	Pupils use ICT to save information and to find and use appropriate stored information, following straightforward lines of enquiry.	the use of ICT to **develop ideas** and **solve problems.**
KEY STAGE 2	1. Pupils should be taught: a. To talk about what information they need and how they can find and use it [for example, searching the internet or a CD-ROM, using printed material, asking people] **(NC, KS2, 1a)** b. How to prepare information for development using ICT, including selecting suitable sources, finding information, classifying it and checking it for accuracy [for example, finding information from books or newspapers, creating a class database, classifying by characteristics and purposes, checking the spelling of names is consistent] **(NC, KS2, 1b)** c. To interpret information, to check it is relevant and reasonable and to think about what might happen if there were any errors or omissions. **(NC, KS2, 1c)**	4	Pupils understand the need for care in framing questions when collecting, finding and interrogating information. They interpret their findings, question plausibility and recognise that poor-quality information leads to unreliable results.	the ability to **combine and refine** information from various sources. Pupils **interpret** and question the **plausibility** of information.
		5	Pupils select the information they need for different purposes, check its accuracy and organise it in a form suitable for processing.	**combining the use of ICT tools** within the **overall structure** of an ICT solution. Pupils critically evaluate the **fitness for purpose** of work as it progresses.

Table 2.1 Progression within the National Curriculum for ICT: 'Finding Things Out' strand (DfEE/QCA, 1999)

database. For children, analogies can be drawn with popular games cards such as *Top Trumps* (Winning Moves).

- Relational databases feature data stored in a number of tables which are linked to one another, such as *Flexidata* (Flexible Software Ltd) and *Access* (Microsoft). The internet and CD-ROMs are also examples of relational databases where organised data are linked together in a variety of ways, and accessed via an attractive user interface, menus, icons and other navigational devices.

The following section indicates how a progression in information-handling skills can be achieved through the use of databases – capitalising upon cross-curricular contexts which promote purposeful use and informative outcomes.

Progression in information-handling using databases

This section suggests phase-appropriate software, activities and National Curriculum 'Thinking Skills'. Case studies provide in-depth examples of classroom information-handling activities.

Links to the National Curriculum

Drawing upon Table 2.1 above, you might expect that at Key Stage 1, children should be able to:

- 'explore information from various sources, showing they know that information exists in different forms' (NC level 1 description); characterised by *exploratory* use (QCDA, 2010); and
- 'use ICT to organise and classify information and to present their findings' and 'enter, save and retrieve work' (NC level 2 description); characterised by more *purposeful* use to achieve *specific outcomes* (QCDA, 2010)

At this stage, the children's use of ICT is likely to be directed by the teacher, and they will benefit from working with a published datafile, or one prepared by the teacher, or perhaps by older children.

A branching database can allow children to develop their skills of 'gathering information from a variety of sources'. For example, using the popular book *Handa's Surprise* by Eileen Browne, (English: Reading, 6d), a prepared branching datafile can support the children in using identifiable features (e.g. shape, colour) to learn the names of the tropical fruits in the story. A branching datafile can also be used to support subject teaching, for example recognising and naming 2D and 3D shapes, reinforcing key concepts such as sides, corners, faces (Mathematics, Space, Shape and Measures, 2b, c). Both examples of ICT use are purposeful and utilise cross-curricular contexts to support learning in both ICT and across the curriculum. Both promote classifying, comparing and contrasting (information processing).

Activities away from the computer are also vitally important to develop information-handling skills. Class discussion might be used to develop enquiry skills – what do the children already know about a particular topic, and what questions would they like to find answers to (enquiry). The popular Key Stage 1 topic 'Minibeasts' provides much opportunity for enquiry. The teacher might need to help children in framing their questions and guide towards appropriate sources of information. Those with closed questions such as 'Where do snails live?' might be directed towards CD-ROMs (e.g. *Oxford First Encyclopedia*, Oxford University Press); while open questions such as 'Which minibeast is the most common in the school grounds?' can be directed towards simple databases or graphing programs (e.g. *Counter*, Black Cat Software, Viglen). Here, children could collate the findings from playground safaris ('locating and collecting relevant information'), adding the number of each minibeast found to a prepared table while the software automatically draws a block graph alongside so that the children can then engage in answering the original question (information processing, reasoning). Repeated over several occasions, stored graphs can be retrieved, and the findings from different days can be compared. Where variability is identified, this might generate new questions, further developing enquiry skills. Such topics are infinitely expandable. For example, if children notice low numbers of a particular minibeast, they might make suggestions about changing their environment to encourage that particular species. This will involve reasoning, enquiry, creative thinking and ultimately evaluation skills.

Links to the National Curriculum

Drawing upon Table 2.1 above, you might expect that at lower Key Stage 2, children should be able to:

- use ICT to 'find and use appropriate stored information, following straightforward lines of enquiry' (NC ICT level 3 description); characterised by the use of ICT to *develop ideas* and *solve problems* (QCDA, 2010).

At Key Stage 2, children can fulfill some of the above requirements using simple graphing programs as advocated for Key Stage 1; however, flatfile databases provide opportunities to develop a broader range of skills. As databases are content free, they can, with a little time investment, be customised to match a cross-curricular topic (for example, see Case Study: The interactive estate agency). Alternatively, databases such as *Junior Viewpoint* (Logotron Educational Software) produce a range of ready-made cross-curricular datafiles which include food, festivals and Britain since 1930.

Whatever the context, children will need time to familiarise themselves with the data and should be involved in generating questions to investigate, although at this stage children are likely to need support in framing questions appropriately (enquiry).

The National Curriculum ICT level 3 description suggests that at this stage children should focus on interrogating, rather than constructing a datafile, focusing upon simple searches to extract information. Children might locate answers by using the forward and back buttons to scroll through each record of the datafile; however, they should be taught to use more efficient strategies by using the tools within the database, which are likely to include:

- sorting;
- searching;
- displaying selected fields;
- graphing.

Discussion should highlight the power of ICT – and you might even stage a race between paper-based records and the database to highlight its speed and efficiency – illustrating why we use technology.

In response to a particular question, children should be directed or guided (dependent upon experiences and abilities) to use the most efficient search strategy to address their query (information processing). Most importantly, once the children have the results of their search, discussion is needed to ensure that the children can articulate an answer to their query – data must become understanding (reasoning). This is perhaps the most challenging aspect. Have they indeed answered their query, or is further investigation required (evaluation)?

Case Study: The interactive estate agency

Whilst conducting a history and geography study of the locality, a Year 5 class teacher, Deborah, collected estate agent particulars for properties in the area and used these to create a datafile of local properties, as part of an estate agency role play.

Step One: Introduction to databases and engaging with the data

Initially, Deborah invited the children to browse through the datafile, using forward and back buttons, to familiarise themselves with its layout and contents. She encouraged them to use terms such as **datafile** – The Interactive Estate Agency file; **record** – each property had its own record; and **fields** – each record contained a number of standard fields, for example property type, price, etc.

Step Two: Finding answers – simple searches

Deborah led a class discussion about property features and how they would choose a property e.g. number of bedrooms, front and back garden, location, etc. (ICT: KS2 Finding Things Out 1a).

Using their knowledge of the fields within the datafile, the children selected one key feature and, using the search tool, conducted a simple search of the datafile, identifying a range of properties that matched this criterion. Deborah used

$\rightarrow$

demonstrations and helpsheets to support the children's independence in selecting the appropriate tools within the database to execute a simple search. Plenary sessions provided an opportunity for the children to discuss the properties they had identified, how they had located them, the limitations of a simple search and what they might do next.

Step Three: Finding answers – more complex searches

Where simple searches identified properties which, while meeting one criterion, did not satisfy the children's other requirements, the stage was set for more complex searches, for example, searching for properties that matched two or three criteria. Deborah invited the children to play a 'Moving House' game. They drew a card from a pack, which identified how much money they had to spend, and then selected several other criteria of importance to them. Demonstrations and helpsheets scaffolded the more challenging expectation of selecting a property which matched several of the children's criteria.

Step Four: Transforming data into understanding

Finally, the children evaluated whether the properties resulting from the complex search met their stated criteria. In some cases, the datafile contained no properties which matched the children's criteria, for example where they had specified a property with many bedrooms in the lowest price band. This led to some useful discussion and a revision of criteria.

Links to the National Curriculum

Drawing upon Table 2.1 above, you might expect that at upper Key Stage 2, children should be able to:

- 'understand the need for care in framing questions when collecting, finding and interrogating information. They interpret their findings, question plausibility and recognise that poor-quality information leads to unreliable results.' (NC ICT level 4 description); characterised by the ability to *combine and refine* information from various sources and *interpret* and question the *plausibility* of information (QCDA, 2010).
- 'select the information they need for different purposes, check its accuracy and organise it in a form suitable for processing.' (NC ICT level 5 description); characterised by *combining the use of ICT tools* and *critically evaluating the fitness for purpose* of work as it progresses.
- The activity links with geography (*Geographical enquiry* 1b; 2d, f; and History: 7, *investigating how a local area has changed over time*).

At this stage, prior experience and familiarity with the search options within a database will promote more independent use. Children should be encouraged to identify their own questions or hypotheses (creative thinking); and phrase these in an appropriate form for investigation (enquiry). Beyond simple searches, children should be able to conduct more complex searches, for example queries which require a combination of search strategies to elicit the answer (information processing). More able children might design and construct a datafile. This might be a branching datafile, perhaps for use by younger children, or a datafile which links to their current topic – see Case Study below: Victorian convicts. Children should be able to take increasing responsibility for interpreting their findings (reasoning); checking the accuracy of the data they enter; and checking their findings for plausibility (evaluation).

Case Study: Victorian convicts

While studying 'the Victorians' (National Curriculum, History: 11a), Clare's Year 6 class investigated convict transportation to Australia, and were fascinated to find that convicts were transported for crimes such as 'stealing bread and cheese' or 'possession of a silk handkerchief'. There are a range of websites which compile such information, listing prisoners by name, crime, length of sentence, place and date of trial, and transportation ship. In some cases physical descriptions of the prisoners are also available. See, for example: Perth DPS (2003), available at: **members.iinet.net.au/~perthdps/convicts/ships.html**

Step one: Engaging with the data

After reviewing some of the data, children were encouraged to ask questions and pose hypotheses. Some questions lent themselves to further secondary research while others required more sophisticated search techniques. Example questions included 'Do similar crimes receive similar sentences?'; 'What is the shortest/longest sentence?'; 'Which crimes were more common?'; and 'Which crimes were most common among the younger convicts?'

Step two: Datafile design

As a whole-class exercise, an attempt was made to answer questions by scrolling down multiple web pages, which served to illustrate the futility of this approach. Reflecting on their earlier ICT experiences children were encouraged to design their own datafile to enable more efficient searching.

At the design stage, relevant questions included the following.

- What information do you want to get from the data?
- What fields will you need?

$\rightarrow$

- What data will you need within each field?

Design considerations, which might vary by software, included the following.

- What is the range of question types (for example, yes/no; number; keyword; date)?
- Is it sensible to have a 'key field and why might you do this (for example, giving each convict a unique identification number)?
- What is the most appropriate question type for each field?
- How will you deal with multiple entries within a field (for example, where criminals are convicted of two crimes)?
- When might it be sensible to limit the field size or range? (This can help to reduce errors at the data entry stage.)
- How can you plan to reduce errors in data entry?

Specific problems with the convict datafile included imperial measurements for height (for which online imperial-to-metric conversion tools were a solution) and the terminology for crimes (where online dictionaries were invaluable).

Step three: Creating the datafile

The children reviewed their planned fields against the list of questions to ensure inclusion of the relevant data to support their enquiries. The children then took turns entering data, taking turns to type or check the accuracy of data input. Given the huge amount of data available and time constraints, a discussion was held to determine how much information should be entered, and the source of this data. Ultimately, one website was selected and the data was limited to three convict ships.

Step four: Finding answers

Working in pairs or small groups, the children selected different questions. They were asked to consider whether their question, as it was written, could be answered by interrogating the datafile. For example, questions such as 'How old were the convicts?' could be more appropriately rephrased to: 'What was the age range (in years) of the transported convicts?', 'How many convicts were there at each age within this range?' More able children reviewed their questions independently.

From the range of strategies available, children were asked to select an appropriate search strategy, or combination of strategies to answer their question, and then proceeded to interrogate the datafile. During the process of finding answers, children reviewed their findings, considering anomalies such as an individual aged 450 (an error in data entry which was subsequently corrected), repeating or correcting searches as appropriate.

$\rightarrow$

Step five: Transforming data into understanding

As a final step, the children created posters illustrating their question, search strategy and an evaluation of this strategy and most importantly the answer to their query. The posters were used to share their learning with the whole class about the Victorian penal system, effective search strategies and 'Thinking Skills'.

Note: In advance of your lesson, you should check websites carefully before allowing children free access. Some pages in the website used above for example contain occasional references to crimes of a sexual nature.

Links to the National Curriculum

This section has suggested how databases can be used to develop information handling and 'Thinking Skills' through the ICT National Curriculum programmes of study. A range of cross-curricular contexts and activities exemplify purposeful practice in detail. Case Study: The interactive estate agency (pages 34–5) supported historical enquiry skills linked to History: 11a, The Victorians. The children found out about the experiences of people in the past (2a) using ICT-based sources (4a, b) and communicated their knowledge and understanding using ICT (5c).

Finding things out with graphs

The following section considers progression in graphing within the ICT 'Finding Things Out' strand.

It is not uncommon to see the walls of primary classrooms displaying attractive computer-generated graphs but all too often these are regarded as an end in themselves rather than emphasising the higher order 'Thinking Skills' described earlier. While computers have vastly simplified the construction of graphs the focus should remain on interpretation rather than production. This is not to say that young children should not have an initial experience of drawing graphs by hand; the skills of measuring, choosing scales and colouring to a line are all important but can consume the greater part of a lesson and leave little time for the more crucial aspects of analysis and interpretation.

The National Curriculum for England (DfEE/QCA, 1999, page 22) outlines the 'information processing skills' as:

- finding relevant information;
- sorting/classifying/sequencing information;
- comparing/contrasting information;
- identifying and analysing relationships.

These skills can be developed though a topic approach; for instance, 'How do children travel to school?'

- Collect data and enter (finding relevant information).
- How many, what is the most/least? (sorting/classifying/sequencing information).
- Why should this be so? (comparing/contrasting information).
- Display charts and explanations (identifying and analysing relationships).

Progression issues

The educational psychologist Jerome Bruner (1966) maintained that young children's learning should begin with motor and sensory experiences. This suggests that children should initially have the opportunity to produce graphs away from the computer, for instance:

1. Encourage the children to line up in columns according to season of birth.
   Ask, 'In which season were most children born?'; 'How many children are in this sample?', etc.
2. Children write their favourite fruit drink on a Post-it then attach to a whiteboard to produce a bar chart.
   Ask, 'Which flavour is the least popular?'; 'How many children preferred citrus fruit flavours?', etc.

Activity

Consider the list of six graph/chart types below. In which order would you introduce these to children? Try and reorder them to provide a logical progression for children.

Graph/chart types
Line graph
Bar chart
Block chart
Pictogram
Scatter graph
Pie chart
You may find that you needed to produce two lists, one which considers the ease of interpretation, and another the ease of production. Pie chart can be particularly difficult to place; while simple pie charts are relatively straightforward to interpret, even for young children, they are complicated to construct by hand, involving as they do angles, degrees and percentages.

Ease of interpretation	Ease of production
Pictogram	Pictogram
Block chart	Block chart
Pie chart	Bar chart
Bar chart	Line graph
Line graph	Scatter graph
Scatter graph	Pie chart

Of course, not all graph types lend themselves to every situation and we need to consider carefully the type of data we are charting.

- *Discrete* data, as we see in Figure 2.1, such as favourite fruits, are regarded as completely separate categories and cannot be ordered. This type of data is frequently represented by pictograms, block charts and bar charts.

- *Continuous* data, which cannot easily be segregated, such as length or temperature, is best represented by line graphs or scatter graphs. An easy way to think about this distinction is that shoe sizes represent discrete data (4, 5, 6, etc.) while foot lengths represent continuous data (26.2mm, 28.6mm, etc.).

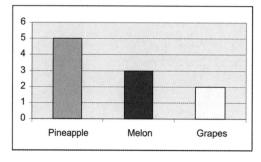

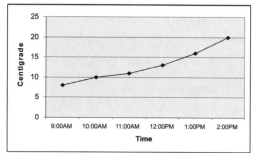

Figure 2.1 Representing discrete and continuous data

Graphing programs

Computer graphing programs allow you to speedily enter and store data which can be shown graphically, often in a variety of forms. The choice of representation generally remains with the user and, as you have seen above, does require some careful thought. Schools often choose to purchase software such as *Counter for Windows* (Black Cat Software, Viglen) or *Pictogram* (Kudlian Software), although there are free alternatives available on the Internet such as *Handygraph*, *Data Handling* and *Line Graph* from the National Strategies section of DCSF website (**nationalstrategies.standards.dcsf.gov.uk**). Alternatively you could use the 'infinite cloner' tool in *Smart Notebook* software (Smart) for interactive whiteboards, to quickly draw pictograms or block graphs.

In summary, computers take the drudgery out of graph construction and allow children and teachers to compare the various methods of representation and understand that different charts are used for different purposes (Mathematics 4, 2c). Computer graphs enable children to focus on the manipulation and interpretation of data rather than the construction of the graph itself.

Links to the National Curriculum

At Key Stage 1, you might expect children to be able to 'gather information' (NC, ICT KS1, 1a) to create graphs, entering this data into tables in the graphing program. Here they are involved in organising and classifying their data (information handling) which the computer automatically converts into a graph. Older or more able children might have some input into selecting the most appropriate type of graph (evaluation and reasoning).

At Key Stage 2 children can also make use of simple graphing programs but when they are working with more complex sets of data the graphing facilities within a database might be more appropriate.

Finding things out with 'Rich Information Sources'

Twenty-first century children are accustomed to very much more than mere electronic words; the world wide web and CD-ROMs, with their text, images, sound and video, may be thought of as 'Rich Information Sources'. However it is this very richness combined with the magnitude of the resource which can often prove such a distraction to learners of all ages. Within the classroom it is essential that we provide focused activities which avoid surface engagement with the material. This section will show how we can ensure that children don't simply browse but buy into the information at a deeper level. Teachers and parents are rightly concerned about the possible dangers associated with access to such wide-ranging resources, and e-safety issues are discussed in Chapter 6.

Research Focus

A recent research study from the University of London of 612 children in five English primary schools showed the children's engagements with ICT to be, 'often perfunctory and unspectacular, especially within the school setting' (Selwyn et al., 2009, page 919). Although over half of the children, both at home and school, were described as using the Internet 'a lot' for playing games, fewer than 15 per cent reported using it 'a lot' for 'general searching/ browsing for information'. The use of CD-ROMs was at a similar low level, although this may reflect the general decline in CD-ROMs as an information medium. In contrast the Becta (2007) survey found that 54 per cent of teachers used 'Internet based resources' in half or more lessons although it is not clear if this was employed as an information source or to provide general teaching resources.

'Rich Information Sources' do not generally manage information in such a clear structured fashion as the flatfile database described earlier. However, there are websites, such as *The Irish Convicts Database*, which are in tabular form and make use of searchable fields and records. The results of a search on the field 'Surname' generates four records and shows 16 defined fields. You may need to reinforce the parallels with the database structure described earlier in the chapter.

Generally the route to desired information on the world wide web may not always be as straightforward and children need to be aware of the quality of the content, its accuracy and currency. A simple search for, 'How old is David Beckham?' might reveal a dozen or more answers depending upon the date that the website was published. Unlike published books, not all websites are moderated and they can be created by anyone with the required skills and access to the internet. It is therefore crucial that children are taught not only how to search the internet but also how to evaluate the credibility of the results.

Kathy Schrock (2001) suggests that children should be encouraged to consider the five Ws of website evaluation:

- WHO?
- WHAT?
- WHEN?
- WHERE?
- WHY?

Activity

Some websites have a professional appearance and seem to be superficially credible but are actually quite fantastical. Access the spoof website: **www.allaboutexplorers. com/explorers/drake** and complete what you can of Table 2.2 below.

WHO?	Who wrote the page(s) and are they an expert? Is some background about the author included? How can I find out more about the author?	
WHAT?	What does the author say is the purpose of the site? What else might the author have in mind for the site? What makes the site easy to use? What information is included and does this information differ from other sites?	

WHEN?	When was the site created? When was the site last updated?	
WHERE?	Where does the information come from? Where can I look to find out more about the publisher of the site?	
WHY?	Why is this information useful for my purpose? Why should I use this information? Why is this page better than another?	

Table 2.2. Activity adapted from Shrock, K. (2001) **kathyschrock.net**

Information overload – translating information into understanding

The amount of freely accessible information available via online or CD-ROM sources verges on the incomprehensible to most of us. Simply finding information on a given topic and faithfully copying it to a different place is not a good model for learning. A key issue therefore is that children need to be taught how to search, skim and scan, engage with and generally make use of the information available.

Activity
Find a suitable website containing information on a topic of your choice; select one or two of the following activities and try them for yourself.
Examples of activities that lead to a high level of engagement with texts:

- reproducing the information in a form suitable for use by younger children (addition of images, simplification of vocabulary);
- producing a condensed version of the text (say 50 words?);
- producing the information in note form, with the main ideas as headings;
- writing one sentence to encapsulate the idea(s) in each paragraph;
- producing a multimedia-style presentation using *Smartboard Notebook* or *PowerPoint*;
- expressing the ideas in the text in diagrammatic form.

Pritchard (2004, page 61) suggests the use of a 'Text Explanation Sheet'. This is a writing frame on an A4 sheet set out in a series of headings which the children are asked to complete and therefore create a new product for a defined audience. The headings used include:

- title;

- space for the original text/images;

- glossary to explain any new words;

- comments or summary in the children's own words.

Case Study: Comic Relief

Mark, a Year 4 teacher, decided to use 'Text Explanation Sheets' with his class as part of a PSHE (personal, social and health education) topic.

Comic Relief by Kevin and Sheila
Original text from: www.comicrelief.com/who_we_are/what_is_comic_relief
Our vision is, 'A just world free from poverty'.
Our mission, thanks to our comedy heritage and the fantastic relationship we enjoy with the BBC, is 'positive change through the power of entertainment'.
And our biggest tool, in trying to achieve these two goals, is the ability to inspire people across the whole country, especially those who don't normally do charity, to do charity.
As the world has changed and become more complex over the last two decades, so Comic Relief has had to adapt and change too but the fundamentals remain the same – a just world free from poverty. In trying to achieve that vision we make this promise to the people who make those efforts possible – our supporters.
'Comic Relief is still able to promise that for every pound the charity gets directly from the public, a pound goes to help transform the lives of people living with poverty and social injustice.'
Glossary or **'What does that mean?'** **Poverty** – not having enough money to take care of basic needs such as food, clothing, and housing. **Mission** – an aim or task that somebody believes it is their duty to carry out or to which they attach special importance. **Charity** – an organisation that collects money and other voluntary contributions of help for people in need. **Social injustice** – unfair or unjust treatment.
Comments on the text Comic Relief works with the BBC and others to try and encourage more people to become involved in giving to charity. This doesn't always have to be money but can be your time. We raised money at school by having a 'No uniform day'. Comic relief promises that all of the money it raises goes directly to good causes.

Table 2.3 Comic Relief 'Text Explanation Sheet'

Mark's approach encouraged children to respect and acknowledge the original material, think carefully about the content and the meanings of the words and to reorganise the information.

Progression issues

When working with Key Stage 1 children, you may wish to initially restrict them to a single vetted website. This gives the opportunity to become familiar with the multimedia nature of the web and provide experience of scrolling, hyperlinks, Forward and Back buttons.

In lower Key Stage 2 you can progress to a safe 'walled garden' where the service provider controls the content and restricts access to non-approved sites. One such commercial provider is *Espresso* (**www.espresso.co.uk**), a library of cross-curricular digital resources which is regularly updated. Alternatively your local authority may offer a search engine and additional safe, appropriate material from within its own site.

Upper Key Stage 2 children should be encouraged to develop more advanced searching techniques, including selecting the most appropriate search engine for a given task as well as developing appropriate strategies for critically evaluating, validating and verifying information.

Case Study: My perfect summer holiday

A class of Year 5 children was approaching the end of the academic year and Khalid decided to involve the class in an internet research activity to plan a family summer holiday. Naturally he was concerned that the class should remain focused and safe so he decided that the children should be restricted to previously vetted websites.

He produced his own single web page ('My Perfect Summer Holiday', available at: **www.staff.ucsm.ac.uk/rpotter/holiday**) which linked only to selected sites.

Over a week the children worked in pairs to research and plan a family holiday. This involved working within a set budget and entering the figures into a spreadsheet template provided by Khalid. (Mathematics: Ma2, 1a, b, c, d, e; 4a, d). Later the children produced a desktop published poster of their destination for display.

Search engines

Searching the internet for specific material can be frustrating for teachers and children alike.

In their research study, *Primary pupils' use of information and communication technologies at school and home*, Selwyn et al. (2009, page 928) found that 61 per cent of children suggested that *teachers could show us how to quickly find information on the Internet.*

Of course, we need to think very carefully before allowing primary children to use internet-wide search engines such as Google or similar. If Google is to be used at all, it is important that strict filtering is applied; this option is available from 'Search Settings'. Search engines such as the BBC's (**www.bbc.co.uk/cbbc/find**) are usually a safer approach for children. Image searches are especially problematic and there may be no need for children to download images if an adult accesses them before the lesson and stores them in a shared folder. Alternatively, you may use Microsoft's clipart library, which automatically adds downloaded images to the Microsoft Office clipart folder on your computer.

For most curriculum-related research, there is no need to use an unfenced search engine; children could be directed to specific websites pre-selected by the class teacher as described earlier. Most local authorities operate some sort of filtering system; however, it is worth noting that no filter-based search engine is completely safe.

Child-friendly search engines include:

Ask Kids (**www.askkids.com**)

Boolify (**www.boolify.org**)

Dibdabdoo (**www.dibdabdoo.com**)

Kids Click (**www.kidsclick.org**)

Yahoo Kids (**kids.yahoo.com**)

Boolify is especially interesting as it is designed to introduce children to search techniques involving the keywords AND, NOT, OR. The search results are presented through Google's 'Safe Search STRICT' technology.

This concept can be introduced to children away from the computer, for instance, by asking:

- all children who are wearing blue AND who are girls to stand up;
- all children wearing blue AND who are girls AND with a name that starts with 'A' to stand up;
- all children wearing blue OR T-shirts to stand up;
- all children wearing blue AND T-shirts OR caps to stand up;
- all children who are boys and NOT wearing trainers stand up.

Ask the children to reflect on the combinations. Challenge them to create a new combination, so that only a single child stands up.

Learning Outcomes Review

This chapter has presented 'Higher Order Information Handling' and 'Thinking Skills', emphasising that these skills are elemental in 'Finding Things Out'. You have been introduced to key issues in finding and selecting information and you should be aware of the distinction between data and understanding and the critical role of the teacher. You have been familiarised with progression through the 'Finding Things Out' strand of the National Curriculum and become aware of ICT applications associated with this strand including databases, graphing programs, and 'Rich Information Sources'. Finally, you have considered activities that allow children to meet the requirements of both the programmes of study and the 'Thinking Skills'.

Self-assessment questions

1. What is meant by 'Higher Order Information Handling' or 'Thinking Skills'?
2. When planning activities for 'Finding Things Out',what **key issues,** identified in this chapter, should you bear in mind?
3. What type of ICT applications are typically associated with 'Finding Things Out'?
4. To 'Find Things Out' at Key Stage 1, suggest a number of activities that would be appropriate, in line with the age-related expectations of the National Curriculum.
5. To 'Find Things Out' at lower Key Stage 2, suggest a number of activities that would be appropriate, in line with the age-related expectations of the National Curriculum.
6. To 'Find Things Out' at upper Key Stage 2, suggest a number of activities that would be appropriate, in line with the age-related expectations of the National Curriculum.
7. Identify a range of contexts that would be appropriate within which children can 'Find Things Out'.

Further Reading

Becta (2007) *How to use ICT for data handling in the foundation stage.* Available at: **schools.becta.org.uk/index.php?catcode=ss_cu_skl_02&rid=647&section=cu** (retrieved: 20 September 2010).
A practical introduction to data handling with young children.

Internet Safety (no date) Available at **www.learn-ict.org.uk/resources/intsafety/int_prof.htm** (retrieved: 20 September 2010).
The Internet Proficiency Scheme is designed to help Key Stage 2 pupils learn how to use the internet and other technologies safely and responsibly.

Potter, R. (2007) An introduction to children's learning, in Jacques, K. and Hyland, R., *Professional studies: primary and early years,* 3rd edn. Exeter: Learning Matters.
An accessible introduction to learning theory for primary and Foundation Stage practitioners.

Primary ICT (no date) Available at: **www.staff.ucsm.ac.uk/rpotter/ict/** (retrieved: 20 September 2010).
Web links and resources to help with your teaching of ICT.

Sales, D. (2008) People Graphs in Primary School. *Teaching Statistics: An International Journal for Teachers*, 30(3): 71–4.
This article describes the use of a novel statistical activity with primary school children.

Webquest UK (2010) Available at: **www.webquestuk.org.uk** (retrieved: 20 September 2010).
An introduction to enquiry-oriented lesson formats in which most or all the information that learners work with comes from the web.

References

Becta (2007) *Harnessing Technology schools survey*. Available at **research.becta.org.uk/index.php?section=rh&catcode=_re_rp_02&rid=14110** (retrieved 20 September 2010).

Becta (2010) *Digital literacy: Teaching critical thinking for our digital world*. Available at **schools.becta.org.uk/upload-dir/downloads/digital_literacy_publication.pdf** (retrieved 20 September 2010).

Bloom, B.S., Englehart, M.D., Furst, E.J., Hill, W.H. and Krathwohl, D.R. (1956) *A Taxonomy of Educational Objectives: Handbook 1, Cognitive Domain*. New York: David McKay.

Browne, E. (2006) *Handa's Surprise*. London: Walker Books.

Bruner, J.S. (1966) *Towards a Theory of Instruction*. Cambridge, Mass: Belkapp Press.

DCSF (2010) *Mathematics ITP: Data handling*. Available at **nationalstrategies.standards.dcsf.gov.uk/node/47751** (retrieved 20 September 2010).

DfEE/QCA (1999) *The National Curriculum: Handbook for Primary Teachers in England*. London: DfEE/QCA.

Govier, H. (2010) *Information handling in the digital age, Sharing good practice*. **www.ictopus.org.uk** (retrieved 20 September 2010).

My Perfect Summer Holiday. Available at **www.staff.ucsm.ac.uk/rpotter/holiday** (retrieved 20 September 2010).

NCET (National Council for Educational Technology) (1995) *Making Sense of Information*, Coventry: National Council for Educational Technology.

Perth DPS (Dead Person's Society) (2003) *Convicts to Australia: A Guide to Researching Your Convict Ancestors*. Available online at **members.iinet.net.au/~perthdps/convicts/ships.html** (retrieved 20 September 2010).

Potter, F. and Darbyshire, C. (2005) *Understanding and Teaching the ICT National Curriculum*. London: David Fulton Publishers Ltd.

Pritchard, A. (2004) *Learning on the Net: A Practical Guide to Enhancing Learning in Primary Classrooms*. London: David Fulton.

QCDA (Qualifications and Curriculum Development Agency) (2010) *Assessment in ICT.* Available at: **curriculum.qca.org.uk/key-stages-1-and-2/assessment/assessmentofsubjects/ assessmentinict/index.aspx#main-tab-2** (retrieved 20 September 2010).

Rose, J. (2009) *Independent Review of the Primary Curriculum: Final Report.* Nottingham: DCSF publications.

Ruddock, G. and Sainsbury M. (2008) *A comparison of the core primary curriculum in England to those of other high performing countries.* National Foundation for Educational Research, DCSF-RBW048.

Schrock, K. (2001) *The five W's of web site evaluation.* Available at **kathyschrock.net/abceval/ 5ws.pdf** (retrieved 20 September 2010).

Selwyn, N., Potter, J. and Cranmer, S. (2009) Primary pupils' use of information and communication technologies at school and home. *British Journal of Educational Technology,* 40(5): 919–32.

The Irish Convicts Database. Available at **www.pcug.org.au/~ppmay/convicts.htm** (retrieved: 20 September 2010).

3. Creating, processing and manipulating information
Debbie Simpson and Jayne Metcalfe

Learning Outcomes

By the end of this chapter you should:
- be familiar with aspects of the National Curriculum for ICT that develops children's ability to capture and organise data, investigate patterns and trends, create and explore models and simulations, monitor environmental variables and control devices;
- understand ways of integrating ICT in thematic, cross-curricular planning;
- understand how to plan for progression in ICT capability;
- be aware of the importance of including all learners in co-operative and collaborative learning activities and assessing individual achievement.

Professional standards for QTS
Q6 Have a commitment to collaboration and co-operative working;

Q7 (a) Reflect on and improve their practice, and take responsibility for identifying and meeting their developing professional needs;

Q22 Plan for progression across the age and ability range for which they are trained, designing effective learning sequences within lessons and across series of lessons and demonstrating secure subject/curriculum knowledge;

Q23 Design opportunities for learners to develop their literacy, numeracy and ICT skills;

Q24 Plan homework or other out-of-class work to sustain learners' progress and to extend and consolidate their learning;

Q25 Teach lessons and sequences of lessons across the age and ability range for which they are trained in which they:

(a) use a range of teaching strategies and resources, including e-learning, taking practical account of diversity and promoting equality and inclusion;

(b) build on prior knowledge, develop concepts and processes, enable learners to apply new knowledge, understanding and skills and meet learning objectives;

(c) adapt their language to suit the learners they teach, introducing new ideas and concepts clearly, and using explanations, questions, discussions and plenaries effectively;

(d) demonstrate the ability to manage the learning of individuals, groups and whole classes, modifying their teaching to suit the stage of the lesson;

Q26 (a) Make effective use of a range of assessment, monitoring and recording strategies.
(b) Assess the learning needs of those they teach in order to set challenging learning objectives.

Introduction

A recent study by Ofsted (2009) found that despite an overall picture of improvement in primary pupils' ICT capability, there are persistent weaknesses in the skills of collecting and handling data and in controlling events using ICT. It is suggested in the report that teachers lack confidence in these areas and prefer to focus on aspects of ICT where they have more experience. Consequently children often have insufficient opportunities to develop their understanding of data collection, modelling and control.

> *Too much emphasis is sometimes placed on pupils using ICT to present their work well, at the expense of developing their skills in handling information, programming and modelling data.*

(Ofsted, 2009, page 8)

This chapter tackles this issue head on. You will discover what is meant by terms such as *modelling, data-logging* and *control,* and how you can use ICT to make learning relevant and exciting for your pupils. Some teachers have been discouraged in the past by the seemingly complex technology used in these areas (spreadsheets, data-loggers, control boxes, etc.) and worried about how they will manage their lesson if equipment fails or behaves unexpectedly. You will discover how technology has changed in recent years to become easier and more enjoyable to use, and how you can integrate it into your lessons. Above all we hope to reassure you that with a positive and confident attitude to technology you and the children will together enjoy lessons that are practical, creative and stimulating.

In the chapter we take a thematic approach, showing through case studies how you can integrate ICT into an integrated whole-school theme of *Weather.* We describe some of the practical ways in which technology can be used in the classroom to capture and organise data, investigate patterns and trends and explore models, simulations and control technology. As you read about these examples, consider how each one demonstrates the underlying principles of ICT capability outlined in the National Curriculum, and think about how you might explore these ideas through other cross-curricular themes.

Capturing, organising and investigating data

Using spreadsheets in the primary classroom

Spreadsheets are powerful learning tools, particularly when used to support teaching and learning in subjects such as mathematics, geography and science.

Spreadsheets can help to:

- perform calculations more easily and aid investigations into number patterns;
- organise and display data in charts and graphs so that it can be analysed, interpreted and presented to an audience;
- model real and imaginary situations and explore the impact of changing variables.

Despite their considerable cross-curricular potential there is evidence that spreadsheets are generally underused in primary schools (Siegle, 2005). Spreadsheet software is sometimes considered too complex to be used by young children, although Williams and Easingwood (2003) recommend that children begin to use spreadsheets to record the results of their science investigations at the earliest opportunity. Software tools such as spreadsheets can be introduced gradually to children using scaffolding strategies whereby you, as the teacher, provide adaptive support for children working towards a given task. Case Study: Feed the birds shows children in Key Stage 1 using a prepared spreadsheet to support a science investigation. Children enter their collected data into a prepared template and use the graphing tool to display their results. Most spreadsheet software designed for the primary classroom includes ready-made templates linked to topics, for example, weather or plant growth. If you are not familiar with spreadsheets, then templates can help you to build your confidence. Begin by using a template, discover how you can adapt it to your needs and you will soon be creating your own spreadsheets from scratch.

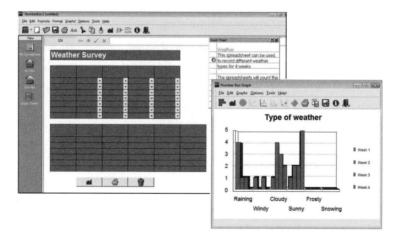

Figure 3.1 A NumberBox Spreadsheet Template (Granada Learning)

Most spreadsheet software can be customised through careful formatting to suit any age of user, even programs originally designed for adult users such as *Excel* (Microsoft). When you are preparing a spreadsheet for children, think carefully about its design. Large fonts, colour and highlighting can draw attention to key areas and present a more child-friendly appearance.

Recording and graphing data

Graphing programs and spreadsheets enable data to be entered, stored, and presented graphically in a variety of forms. If children have previously used graphing software, for example *Counter Plus* (Black Cat, Granada Learning) or *2Graph* (2Simple), then progression to spreadsheets should be relatively straightforward. The following two case studies show spreadsheets used to record and compare numerical data to aid children's investigations in science and geography.

Case Study: Feed the birds

At the beginning of January Beccy's Year 2 class were concerned that the cold weather would make it difficult for birds to find enough food to eat. The children used books and the internet to research how they could help the birds. They set up some bird tables and feeders and prepared a variety of food to attract different species of birds. The children took great delight in seeing the birds visiting and Beccy saw an ideal opportunity to carry out meaningful data handling and investigative work with her class.

The children used digital video to record the numbers and species of birds that visited the feeders after morning break time and after lunch. The children played back the video and recorded the numbers and types of visiting birds. Data was transferred into a simple spreadsheet, which Beccy had created. Children graphed their data to identify the total numbers and types of birds that visited at particular times each day. They could see from the graphs that total bird numbers were highest in the morning and they began to suggest reasons for this finding; for example the extra availability of food after the children's snack time. This led on to further investigations, such as whether some species preferred particular foods.

Beccy registered her class to take part in the Big Schools' Birdwatch project organised by the RSPB, **www.rspb.org.uk/schoolswatch/about**, and the children contributed their data to a national project.

Links to the National Curriculum

The investigation above began with a question: 'How can we help the birds in wintertime?' Beccy was quick to build on children's interests by adopting an enquiry approach. Through collection and analysis of data children were able to find answers to their questions, and plan new investigations arising from their findings. Digital video was useful for data capture, and a simple spreadsheet program was used to record and present the data (ICT 1a, b, c; 2a). The children had opportunities to observe, explore and ask questions. They worked together to collect evidence to help them answer questions and linked this to simple scientific ideas about how birds are adapted to their environment. These activities have contributed to the development of children's knowledge, skills and understanding, in relation to Scientific Enquiry (Science 1, 2a, b, c, f, g, i); Life Processes and Living Things (Science AT2 1 b, c; 2b, e, 5a, b) and Data Handling (Mathematics 2, 5a, b).

Case Study: Is it raining in Alice Springs?

Laura's Year 4 class developed links with a primary school in Alice Springs, Australia. Children planned to compare and contrast different features of the two places, including the weather. To ensure the class obtained the best possible data, a weather vane, thermometer and rain gauge were sited carefully and the children were taught how to take measurements and record the data (NC: Geography, 2b). A class rota was set up and each morning at 9 a.m. over a two-month period they collected and recorded weather data.

Laura downloaded and adapted a spreadsheet template from the *weather for schools* website **www.weatherforschools.me.uk/index.html**. Embedded graphs on the worksheet meant that the children could see immediately how entering or amending data affected the graph. Children were able to find out for example the windiest and wettest day, the usual direction of the wind when it rains and the highest, lowest and mean average temperatures. Laura's class summarised their key findings and e-mailed it to their link school. Once they had received data from the other school they were able to compare and contrast the weather conditions for the two locations and begin to draw conclusions.

Links to the National Curriculum

Throughout the activity children were involved in asking geographical questions and using geographical vocabulary about the weather (Geography: 1a, 2a). They were able to use weather instruments to collect, record, and analyse evidence and draw conclusions (Mathematics 4 1a–d, 2a–d, Handling Data and Measures; and Geography: 1b, c, 2b). Children developed knowledge and understanding of weather features, patterns and processes in their own locality and discussed similarities and differences with the contrasting locality (Geography: 3a, d, f; 4a; 6a, b). ICT was used to support geographical investigations (ICT AT: 1a–c, 2c, 3a, 5a; Geography: 2f).

In both these case studies the graphing facility of the spreadsheet software enabled the data to be represented quickly and easily in a graphical form. In the Key Stage 2 case study this included comparative line graphs of the mean and maximum temperatures; spreadsheets are a particularly useful graphing tool when continuous data is involved. The automatic functions in a spreadsheet meant children were also able to update their data easily and see the immediate effect of the changes and could concentrate on the interpretation of data rather than the construction of graphs and charts. For a more detailed discussion of this topic see Chapter 2.

The case studies both used the outdoors to provide high-quality learning experiences in line with the aims of the Learning Outside the Classroom Manifesto (DfES, 2006) **www.lotc.org.uk/**.

Activity

You should be able to choose and use the most suitable and most effective resources, including ICT, to support your teaching. Follow this link to the Primary Mathematics Framework and choose a spreadsheet resource to explore. **nationalstrategies.standards.dcsf.gov.uk/search/primary/results/nav:49919**

Consider the following questions:

- What mathematical and ICT skills and concepts would the resource support?
- Where might you use the resource in your mathematics lesson – as part of a mental/oral starter, in the main part of the lesson or in the plenary?
- Would you use the resource with the whole class, groups, pairs or individuals?

The use of spreadsheets for modelling will be explored later in this chapter but you should now have some appreciation of how spreadsheets can support teaching and learning in the classroom.

According to Beare (1993, cited by Baker and Sugden, 2003), spreadsheets

- *are interactive: they give immediate feedback to changing data or formulae;*
- *enable data, formulae and graphical output to be shown together;*
- *give children control and ownership over their learning;*
- *can solve complex problems and handle large amounts of data.*

(Baker and Sugden, 2003, page 22)

Modelling

What is modelling?

In the simplest sense modelling is trying things out and exploring questions that begin: *What happens if ...?* Children are natural modellers and develop mental models during their play to help them make sense of the world around them. Through role play children explore the consequences of different decisions and actions; they try things out and explore situations.

Children can use computers to explore real and imaginary situations safely. Interactive storybooks, that let the reader choose between alternatives in order to progress through a story in different ways, are among the earliest examples of modelling software children will encounter. Adventure and simulation games are particular types of computer models that are discussed in more detail later in the chapter.

Computer models and simulations are widely used for training and research by the military, in medicine, and in the nuclear and airline industries, as they are quicker, cheaper and safer than trying things out in real life. In our day-to-day lives computer models can help us reach a decision in a virtual world before we commit ourselves to the real thing. For example, when planning a kitchen, modelling software allows us to try out a range of different layouts and colour combinations to find the best design for our needs. Computer models help us to solve problems and identify patterns and relationships to develop our understanding of the world.

Modelling in the National Curriculum

Exploring and developing models and simulations is part of the *Developing Ideas and Making Things Happen* strand of the ICT National Curriculum. At Key Stage 1 children try things out and explore what happens in real and imaginary situations (2d) and at Key Stage 2 adventure games, simulations and spreadsheet models help children to identify patterns and relationships and to evaluate the effects of changing variables (2c).

Case Study: Dress teddy

As part of their topic on the weather, and to support work in ICT and PSHE, Jen's Year 1 class is exploring appropriate clothing for different weather conditions. They use the *Dress Barnaby Bear* activity available at **www.ngfl.northumberland.gov.uk/ict/mouseskills/barnaby.html**. Children decide whether Barnaby would like to fly a kite, build sandcastles or a snowman or play in puddles; and choose appropriate clothing from a selection on screen. They *dress* Barney using onscreen *click and drag* actions. Children are encouraged to name the various items of clothing and talk about their choices.

Figure 3.2 Dress teddy (Key Stage 1 modelling activity)

Jen then introduced the class to the program *Do It Yourself* (2Simple) and showed them how they could draw their own teddy bear and a selection of accompanying clothes for different weather types. An example can be viewed at:
www.2simple.com/2diy/examples/samples/adress%20teddy.html.

Jen talked to the children about whether the program was a good representation of reality. Children shared their experience of putting on different items of clothes and how this differed from dragging and dropping items of clothing on screen. Children recognised that the computer model allowed them to make choices and that different decisions produced different outcomes. They learned that models can represent the real world, but they have limitations. The use of simulations and models to support work in science will extend their learning in this area. Jen now plans to give the children opportunities to explore and then create their own fantasy worlds and explore simple adventure games.

Research Focus: Modelling through computer games

Computer games are now part of everyday life for many children; however, for some people associating games with education creates discomfort. Research into computer games in education is not well established, although according to Kirriemuir and MacFarlane (2004) the role that games can play in skills development and the formation of learning communities is increasingly recognised by teachers and parents.

The Computer Games in Education (CGE) project was established to investigate the educational potential of computer games. The project found that gaming requires children to develop a wide range of ICT skills and concepts. Children use prediction and hypothesis in order to devise and evaluate different gaming strategies, and this supports development of critical thinking and problem-solving skills. Motivation is a well-documented strength of computer games and is sustained in and outside of lesson times. Game playing, like learning, can be a social and participatory process and games can provide platforms for social interaction; encouraging teamwork and collaboration as children share ideas, expertise and resources.

According to Oblinger (2004) computer games have pedagogic value in requiring players to activate prior learning and transfer existing knowledge to new contexts and learn from feedback. Games are also learner centred and intrinsically experiential. *Adventure* and *Sim* games, where children build, explore and manage an imaginary environment, can support learning effectively; however MacFarlane et al. (2002) note that teachers need to investigate the relationships between game activities and desired learning outcomes before embedding computer games into a learning context.

Computer simulations

As we have seen, a model is a simplified representation that helps us to understand a real system. A *simulation* is a model that we can interact with outside the constraints of time or space. For example, simulation games such as *SimCity* (Maxis) allow you to create, maintain, populate and unleash natural disasters upon a virtual city. You can watch, in a couple of hours, the consequences of your decisions as they unfold over years or even decades in *game time*. In school children can use simulation software to investigate during a single lesson phenomena that in real life would take much longer: the changing phases of the moon, the number of times heads would win if you tossed a coin ten million times, or how an animal population evolves in response to a changing environment.

Models and computer simulations can describe and depict activities or events which would be difficult, abstract, time-consuming, expensive or dangerous to carry out in real life. There are many examples available online and some are listed at the end of this chapter. As a teacher you should evaluate the extent to which simulations can help to describe and depict a real event and identify, and plan how you will address, any misconceptions which may arise. However, while models and simulations are valuable resources they should not be seen as a substitute for practical investigative work in science or geography.

Activity
The following two links take you to water cycle simulations.
www.crickweb.co.uk/assets/resources/flash.php?&file=watercycle
Click on *play* to run the simulation.
teacher.scholastic.com/activities/studyjams/water_cycle
Click on *play video* to access the simulation.
Explore both simulations carefully and then compare and critically evaluate them in relation to the questions below:

- How successful is each simulation for helping children visualise scientific ideas and aiding their understanding of the key concepts?
- What are the strengths of the simulations? Which features are particularly helpful?
- Are there any misconceptions or misunderstandings which could result from using the simulation? Which features are particularly problematic?
- What would improve the effectiveness of the simulation?
- How might you use these or other simulations with children in your classroom?

Modelling with spreadsheets

In Key Stage 2, spreadsheet models can be used for exploring mathematical problems where calculations are performed and variables changed to observe the effects. One of the most common uses of spreadsheets is financial modelling, where children plan expenditure within a particular budget or predict costs and profits from a school disco or snack bar.

Activity

In Chapter 2, the Case Study: My perfect summer holiday referred you to the following website **www.staff.ucsm.ac.uk/rpotter/holiday**. Follow the link and click on *See the spreadsheet* and open the Excel file. This is an example of a spreadsheet being used for financial modelling. Can you plan a holiday and stay within budget?

Note how the spreadsheet is used to calculate the available spending allowance and the remaining balance as you pay for different holiday items. Note how easily the data can be changed to explore the effects of different choices. By keeping the data simple it is possible to demonstrate to children how the spreadsheet manipulates the data. They may be able to predict and check some of the outcomes using mental strategies.

Think of other topics you could use as the basis for a financial modelling spreadsheet.

Graphical modelling

Modelling can involve developing ideas visually. Children learn to combine and manipulate graphics elements such as shapes, lines and colour to model different outcomes, for example in planning the layout of a playground or designing pizzas.

Object-based graphics software is used for graphical modelling. With these the separate graphical elements which make up an image can be moved, replicated or resized without affecting other onscreen elements. Compare this to Paint packages where an image is saved as a whole and any changes, for example repositioning, impact on the entire image rather than a particular section. Objects can also be *layered*; that is, arranged above or behind each other on the page. The 'Draw' tools in Microsoft Word or Publisher can be used for graphical modelling. Specific software for primary graphical modelling includes *Textease Draw* (SoftEase) and *Spex+* (Aspex Software).

Modelling projects include designing room or garden layouts, providing opportunities for children to try things out and to ask and answer the question, *What will happen if?* in a practical and familiar context. These types of activity help children to understand that graphical models can be used to explore alternatives and identify patterns and relationships. Some graphical modelling tools such as *Spex+* (Aspex Software) include a spreadsheet so that children can see the financial consequences of their choices.

Computer models can be used to broaden children's experiences by helping them extend their ideas or transform their thinking to formulate and test hypotheses and find solutions to problems. Sharing ideas and mental models with others enables children to try things out and explore the effects of making different choices in a safe environment. When using simulations, children can observe the effects of changing variables in an environment where time and space can be compressed.

Data-logging

What is data-logging?

Data-logging has been described as *the capture and storage of variables as they change over time* (Becta, 2003, page 1). Our own bodies constantly measure changing conditions in the environment so that we can respond and stay safe and comfortable. Our eyes monitor light levels; our ears detect changing levels of sound and our skin monitors differences in temperature. We can also use technology to monitor and record variations in light, sound and temperature. We do this in order to better understand and manage our environment, predict how things might change in the future and plan our responses. This process has close links with investigative science.

> ## Case Study: How loud is thunder?
>
> Firdos is teaching her Year 2 class one afternoon when there is a thunderstorm. The children are excited and distracted so she decides to use the event to explore some scientific concepts. Thinking quickly, Firdos plugs a hand-held data-logger into the USB port of a laptop connected to the interactive whiteboard (IWB). The data is automatically displayed as a line graph on the whiteboard and the children are fascinated. They want to know why thunder 'makes the line jump', and if thunder is louder than the school bell. They notice that the sound of the thunder becomes quieter as the storm travels farther away.
>
> Firdos uses the unexpected event and the children's questions to plan future lessons related to the Key Stage 1 National Curriculum for science (AT4 3 c, d). The children measure sounds around the school using sound sensors on a hand-held data-logger. They can see data on the data-logger display screen and download them to the IWB back in the classroom. They make predictions and suggest reasons for their findings. Technology enables children to measure and record data easily in order to explore scientific phenomena such as sounds becoming fainter the further they are from their source.

Firdos was able to respond quickly to maximise the learning potential of an unexpected event because she already knew how to use a data-logger. The data-logger Firdos used is a hand-held device with sensors to measure sound, light and temperature. It has an integral display and can also be plugged into a computer so that data can be analysed using graphing software. It can record and store data over a period of hours or days. This means that data can be collected on field trips and then downloaded and analysed back in school.

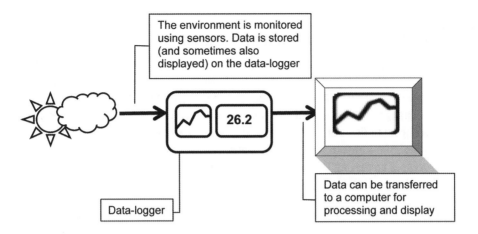

The environment is monitored using sensors. Data is stored (and sometimes also displayed) on the data-logger

26.2

Data-logger

Data can be transferred to a computer for processing and display

Figure 3.3 The data-logging process (not to scale)

Activity

Borrow a data-logger from your placement school or training provider and find out how it works. Most models are only a little larger than a mobile phone and just as easy to use. If there are no instructions with the device try searching the internet; most manufacturers provide instructions and sometimes lesson ideas and other resources on their websites. If you have seen data-loggers before and found them confusing or difficult to use, you will be pleased to know that newer devices for primary schools are robust, reliable and user-friendly.

Plan and carry out your own mini-investigation linked to Key Stage 1 or Key Stage 2 knowledge and understanding in science. For example, you might use light sensors to investigate the opacity of materials by measuring how much light passes through different fabrics (Sc4: 3a, b); or measure the light levels of minibeast habitats to investigate environmental factors affecting life processes and living things (Sc2: 3, 5).

Characteristics of data-logging that support learning

The data-logger enabled the children in Case Study: How loud is thunder? to carry out activities that would have been more difficult or impossible to achieve without it. Without a data-logger children would have had to estimate by ear which sounds were louder or fainter, and it would be difficult for them to present their findings graphically.

A lesson enhanced by technology undoubtedly offers potential benefits for children; however, for inexperienced teachers the risks and challenges can seem daunting. There are a number of things you can do to ensure your lesson is successful, however, and in the next case study we follow Catherine as she plans a Year 6 science lesson.

Case study: Why do penguins huddle?

Catherine's Year 6 class have watched videos of different weather conditions around the world, including some time-lapse video footage of huddling Emperor penguins in Antarctica. The class noticed that the huddled groups constantly shift and change as each penguin tries to make his way to the centre. They decide to investigate to find out why this is, and predict that it is warmer in the centre of the huddle. The context of the investigation is set within the science strand, Life Processes and Living Things (Sc2); considering how different organisms are adapted to their environment.

Catherine begins by identifying the learning objectives for the lesson:

- To know how penguins' behaviour is adapted to their environment (Sc2 5c);
- To make a fair test by changing one factor and measuring the effect while keeping other factors the same. (Sc1 2d);
- To use observations, measurements or other data to draw conclusions (Sc1 2j);
- To identify risks and take action to reduce risks to themselves and others. (Science: breadth of Study, 2b);
- To explore a range of information sources and ICT tools (ICT 5a, b).

Catherine decides to fill plastic drinks with hot, but not boiling, water to represent the penguins. Children have investigated thermal insulation beforehand, when they tested the best material to keep potatoes warm on bonfire night, but they have not used data-logging equipment before. Catherine checks her resources to make sure that she has enough temperature sensors, and that graphing software is installed and working on the class computer, and she performs a quick test of the investigation. As the children are unfamiliar with data-logging equipment Catherine creates some prompt sheets to refer to during the lesson.

Catherine has enough data-loggers to allow the children to work in groups of five. She plans differentiate the activity by asking one group to design a fair test to measure the effect of wind chill on the penguins, using a desk fan. Catherine decides to ask children to record the investigation in groups whilst the data is collected, using drawings, notes and digital cameras. The use of technology offers good opportunities for collaborative work, but group products can be difficult to assess and may not give a true picture of individual progress.

Activity

Draw up a list of the resources you think Catherine used for this lesson. Consider what short, whole class activity Catherine might plan for the beginning of the lesson to demonstrate how the data-logging equipment works.

Consider other ways in which Catherine might differentiate this lesson.

How might the use of technology mask children's individual achievements? Which strategies can Catherine use to assess and record the achievements of individual pupils in this lesson?

Through planning and preparing for her lesson thoroughly, and testing the equipment beforehand, Catherine has minimised the risk of things going wrong. She also plans how to make best use of the help of a teaching assistant or other adult if one is available. She *could* be extremely cautious and ensure that she has some standard thermometers and stopwatches to hand, so that in the unlikely event of total technology meltdown the investigation could still go ahead. You might ask why Catherine bothers to use technology if she has alternative resources. Below, some of the differences between traditional and technology-enhanced investigations are identified, demonstrating how the use of data-loggers can benefit both children and teachers.

The impact of using data-logging technology in investigative science

- Data-loggers overcome constraints of time and distance. Data can be collected over hours or days and from different locations. Data-logging can continue through break time, overnight or during the weekend. Automatic logging also allows for safer data collection; for example, when hot materials are involved, as in the case study above.

- Data collected and graphed automatically allows children to concentrate on their analysis and interpretation. This is not to say that children shouldn't learn how to record data systematically and construct their own graphs; however, this can sometimes become an end in itself. You will decide within the context of your learning objectives whether children's time is best spent on collection and presentation of data or on analysis and interpretation.

- Data-loggers can show data graphed simultaneously or one variable at a time. Children can switch between graph types and discuss which best represents the information. Graphing of events in real time can also help children to understand the purpose of graphs. This supports data-handling skills in mathematics (Ma4: 2).

- Ease of data collection may motivate children to repeat investigations to test different hypotheses. Higher achieving children in particular will appreciate opportunities to set their own challenges and develop higher order thinking skills. This supports investigative skills in scientific enquiry (Sc1).

- Data-logging promotes interest and talk about what is happening. Using a large display such as an IWB means the whole class can be involved in a discussion. Whole-class teaching can also allow teachers to promote open attitudes to scientific enquiry through modelling experimentation and learning from mistakes.

LOGO and control

Research Focus: Inclusion – challenging gender stereotypes in ICT

There is evidence to show that women remain underrepresented in technology-based careers (Beisser, 2006); recent estimates suggest that women make up only a quarter of the IT workforce, and are six times less likely to hold leadership positions in technology industries (McKinney *et al.*, 2008). Denner *et al.*, (2005) suggest that while women are successful in IT work, the problem is on the 'supply side'. Lack of early positive experiences and role models, and social barriers such as gender stereotyping, are blamed for the reluctance of women to pursue IT-qualifications or explore IT related jobs (Mammes, 2004; Denner *et al.* 2005). Mammes (2004) argues girls have fewer opportunities than boys outside school to work with tools, or play with technological toys, an inequality that can be addressed in school through encouraging all children to take equal roles in activities. Denner (2005) suggests that Key Stage 2 is the beginning of a *critical time for intervention* to help girls develop positive attitudes to technology (page 91).

As you will see in the following section, control technology presents opportunities for developing the skills of thinking, problem-solving, teamwork and independent learning that are essential for both sexes in the twenty-first century.

LOGO: A constructionist tool

Constructivist theories of learning suggest that children learn by actively constructing new knowledge, not by having information dispensed to them (Piaget, 1928). *Constructionists* suggest that children learn most effectively when engaged in *constructing personally meaningful artefacts ... such as computer animations, robots, plays, poems, icons, objects, or pictures* (Beisser, 2006, page 10). Theorists of both schools would agree that making time in the curriculum for practical *design and make* activities is of crucial importance.

One aim of the ICT curriculum is to develop children's ability to use technology to achieve planned outcomes. *LOGO* is a computer language developed in the early 1980s by Seymour Papert, a leading constructionist. Using *LOGO*, children can choose and combine simple commands to control robots, screen turtles and other devices. In the next case study Mohammed begins teaching control concepts to his mixed Reception/Year 1 class, using a programmable floor turtle.

Case Study: Big Barn Farm

Basing his idea on the popular BBC children's programme *Big Barn Farm*, Mohammed uses a floor mat which is marked out in squares and Reception/Year 1 children add simply decorated cardboard boxes to represent farmyard buildings, with a pond, barns, and pigsty etc. The *Roamer* floor turtle (Valiant) is placed on the mat and children use its directional buttons to program it to move forward, backwards, left and right. Mohammed pre-programs the floor turtle so that the left and right buttons turn the turtle through 90 degrees on each press, so children do not need any prior knowledge of degrees and angles.

The children decorate the floor turtle with fabric ears and a tail to represent *Dash the Donkey*. Working in teams, they build stories around Dash's travels around the farmyard. They use cards with commands printed on them to plan and record the journey. Mohammed supports children who find this difficult by walking them through the journey themselves, so at each stage they can decide what to do next; for example, move forward three [squares], turn right, then forward one to visit Petal the piglet in her sty. Some children draw or write out a record of the journey.

Figure 3.4 Floor turtle instruction cards for planning routes

Following this activity, Mohammed shows the children how to use the floor turtle to make sounds. He demonstrates how to press the music note (see Figure 3.5) to access the sound feature, and then choose two numbers to press. The first number determines the length of the note: 1 makes the shortest note, 8 makes the longest note. The second number determines how high or low the note is: 1 makes the lowest note, 13 makes the highest note. This means that 1, 1 makes the shortest lowest note, and 8, 13 makes the longest highest note. To begin with Mohammed restricts children to choosing two single digit numbers between 1 and 8. Children talk about the sounds that the floor robot makes and describe which farmyard animals the sounds might represent, for example 8, 1 reminds them of the mooing of a cow.

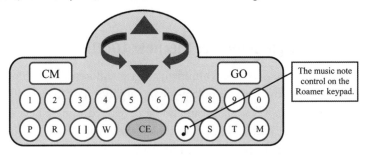

Figure 3.5 The floor turtle keypad

> ## Links to the National Curriculum
>
> Children have the opportunity to develop skills in a number of different cross-curricular subjects during this case study. Working through a narrative to support the robot's journey the children explore speaking and listening (English En1), group interaction and some aspects of drama in role play. Design Technology skills of developing, planning and communicating ideas (DT1a, b, c, d, e) are explored through the design and recording of the robot's route (and also, optionally, through the design and making of the farmyard setting). The activity develops ICT skills within the strand of Developing Ideas and Making Things Happen (ICT 2c) and mathematical skills linked to Mathematics Ma3: 3, understanding properties of position and movement.
>
> Using the sound facility of the *Roamer*, children learn how to control sounds (Music 1b) and explore, choose and organise sounds and musical ideas (2b). They learn how to listen with concentration to sounds made in different ways and begin to understand how pitch and duration can be combined to produce different effects (4a, b, c).

Progression in *LOGO*

Once children have experienced *LOGO* through using floor turtles they are ready to move on to more abstract onscreen activities. Most *LOGO* software has a range of different *turtle* designs for children to control, for example space rockets, racing cars, people or animals. Children can even design their own turtles and set them to exploring a preloaded environment. This links well with the activity designed by Mohammed in the case study above. Using the commands *penup* and *pendown* the children can make the turtle trace its route onscreen.

As they become confident children will learn that commands can be combined to create *procedures*. Imagine a group of children teaching their turtle how to draw a square. They begin by entering each individual command separately using *forward* and *left 90°* commands. They then *teach* the turtle to treat this sequence of commands as a single instruction, which they call *square*. Now they can type in the instruction *square* and the turtle will draw a square using the command it has *learned*.

Computer game design software: the new *LOGO*?

Seymour Papert designed the *LOGO* environment to give children simple tools to control computers and develop creativity and problem-solving abilities. For further discussion of Papert's ideas, see Chapter 1. These skills can also be developed using a new generation of programming languages that enable children to design their own simple computer games. One example is *Scratch*, which was inspired by the popularity of *Lego*™ bricks. Each *Scratch brick* is a block of program code that looks rather like a jigsaw piece. The connectors on the pieces suggest how they should be put together. In *LOGO* children need to type in their commands very precisely and sometimes they make mistakes. *Scratch* is a visual environment that demands very few typing skills. It is designed to enable children aged from six to 16 to design, create, modify and share programs with the minimum of instruction. The online *Scratch* community is a good source of ideas, tutorials and examples of children's projects (**scratch.mit.edu**).

For an example of how one teacher uses Scratch with his Year 2 class see Case Study: Brendan (Chapter 5).

A game design program that develops some similar skills and concepts to *LOGO* and *Scratch*, and is suitable for both Key Stage 1 and Key Stage 2 children is *2DIY* (2Simple), as discussed in the Case Study: Dress Teddy (above).

Controlling models

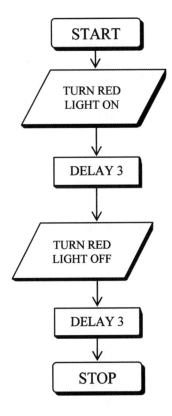

Figure 3.6 A simple flow diagram

Activity

What process does the flow diagram show (Figure 3.6)?

As you probably guessed, the flow diagram above shows a set of instructions for switching on a red light for three seconds then turning it off again.

On paper, sketch out a flow chart for a set of red, amber and green traffic lights.

Add an arrow to connect the last instruction to the first, to loop your instructions so that the lights work continuously.

Think about other processes that you could chart in a similar way, to introduce flow charts to children; for example, moves in a line dance or clapping game.

Explore the National Curriculum for English to identify cross-curricular links with use of procedural language.

Flow diagrams make computer control easier to plan and to explain to others; and they can be kept very simple for younger children. Compare the flow diagram above with the floor robot sequence that Mohammed used with his class in Case Study: Big Barn Farm.

Key equipment for ICT control work

Control box

A control box usually acts as an intermediary between a computer and the model you want to control, for example a (toy) railway crossing. On the control box you will see a set of connectors labelled *outputs*; the computer sends a message through these via the control box to power the bulbs, buzzers and motors on a model.

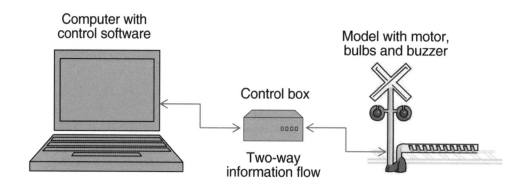

Figure 3.7 Computer control equipment (not to scale)

Some control boxes are free-standing and instructions to control models can be entered directly through the box, without the need for a computer or special software. Examples include *Egg-box* (TTS) and *Learn and Go* (Data Harvest).

Control software
Control software allows you to create and link together instructions to control your model. The software usually includes onscreen simulations, so that children can develop and test their programs on screen before moving on to controlling actual models.

Control models
Many schools will have complete control kits that also include a few preassembled models such as traffic lights, a clown face, lighthouse or fairground ride, but children will also enjoy the challenge of designing and making their own models. These can be made using standard design technology equipment, or assembled from *Lego* or *K'nex* kits.

Links to the National Curriculum
Control technology combines aspects of the National Curriculum Programme of Study for Design Technology (4c: how mechanisms can be used to make things move in different ways, using a range of equipment including an ICT control program) and ICT (2b: how to create, test, improve and refine sequences of instructions to make things happen). It can also help to develop children's use of instructional language (English En3, 7b). It is particularly important that children have a clear purpose for the use of control technology; otherwise the activity becomes purely skill-based without parallel development of the underlying concepts of problem-solving and logical thinking.

Inclusion

The practical and kinaesthetic characteristics of control technology support an inclusive approach to learning. The research focus at the beginning of this section raised issues of gender inclusion through the development of positive attitudes to technology among girls. Children for whom English is an additional language will also flourish where a visual, hands-on approach and collaborative project development is encouraged.

Putting it all together: control and monitoring

Look closely at a control box in school or your training setting. You will see that it has input sockets as well as output sockets; these can be used to send messages through wires, from the sensors on your model to the computer. Sensors can detect and measure light, sound, pressure and temperature, just like the sensors on a data-logger. The computer can be programmed to instruct a model to respond to these inputs in particular ways; for example to change a traffic light, raise or lower a barrier and sound a buzzer when the model train crosses a light sensor or a pressure-sensitive section of track.

Monitoring and control is an important aspect of everyday life and children will be able to think of many examples. Burglar alarms that use motion and heat sensors to detect an intruder and respond with an alarm, pedestrian crossings that respond to a button press to change the traffic lights and supermarket doors that use pressure or motion detectors to open doors automatically, are some systems they will have seen. Encourage children to spot examples of control and monitoring systems on field trips to supermarkets, museums, theme parks and other settings.

Case Study: The weather house

Naomi brought a weather house into school for her Year 6 pupils to examine. A weather house is a pre-computer example of monitoring and control technology that responds to changes in humidity. When the air is moist, a man with an umbrella comes out of the house. When the air is dry, the woman with a sunshade comes out. The principle behind this device is that the man and woman are fixed to a support that is attached to humidity-sensitive material. The material stretches when moist and shrinks when dry.

The children plan and design their own weather houses to respond to environmental conditions. They use light and temperature sensors to control a small motor inside a model house. The children design and make appropriate animal figures for hot and cold conditions. As light and temperature levels rise or fall, motor outputs move the figures in and out of the house.

Taking it further

The case study ends here but the children's learning didn't. Naomi helped the children to continue to explore aspects of control and monitoring technology through researching and developing their own ideas, sparked by the original project. They used the internet to discover other uses of sensors to control devices, and devised real-world problems to solve. Two children developed light-sensitive headlamps for a model car; another group designed an *automatic umbrella*. Others created a driverless bus that navigated using a light sensor. Placed on a white surface with a black border, the bus changed direction whenever it reached the border, moving back onto the white mat.

Naomi supported learning through suggesting and providing resources, and by helping the children to plan, develop, communicate and evaluate their ideas. She fostered each child's self-image as *expert consultant*. The children wore *Ask me about ...* badges: *Ask me about motors; ... about electrical circuits; ... about my Lunar Buggy.*

Teaching simple computer languages such as *LOGO* to children, and encouraging them to design and build computer-controlled models, is not primarily intended to train them to become programmers or robotics engineers, although these are interesting and rewarding careers. The underlying rationale is twofold.

Firstly, age-appropriate grounding in computer programming and control technology helps children to better understand a society which is increasingly dependent upon technology. If children's natural curiosity about the world and technology is nurtured, then they are likely to grow into adults who can question and evaluate the uses to which we put technology, even if they do not themselves become scientists or engineers. Through teaching children how to design, develop and program simple models you will foster their understanding of technology as a phenomenon subject to human responsibility and control.

The second reason for engaging with technology in primary school is pedagogical. To control technology we need to be clear about our goals, think logically, be persistent and choose appropriate resources for a task. Most developments in technology are the result of teamwork, so we also need to develop the ability to share ideas and resources with others, communicate ideas and manage projects effectively. With your help children will take their first steps towards developing these skills in your classroom.

Learning Outcomes Review

In this chapter you have familiarised yourself with aspects of the National Curriculum for ICT that develop children's ability to capture, organise and investigate data, create and explore models and simulations, monitor environmental variables and control devices. You also noted ways in which children's learning in the classroom can be linked to their understanding of the wider world. You have explored different resources and teaching activities that would support the delivery of these areas of the ICT curriculum. The use of *weather* as an integrated theme illustrated how ICT can be embedded in other subjects and support a creative, cross-curricular approach to teaching and learning. You have had opportunities to consider how you might apply this approach to your own teaching, and examples of practice at both key stages have highlighted how you can plan for progression when developing children's ICT capability. You considered ways in which all learners can be included in co-operative and collaborative learning activities, and how individual achievement can be assessed.

Self-assessment questions

1. What type of resources would develop children's ability to:
   (a) capture, organise and investigate data;
   (b) create and explore models and simulations;
   (c) monitor environmental variables and control devices?

2. (a) Identify how you might integrate the above aspects of ICT into a cross-curricular theme such as 'transport'.

   (b) With which curriculum subjects do the above aspects of ICT have particularly strong links?

3. (a) How will you ensure you plan for progression in ICT capability?

   (b) What are some of the ways in which ICT can facilitate collaborative working and how will you ensure all learners are included?

   (c) What must you consider when assessing individual achievement in group work?

Further Information

Spreadsheets

www.kenttrustweb.org.uk/kentict/kentict_subjects_sc_spreadsheets.cfm Ideas and resources for using spreadsheets in science.

Modelling

BBC Schools Science Clips
www.bbc.co.uk/schools/scienceclips/index_flash.shtml includes a range of computer simulations for both Key Stage 1 and 2.

The Northumberland Grid for Learning
ngfl.northumberland.gov.uk/ict/qca/ks2/unit5A/default.htm provides a complete set of resources and teacher notes for teaching children about graphical modelling.

www.kenttrustweb.org.uk/kentict/kentict_subjects_sc_simulations.cfm Links to a range of science simulations on the Internet.

Data-logging

rogerfrost.com/primar.htm Roger Frost's data-loggerama site includes data-logging ideas and links to resources.

www.educationict.org.uk/dataloggers.htm includes an introduction to using the LogIT Explorer data-logger, lesson plans and teacher notes, all from the Scottish Border Council.

Logo, control and monitoring

ngfl.northumberland.gov.uk/english/littleredship/LRS%20control/LRS%20control.htm Simple onscreen control activities for Key Stage 1.

www.bbc.co.uk/schools/gcsebitesize/ict/measurecontrol/1logocontrolrev1.shtml provides an overview of LOGO and includes simple practice activities. Highly recommended as a LOGO introduction or refresher.

www.softronix.com/logo.html Download a free version of LOGO.

Further Reading

simonhaughton.typepad.com/ict
Simon Haughton's ICT blog is well worth a visit, with practical and exciting ideas trialled in his own classroom. Examples of Simon's resources include a scheme of work and resources for teaching spreadsheets, and using simulation software with a Year 3 class and *Scratch* programming.

References

Baker, J. and Sugden, S. (2003) Spreadsheets in Education – The First 25 Years. *eJournal Of Spreadsheets in Education*, 1(1): 18-43.

Becta (2003) Technical paper. *Datalogging*, 35(1): 1–10. Available at **www.becta.org.uk/**.

Becta (2006) *Computer games in education project.* Available at **research.becta.org.uk/index.php?section=rh&catcode=&rid=13595&pagenum=1&NextStart=1**, (accessed 23 August 2010).

Beisser, S. (2006) An examination of gender differences in elementary constructionist classrooms using Lego/Logo instruction. *Computers in the Schools*: 7–19.

Denner, J., Werner, L., Bean, S. and Campe, S. (2005) The Girls Creating Games program: strategies for engaging middle-school girls in information technology. *Frontiers: A Journal of Women Studies*, 26 (1): 90–98.

DfES (2006) *Learning Outside the Classroom Manifesto*. Nottingham: DFES.

Kirriemuir, J. and McFarlane, A. (2004) *Literature Review in Games and Learning*. Graduate School of Education, University of Bristol.

Mammes, I. (2004) Promoting girls' interest in technology through technology education: a research study. *International Journal of Technology and Design Education*, 14 (2): 89–100.

MacFarlane, A., Sparrowhawk, A. and Heald, Y. *Report on the educational use of games, TEEM*, available at **www.teem.org.uk**, (accessed 23 August 2010).

McKinney, V.R., Wilson, D.D., Brooks, N., O'Leary-Kelly, A. and Hardgrave, B. (2008) Women and men in the IT profession. *Communications of the ACM*, 51(2): 81–4.

Oblinger, D. (2004) The next generation of educational engagement. *Journal of Interactive Media in Education*, 2004 (8): 1–18.

Ofsted (2009) The importance of ICT: information and communication technology in primary and secondary schools, 2005/2008. Available at **www.ofsted.gov.uk/**, (accessed 24 August 2010).

Piaget, J. (1928) *The Child's Conception of the World.* London: Routledge and Kegan Paul.

Siegle, D. (2005) An introduction to using spreadsheets to increase the sophistication of student projects technology. *Gifted Child Today,* 28(4): 50–55.

Williams, J. and Easingwood, N. (2003) *ICT and Primary Science.* London: Routledge Falmer.

4. Collaborating, communicating and sharing information
Ed Tyson and Eamonn Pugh

> ### Learning Outcomes
>
> By the end of this chapter you should:
> - understand what is meant by the term 'collaborative tools';
> - be able to identify the potential benefits and risks associated with children's use of Web 2.0 technologies;
> - be aware of the means by which information can be exchanged and the alternative approaches to meeting the needs of other audiences and participants;
> - recognise ways in which collaborative and communication tools can support children's learning across the curriculum and outside the classroom.
>
> **Professional standards for QTS**
>
> Q8 Have a creative and constructively critical approach towards innovation, being prepared to adapt their practice where benefits and improvement are identified.
>
> Q17 Know how to use skills in literacy, numeracy and ICT to support their teaching and wider professional activities.
>
> Q23 Design opportunities for learners to develop their literacy, numeracy and ICT skills.
>
> Q24 Plan homework or other out-of-class work to sustain learners' progress and to extend and consolidate their learning.
>
> Q25a Use a range of teaching strategies and resources, including e-learning, taking practical account of diversity and promoting equality and inclusion.
>
> Q30 Establish a purposeful and safe learning environment conducive to learning and identify opportunities for learners to learn in out-of-school contexts.

Introduction

In this chapter you will read how the use of collaborative tools such as wikis, blogs and podcasts can be used effectively to develop children's skills, knowledge and their learning while also providing appropriate and relevant contexts to communicate with others within a safe environment. The revised National Curriculum (1999) amended the former title of Information Technology to the expanded Information Communication Technology. This placed greater emphasis on the increasing role the internet was playing in helping schools to communicate outside of the classroom, principally with e-mail, and early forms of video conferencing.

Web 2.0 technologies have the ability to transcend the walls of the classroom, to enable children to reach out to other audiences and to be able to work with other pupils around the world (see Chapter 9), using collaborative tools that allow several users to develop and enrich the online content. This is likely to significantly enhance the authoring experience for both the pupils and ultimately the teacher.

Digital technologies allow increasingly flexible arrangements and with the ease of sharing information and/or files; children are more able and willing to engage in learning outside of normal schooling by using school learning platforms. The low cost (or freeware) of socially collaborative tools like wikis and blogs enables many more learners to engage with activities at home, which may be initiated in school. This does depend on the children accessing a computer and network connection or other mobile wireless technologies. The dependence on costly software and a fixed location such as a desktop computer based in the classroom has been removed. Now sharing and collaboration can take place at any time and almost anywhere.

While this chapter deals with collaborative technologies and their potential impact on teaching and learning, it is important that we consider *how* and *when* the digital tools should be employed. Creating a wiki in class might seem a *cool idea*, as it will undoubtedly have great initial appeal. However, if the content or methodology for the chosen application is ill-suited the project will end, without reaching the level of engagement and quality that the teacher had initially intended. This has often been blamed in the past on the failure of the technology to deliver, but pedagogical practice needs to be carefully considered. John and Wheeler (2008) urge the use of the right tools for the right job.

> *Outside of the classroom, social technologies such as wikis and blogs are providing the impetus for expert communities of practice to evolve, emerge and connect together, and this movement is set to become even more influential...The onus is now on teachers to attempt to exploit these technologies to promote new forms of interactive learning.*

(John and Wheeler, 2008, page 128)

Children are often engaged in group work or working collaboratively. Therefore the emphasis in this chapter is the impact that digital technologies can have on the widening role of peer feedback. In Chapter 5 the focus is on refining and improving work related to the individual's need for formative assessment. Issues concerning e-safety and online social networking are covered in Chapter 6 but some reference will be made in this chapter to safeguarding children when using collaborative tools and when sharing or communicating with others.

Collaborative tools

Until relatively recently there have been few collaborative tools for use within the school context. This did not stop creative teachers developing collaborative practices within the classroom using existing tools both in school and between schools. The main vehicle for children communicating and file sharing (using the file attachment option) was e-mail; further back in time it relied on postal communications (letters). This limited form of collaboration was linear as it relied on the trafficking between recipients or groups; and changes made to a single file were not easily communicated to others without multiple copies flying about via the internet.

Along with the development of social networking sites like *Facebook* (**www.facebook.com**) and *Bebo* (**www.bebo.com**) has come a range of Web 2.0-related tools such as **wikis**, **blogs**, and **podcasts**; we will look at the features of each of these tools in order to gain a deeper understanding of their capabilities.

Wikis (What I know Is) are essentially web pages that can be quickly edited on the screen and then posted on to the internet. Each page comes with an important feature of a 'page history'; this allows you to view the changes that have been made, by whom and when. The most well-known wiki is the online digital encyclopaedia, *Wikipedia* (**en.wikipedia.org**). Many thousands of users contribute to the ongoing development of information; its strength and weakness relies on the contributions its collaborators make and the accuracy of their information.

Weblogs, often referred to as **blogs**, are easily created and allow the user to publish their material to the internet. They vary considerably in type and format and while often considered as an individual activity they can be highly interactive or have more than one person involved in their construction. People have occasionally confused blogs with online diaries; however, while some blogs exist in this form, many do not. The confusion probably arises from the fact that blog entries are chronological in order. Blogs can be enhanced with the inclusion of hyperlinks, digital images and video to enliven the text. Most text content on a blog is short and concise and features articles about current issues or themes in the world that the *blogger* is interested in. Part of the fascination of blogging relies on the blog being read by an audience and having someone *post* a comment. An example of a current blog can be found at *Mashable* (**www.mashable.com** or try the *Guardian* news blog (**www.guardian.co.uk/tone/blog**).

Podcasts differ from the two previous digital tools as they are essentially sound recordings or audio files. What makes a podcast different from a simple audio file is that the podcast is shared with many different users rather than sitting forlornly on a desktop computer. Podcasts can be created on a wide range of software utilising an *mp3* player and/or recorder. A source of free software that enables people to record and store podcasted material is *Audacity* (**audacity.sourceforge.net**). You can also utilise *Skype* software (**www.skype.com**) for creating and generating video podcasts or for video conferencing. It is important to remember that podcasts need a site to be hosted on like a blog or other social networking service; otherwise they remain simply an audio file.

There is an ever increasing range of social networking tools, and the development of audio- and video-based products like podcasting and video publishing and their related sites like Flickr (**www.flickr.com**) and YouTube (**www.youtube.com**) will continue to proliferate. The task for teachers and educators, as noted earlier by John and Wheeler (2008), is to select and use the tools when and where appropriate. This is a skill that the next section will develop.

Activity

Reflect on your own use and engagement with Web 2.0 (interactive) technologies by using the table below as a framework for developing your own practice.

Web 2.0 technologies	Wikis	Blogs	Podcasts
Personal usage Have you used this type of digital tool before? If so, list the sites that you are familiar with for each of the technologies.			
Personal creation Have you ever constructed a site or file that used this type of digital tool before? If so, list the things that you have created and the frequency with which you use them.			
Professional usage Have you used any of these tools professionally either for your own use or with a class/group of children? List the type of activity you have done in the corresponding columns.			
Professional creation Which of these technologies have you used with pupils in order to create social network resources within either the classroom or school environment?			

Table 4.1: Auditing own and professional engagement with Web 2.0 technologies

You may find it beneficial to view the potential of one of the collaborative tools; do this by either going to the website directly or looking for video examples on *YouTube* (**www.youtube.com**).

Research Focus: Digital literacy

This research section focuses on some of the issues related to the need for both teachers and children to develop digital literacy skills. Owen et al. (2006) raise the concern that teachers will lag behind pupils in their ability to professionally utilise digital technologies in the classroom. They caution that many professionals will not acquire the knowledge themselves due to lack of time for professional development and the resistance to change, especially related to ICT, that pervades some schools.

$\rightarrow$

The Technology Enhanced Learning phase of the Teaching and Learning Research Programme (TLRP-TEL, 2008) commentary on *Education 2.0* suggests that teachers and educators should move beyond asking whether the current Web 2.0 technologies work in the classroom. They believe we should be focusing on how education might be reshaped by the use of these digital tools and how we can blend technology and pedagogy to address the learning needs of today and the near future.

The Rose Review (2009) of the Primary Curriculum commented that all children would need to be familiar with *digital literacy* if they were to become successful future citizens. In the most recent report from Becta (2010) on digital literacy, research has shown that some pupils lack sufficient digital skills to engage critically with the technology and to use it effectively, and that there is a need for all teachers to embed digital technologies into the curriculum. However, currently it is unclear how teachers will be supported in their developmental needs and what the implications are for both the funding of technological change in the classroom and research into effective practice.

Children's use of Web 2.0 technologies: potential risks and benefits

One of the most significant benefits of using Web 2.0 digital tools is the increased collaborative element that they bring to the classroom and the ease with which children can access them at home and in out-of-school activities. The fact that information can now be stored *in the cloud*, a reference to the functionality of the wireless internet, makes it possible to work anywhere using a laptop or other mobile technology. This freedom from the classroom does come with a cautionary reminder about the need to safeguard and protect pupils from accessing unsuitable material and emphasises the need for them to understand safe operating procedures, such as not revealing personal details, as recommended in the Byron Review (DCSF, 2008). One criterion for considering the potential benefits will be the degree of *collaboration* that a specific tool can support and this should also be set against a continuum of *how secure* the resource is, or can be made to be. You also need to be aware of the term *digital literacy* which Becta (2010, page 4) defines as a combination of:

- functional technology skills;
- critical thinking;
- collaboration skills; and
- social awareness.

Digital literacy is, therefore, knowing about how and when to use ICT effectively; from gathering and presenting information and being critically able to analyse and evaluate it, to using media online in a safe and sensible manner and being able to work and collaborate with others.

Wikis (What I Know Is)

Wikis are essentially web pages that can be quickly edited on screen and then posted on to the internet; they are easy to set up and are virtually cost free. Like *Wikipedia* (**en.wikipedia.org**), their strengths lie in their ability to allow contributors to add and develop material in a collaborative process. The criticisms of *Wikipedia* have been that it contains many inaccuracies or unsubstantiated articles. Some schools and institutions have banned its use by their pupils, yet the fact remains that for many people it is a first point of call, and has increased young people's engagement in looking for information in an encyclopaedia. Recent research into *Wikipedia* has revealed that it is no more inaccurate than any other online encyclopaedias, even those which have subscription charges (Carrington and Robinson, 2009). The point is that wikis in themselves are tools to be used by groups of individuals and it is up to that *community* to police the systems, to generate their own level of *appropriateness* and *validity*. Within the classroom there is an opportunity for the children to set their own rules and to establish the *correctness* of the content. Equally, being critical of the material and cross-referencing information sources are essential research skills that all lifelong learners need to develop (see Chapters 2 and 8).

Wikis are probably best used with a group or for a class activity to enable several users to collaborate and develop the content. A class wiki on *Harry Potter* may be more useful than individual blogs about 'favourite characters' from the series of novels, as pupils could collaborate and develop a knowledge base. Carrington and Robinson (2009, page 73) define four types of *core uses for wikis*, these being:

- *knowledge management;*
- *narrative builder;*
- *resource aggregator;*
- *value adding.*

It is important to reflect that wikis and blogs are *multimodal* and that it is not just the text that is important; careful thought has to be given to the presentation and other features such as interactive elements. These include hyperlinks, comments or feedback boxes; digital images, both photographic and video; plus sound files including music and podcasts. An excellent example is Room 25 at Katikati Primary School in New Zealand (**kkps-r25.wikispaces.com**), or why not start your own wiki at *wikispaces.com* (**www.wikispaces.com**)?

As mentioned earlier, care must be taken in selecting software and hosting sites that allow you to feel secure about protecting and safeguarding children. Therefore you need to consider what levels of security are needed or appropriate. There are a number of web-based wiki sites that feature password or login systems which restrict access to ensure that only pupils and teachers, or invited groups, can interact and collaborate within the site. This is sometimes referred to as a *walled garden* approach.

One of the unique features of a wiki is the *edit page* and its facility to recall previous amendments and also to record who made the changes. While this doesn't prevent all the problems of children deleting the content or adding hurtful comments, it does reduce the tensions as the wiki can be monitored by the teacher and the children who are contributing. Remember, the point of using a wiki is to develop collaborative practices and the group will need to develop their own strategies for appropriate academic and social behaviour.

Wikis score highly on collaborative practices when used with a class or group of children and their security can be improved if only selected users are given access. While this enables a high level of safety it also reduces potential interactions and collaborations that might exist if they are based openly on the web. Children and teachers in Key Stages 1 and 2 will probably feel more secure using a protected, walled garden approach, with limited and controlled access to a class- or school-based wiki.

Case Study: Collaborative Year 5 class wiki

Ciara and her Year 5 class decided to create individual blogs on the school's learning platform *Moodle* (**moodle.org**), about the lives and music of famous composers. After a discussion with the ICT subject leader Ciara altered her approach by setting up a wiki site to allow children to work in small collaborative groups. In addition, they would be able to add to the knowledge of the whole class through making changes to other pages. Ciara used the features within *Moodle* to create the class wiki and to develop her own knowledge of how wikis work. As an administrator for the site Ciara was able to give herself permissions to ensure the security and to manage the children's creative inputs.

To develop children's understanding of what wikis look like and their functions, Ciara and her class studied Wikipedia, and then looked at some examples of class-based wikis (see kkps-r25.wikispaces.com). She divided the class into mixed-ability groups and gave them each a composer to find information about. The initial information gathering was done in the school's library as Ciara thought it was important that the children recognise that information comes from different sources, including books, CD-ROMs, etc. She also designed a page template on the wiki as a framework for children's writing and to scaffold their learning.

The children quickly engaged with the information-gathering process, using a variety of sources including the internet, and then began the process of checking and editing the content collaboratively on their wiki page; Ciara checked the content before it was published. The children were keen to upload images and examples of the composer's music and create their own podcasts. After investigating copyright issues, Ciara explained to the class that they must state where the image had come from and/or the creator's name, including a hyperlink to the original source. Only short musical extracts could be used and again the

$\rightarrow$

source and owner of the music must be displayed. She found that a lot of this information was displayed on Wikipedia.

Because the materials and programs being used were Web 2.0 tools the children were able to access their work at home and collaborate outside school time through the school's learning platform. This gave rise to more material and pages being added. Ciara did spot after a while that content and engagement were dropping, so she invited the class to review the work of other groups, after carefully reminding them about the *two stars and a wish* approach to evaluating other pupils' work. This evaluation process also prompted checking for errors and omissions. At this point Ciara felt that the children were responsible enough to make minor changes as these could be tracked using the *page history* tool to ensure that vital information was not lost. This led to a further wave of engagement, with different groups and individuals cross-checking information and searching for meaning and consensus.

After reviewing the wiki project Ciara felt that the children had gained much through working collaboratively both in school and at home. They had learned to engage with information and display it effectively, rather than just 'cutting and pasting' chunks of information from an online encyclopaedia. The children's critical thinking skills had been engaged and while the technology had a motivating force it was primarily the vehicle through which children engaged with their learning and developed digital literacy skills.

Links to the National Curriculum

During this activity Ciara's class were engaged in reading for information (English, En2, 3a, b, c, d, e) using print- and ICT-based sources (En2 9b). They recognised that information can exist in different forms, through their use of multimedia texts and internet sources (ICT, Finding Things Out 1a), and prepared and checked their information using ICT tools (ICT 1b, c). In the children's writing they focused on the subject matter and how to convey it in sufficient detail for the reader (En3 9b), using language and style suitable to the reader (En3 1c). They developed their musical understanding of a range of composers and their music and edited and combined sounds using their ICT skills (Music 5 d, e). The children were able to create and refine their work (ICT 2a) and were able to exchange and share information (ICT 3a, b) as well as being sensitive to the needs of their audience and the need to be accurate and factual. The children were also able to review and discuss their work to improve it further (ICT 4a, b, c).

Activity

Consider the following questions, with reference to Case Study: Collaborative Year 5 class wiki and what you have already read about wikis and Web 2.0 technologies.

- Evaluate Ciara's approach. How might you have done it differently and what do you think the outcome might be?
- This project was carried out over a half-term; do you feel that this is an appropriate amount of time to engage with all the aspects of learning? How might you approach a similar project?
- Using Carrington and Robinson's (2009) definition of *core uses for wikis: knowledge management; narrative builder; resource aggregator; and value adding*, analyse the case study above. Which definition(s) do you think are most suitable for the class wiki Ciara designed?
- Familiarise yourself with the term *digital literacy* by considering the four elements that Becta (2010) defines as:
  - functional technology skills;
  - critical thinking;
  - collaboration skills; and
  - social awareness.

Apply these criteria to the case study above. Do you feel that they were all equally addressed and if not, why not?

Weblogs (Blogs)

Blogs are extremely popular and are used by a wide variety of people, from children to amateur and professional news reporters, and they vary hugely in their style and format. The main thing that keeps blogs alive and *bloggers blogging* is the feedback they receive, usually in the form of comments or *postings*. You may want to look at some popular blogs like *Reading Matters* (**kimbofo.typepad.com/readingmatters**). If you intend to use them with a class of children and want to get them reading and possibly posting comments, try *Puffin* (**www.thepuffinblog. typepad.com**) or *Harry Potter* (**harrypotter.savvy-cafe.com**). These sites are suitable for children to read, and post comments to, provided they are aware of e-safety guidelines (see Chapter 6).

Blogs offer similar opportunities to wikis, but the focus is perhaps slightly different. Wikis are more about a *community* developing knowledge on a subject or topic. Blogs tend to be more individualised (although there is nothing to stop you having a class blog) and give the 'blogger' a great sense of ownership of their site or page. Bloggers can design the look of the site, adding various tools and links to give it a personalised feel. This is something that is more difficult to achieve with a Wiki, as groups will need to agree on the layout and the appropriateness of tools and content. It is possibly and probably desirable for children to set up a *blogroll*, which is a simple collection of links to other sites and/or blogs. This helps to establish a sense of identity with individuals and groups who share similar interests or ideas. The most important feature of a blog is the comments facility or *postings*. Bloggers rely on the feedback they receive, as it enables the individual to respond to fresh ideas from others, and acts as a motivational device to encourage them to keep adding more authored text or related media, e.g. podcasts. Equally it is important for the person *posting* as this interactive element serves both the individual who is posting comments and the blogger who is receiving them. This is similar to an e-mail dialogue, but the difference is that the blogger is able to use a wider variety of media, making the blog visual rather than purely text based. You could set up a blog of your own; it is easy to do, and this is the best way to get to grips with the concepts of blogging: try *blogger.com* (**www.blogger.com**)

The security of blogs is important and you will need to refer to the school's policy on acceptable use of the internet (see Chapter 6) before you start signing your class up for individual blogs. As with wikis, blogs can be designed to give restricted access so that only selected users can post comments, and some blog services include features that restrict postings until cleared by the teacher. Hosting blogs on a school-based intranet or learning platform reduces the risks and provides a safe environment for children to develop their blogging skills. Blogs score lower on the collaborative scale, but they are an important tool for developing the authoring skills of the individual and can be designed to develop a sense of community identity.

Podcasting and podcasts

Podcasts are considerably different from either blogs or wikis. They rely on either individuals or small groups creating an audio file and then adding it to a wiki- or blog-based site. The level of collaboration can be quite low unless children are working in groups to produce a radio-style programme. That said, podcasts do address a different aspect of learning which would aid children's development of their speaking and listening skills. Blogs and wikis essentially help to develop a range of writing styles; podcasts enable children to express their ideas through speech and/or music and sound effects. It is also possible to create video podcasts, which allow another set of presentation skills to be engaged with and developed. Examples of podcasts are available on the *BBC* site (**www.bbc.co.uk/podcasts**) like *Time and Tune* (**www.bbc.co.uk/podcasts/series/timeandtune**). You can also download *Audacity* (**audacity.sourceforge.net**) to help you record your own. It is also worth checking your own or your school-based computer as it may already contain software that will enable you to record and play audio files in *mp3* (podcasting) format.

From a security point of view, podcasts in themselves present a low-level threat; however, they will need a site host, and this presents increased risk (as discussed earlier). Podcasts also need to be checked to ensure the content is appropriate and not offensive. Their greatest value is in the use of recorded speech and sound to enable children to develop their skills in speaking and listening.

Case Study: Looking after the school environment

Jasmine and her Year 2 class were keen to present some information relating to their environmental geography and science topic where they looked at the wildlife in the school grounds and considered how they could help establish better conditions for the animals they had found. Initially Jasmine thought about the children writing some text to accompany a series of digital photographs the children had taken. She decided against this as she felt that the class would benefit from an activity more related to the speaking and listening strand of the English curriculum (EN1). The class listened to some examples of podcasting by the RSPB (**www.rspb.org.uk/podcasts/naturesvoice.aspx**). Having researched the *National Strategies* website (**nationalstrategies.standards.dcsf.gov.uk**), Jasmine found an article on *ICT application in literacy* about podcasts related to Key Stage 1, and she felt that a podcast was a suitable medium for the children. She also understood that recording a podcast and placing it on the internet was an activity suggested for upper Key Stage 2. Jasmine felt that with some care and attention she could modify the activity and host it on the school's learning platform as this would provide a secure and safe environment.

Jasmine organised the class into small groups, giving them each an activity card related to a digital photograph that had been taken previously in the school grounds, and asked the children to create a 30-second talk on a topic such as litter or nest boxes. The children made simple storyboards and wrote down key words and phrases. They practised in their groups the parts they would say and the order of who would speak. With the help of a Teaching Assistant (TA) each group recorded their podcast using software similar to *Audacity*. The recordings were played back to each group and there was a further opportunity to edit out some of the pauses, giggles and interruptions, again with the help of an adult. When all the podcasts were completed Jasmine and the TA created pages within the class folder of the school's learning platform and with some help from the children they added the photographs and accompanying podcasts. This was then replayed to the class over the week.

Later on in the term during a parents' meeting Jasmine and her class were congratulated for their digital presentation, which the children had been very enthusiastic about, by many of the parents, who had been able to view the materials online through the school's learning platform.

Links to the National Curriculum

Jasmine's use of technology was the result of considering how best to record the children's use of speaking and listening (EN1 1a, b, c, d, e, f; 2a, b, c, d, 3a, b), as well as developing aspects of their written work by making plans and drafting out their ideas (EN3 2a, b, c). The use of digital photographs gave her the impetus to consider recording the children's speech and creating a podcast (ICT 1a, b, c; 2a; 3a, b; 4a; 5a, b). Due to the nature of the children's topic, 'caring for the environment', it also provided cross-curricular links with science, geography and PHSE (Science Sc2 2b, e; Geography 1b; 5c; PHSE 1b; 2e, g).

The use of the ICT facilitated the children's learning and enabled them to learn more effectively and efficiently. The hosting on the school's learning platform, while initially chosen because of e-safety concerns, enabled the parents to see and hear for themselves the work that the children had done in class.

Activity

Jasmine's work with the children benefited from her research and her willingness to try out technologies that were unfamiliar to her. In the previous activity you were asked to complete an audit of your personal and professional engagement with four types of Web 2.0. From your reading in this section of the chapter, including Case Study: Looking after the school environment and your own personal experience, consider the questions below.

- When would the use of a class-based blog be most appropriate and which aspects of the National Curriculum do you think it would cover most effectively?
- What security protections might be needed with setting up individual class blogs and how would you attempt to reduce any malicious postings?
- How might you host children's podcasts without a school-based learning platform?
- Jasmine thought about the speaking and listening needs of the children (EN1) and how she could develop their skills. Do you feel this approach was justified or could she have achieved a similar outcome without the use of ICT?

Are there any of the tools discussed above that you are still unfamiliar with? If so you may like to select one of the technologies and develop your own practice. Select one that might be best suited to your situation and reflect on previously taught topics. Consider how one or more of the technologies above may have enhanced these topics.

Research Focus: Pedagogical issues

This research section focuses on the need for teachers to consider how they might incorporate digital literacy tools into their classroom practice. Higgins' (2003) review of research concluded that the changing nature of ICT offered many new possibilities for teachers and that 'digital literacy' has the potential to make learning more effective and efficient. However, change of cultural practices within

→

school may impact more slowly due to the nature of the curriculum and existing classroom practices such as assessment. The DfES (2005, page 28) report *Harnessing Technology* stated that: *new technology can transform the experience of learning for all learners,* a point that Grant (2006, page 10) develops in a small-scale study of wikis, saying that they had the *potential to support knowledge-building networks* and are able to help classrooms *engaged in collaborative learning.* She also pointed out that wikis themselves don't build communities of practice; this is a skill that teachers need to develop and nurture in their children.

Owen *et al.* (2006) have commented that along with the development of text-based tools on the internet there is a shift towards collaborative use of online documents and an ever growing use of podcasting and video media. They also expressed concerns regarding children blogging on the internet and their relatively poor understanding of e-safety. The Technology Enhanced Learning phase of the Teaching and Learning Research Programme (TLRP-TEL, 2008) also reminds us that the growing use of Web 2.0 tools by children and young people in the home presents a range of challenges. There is obviously a growing need for children's informed use of digital literacy skills so that they can recognise issues of copyright alongside the development of their critical thinking and internet safety skills.

Information exchange and meeting the needs of other audiences

Ever since the humble arrival of the computer in the primary classroom back in 1981 and its ongoing transformation into the networked and internet-enabled device of today, teachers and children have had choices to make over how might they present their work. Initially these choices were quite limited but with the development of simple word processors into multimedia programs which can handle images and sounds, the choices have continued to widen. In some cases children have been restricted by the teacher's own abilities and understanding of the capabilities of particular programs.

Work completed on a computer is stored digitally and it can be easily transformed into another format. This *provisionality* (see Chapter 5) is at the heart of the transformational nature of ICT. A child's work created in a desk-top publisher like *Textease* (Softease) can be easily transferred into a presentation program like *Smart notebook* (Smart) simply by copying and pasting the relevant information between the two programs. The ability to recreate material in different forms also makes it easier to adapt and alter the content for a range of audiences. A poem can be typed out in *Word* (Microsoft) and then stored, reopened and the text copied and pasted into *Photostory* (Microsoft), with the inclusion of suitable digital images, for a presentation to another class. It could be altered again with the text from *Word* being combined with the digital photographs into presentation software like *PowerPoint* (Microsoft) and this time enhanced with the use of animations to make the poem more engaging for a younger audience.

The growing range of tools and software makes the choices of both the teacher and the children more difficult, as a certain level of skill and familiarity with the programs is more likely to draw out a higher quality outcome. Sutherland *et al.* (2009) suggest that limiting choice can be more effective for meeting the learning outcomes, but that this can impact on the overall quality. Bennett *et al.* (2007, page 21), in their model for *ICT capability – the global level,* believe that initially young children will need to be guided in order to develop their skills and techniques. This, however, should diminish over time, as the children's *independent choices* increase.

The principal development in computing in recent times has been the ability to communicate and collaborate more effectively. You may remember we discussed earlier that e-mail and video conferencing initially opened up new audiences between schools and between trusted individuals or organisations. Some schools have also projected their presence onto the internet and others have developed learning platforms for access outside of the normal school day; all of these are methods of communication. Web 2.0 tools have greatly increased the range of options that exist; we have looked at **wikis, blogs** and **podcasts,** and have considered their advantages and weaknesses. It is time to look at a number of collaborative programs currently available and consider how these might be used for different audiences.

You may be familiar with other web-sharing sites like *Flickr* (**www.flickr.com**), or *YouTube* (**www.youtube.com**), where you can distribute your own digital images and video, but these sites have limited regulation and care should be taken when viewing the content with children. Sites which promote collaborative working and have a good level of security that are designed for use with primary age children include *j2e* (**www.j2e.com**), *Storybird* (**storybird.com**) and *PrimaryPad* (**www.primarypad.com**). *PrimaryPad* is explored further in Chapter 5.

Case Study: Year 4 healthy living newspaper articles

Ibrahim and his class of Year 4 children combined a science topic on 'Healthy Living' with the ICT scheme of work for Unit 4A: Writing for different audiences (**www.standards.dfes.gov.uk/schemes2/it/itx4a/?view=get**), to produce a class newspaper with articles about healthy eating, exercise and staying healthy. In their science and PHSE lessons the children learned the scientific knowledge and in PHSE they discussed issues of drug taking and lack of exercise. In their ICT sessions they learned how to use the spelling and grammar checker along with tools such as the thesaurus. Once the class had mastered the basics of onscreen editing and enhancement, Ibrahim introduced the children to *j2e* (**www.j2e.com**). As the pupils had already been using the desktop publishing software *Textease* (Softease) they made the transition quite easily, as they were already familiar with a similar product. The class was organised into teams of four and asked to engage collaboratively to produce a newspaper-style report for the school website. The *j2e* program enabled them to work individually, but they were able to edit and make comments about the work as it developed within the group. *J2e* includes a speech engine, which enabled some of the children, who were less confident at reading, to

→

be supported both in school and at home. As the material was hosted on the school learning platform many of the children chose to work on their tasks outside of school. This enhanced the quality of the articles, as the children often found useful links and images which they discussed before adding them to their work. The work was laid out in columns to give a newspaper feel, and the text was reviewed by the class to approve its suitability and style.

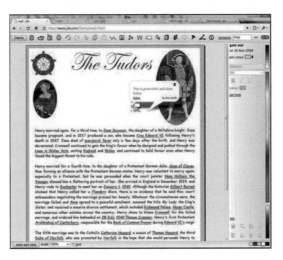

Figure 4.1 j2e screenshot (**www.j2e.com**)

Screenshot taken with kind permission from *www.j2e.com* from their demonstration video 'What is j2e?'. The text shown is taken from *Wikipedia* (**en.wikipedia.org/wiki/Henry_VIII_of_England**) and reproduced under *creative commons* licence (**creativecommons.org/licenses/by-sa/3.0**).

When the articles were completed and checked by the teacher they were uploaded to the school website; any personal details having been removed for safeguarding purposes. This enabled the materials to be viewed by a wider audience. The class were excited about their work being posted onto the internet; something which their parents and extended family members could also enjoy.

In a follow-up activity some of the children asked if they could take their newspaper articles and translate them into German, which was the school's preferred choice of Modern Foreign Language (MFL). As the software in *j2e* supports this, the children were able to easily alter some of the articles and, having gained the approval of the languages specialist, these pages were also added to the school's website. Some of the children also asked if they could alter the articles to make them suitable for children in Key Stage 1. Ibrahim considered this and set up accounts on *storybird* (**storybird.com**) for the children to work on after school at home. He controlled the site by using the *guardian* facility and approved the final product before it was hosted on the site for others to look at on the web.

Activity

Ibrahim's approach varied from Jasmine's, yet the overall outcomes were quite similar. Both used the technology to support the children's learning, but also to deepen and engage the children's interest. Consider the following questions as you learn to appreciate the benefits of a planned approach to learning which includes ICT as a motivational force'

- What was the curriculum focus in each of the previous two case studies?
- What function did the ICT have and what was the primary difference in its use?
- How might you have developed and extended home–school links?
- What enabled Ibrahim in particular to develop the children's learning?

Links to the National Curriculum

Ibrahim began with linking the QCA schemes of work for ICT and the POS (ICT) 1a, b, c; 2a; 3a, b; 4a b, c; 5a, b), combining these with a healthy living topic which was linked to the science POS (Sc2: 2a, b, c, d, e, f, g). As the children were actively reading and writing they also covered several aspects of the English curriculum (EN2: 3a, b, c, d, e; EN3: 2a, b, c, d, e, f). They discussed aspects of the topic in their PHSE sessions (PHSE: 1a; 2a; 3a, d; EN1: 1a, c, d, e, 2b, c, e, 3a, d, f). The combination of these elements was mutually supportive as the focus of the ICT was to create and amend text for different audiences. Some children went on to present their materials in German and others altered their newspaper articles into story books for younger children (MFL: 2f). The teacher uploaded their final pieces onto the school website which enabled a much wider audience to view their work.

Supporting children's learning across the curriculum and outside the classroom

Previously in this chapter you will have read about the potential that Web 2.0 technologies offer; especially in relation to collaboration both within and outside of the classroom. The motivational aspects of the computer on children's learning, especially for boys, has been researched by Becta (2003) and by Sutherland *et al.* (2009). In this age children need to develop a range of digital literacy skills and as Richardson (2009) explains:

> *We are no longer limited to being independent readers or consumers of information;… we can be collaborators in the creation of large storehouses of information. In this process, we can learn much about ourselves and our world. In almost every area of life, the Read/Write Web is changing our relationship to technology and rewriting the age-old paradigms of how things work.*

Richardson (2009, page 2)

The generic nature of collaborative tools like wikis, blogs and podcasts enables both the teacher and children to engage with their learning and curriculum in an *open-ended* and *open-minded* approach. The skills level involved in many of these digital tools is quite low, yet they are capable of developing deeper learning, thus transforming children's work. While such tools have a relatively high literacy component of reading and writing (and speaking, if you include podcasting), the tools are essentially *generic*, you can do what you like with them. You do need to supply a meaningful and appropriate context with which to engage children in their gathering, sifting and analysis of the information. The 'multimodal' nature allows for choice and personalisation of the material, alongside a high visual presentational element. This enables all children and learners to represent their ideas and thoughts in a dynamic way that pen and paper do not (Sutherland *et al.*, 2009). The combination of elements and the characteristics of ICT (see Chapter 5), especially the provisional nature of digital text, make it appealing to many children, particularly boys, who have sometimes struggled with more traditional methods in schools, when compared to their digital lives within the home environment (Carrington and Robinson, 2009).

Research Focus: motivation and extending work beyond school hours

In the case studies above we have seen that extending learning beyond the classroom into the home and wider community can help to engage and motivate children. It is also possible, even desirable, to enable parents and the child's wider family to be able to view and/or assist in the children's work, so long as safeguarding procedures are in place (Byron, 2008). It is important that we consider the implications of research into motivation and into work beyond the normal routines of school (homework).

Becta (2003) reported that there was an increased commitment in children's attitudes towards learning and this motivation continued beyond the school day to outside of school where internet-based resources were being used. Sutherland *et al.* (2009) found that patterns of similar use existed both in school and within the home environment when children were using computers and/or the internet. They advocate teachers' need to establish effective communication links between 'official' and 'unofficial knowledges', so that *valuable learning experiences* can be developed (page 176). John and Wheeler (2008) also point out that home-school links have always existed and that the continuing use of technology is enabling information to be shared between schools, parents and the wider community more efficiently and effectively. They also recognise that technology is extending learning beyond the boundaries of the classroom, and go further by suggesting that there could be a blurring between home and school to provide flexible learning spaces that are not dependent on time and location.

Learning Outcomes Review

You will now have a wider appreciation of the nature of collaborative Web 2.0 tools such as **wikis, blogs** and **podcasts,** and of how these tools can be used effectively to develop children's skills and knowledge throughout the curriculum. You have explored, through research and case studies, the importance of planning and effective engagement with both the tools and the learning outcomes and how digital literacy can aid learning. You have looked at a range of ideas for information exchange and seen how children can use the provisional and multimodal nature of digital text to alter and create new materials for different audiences. You have considered the nature of *digital literacy* and how this can be developed through children's safe use of child-orientated programs available on the internet, such as *j2e* and *Storybird*. You have considered how work begun in the classroom can be continued at home, and the benefits of involving the parents and the community in this process, while acknowledging the importance of risk management. You should now have some awareness of how technology facilitates children and teachers to learn more effectively and efficiently with increased levels of motivation and engagement.

Self-assessment questions

1. Which collaborative tools could you use to facilitate a piece of writing about a famous composer?
2. What are the potential benefits of using Web 2.0 technologies in the classroom?
3. What are the main characteristics that enable digital text to be altered and adapted for different purposes and audiences?
4. How might you use ICT to support children's learning at school and at home?

Further information

Wikis

wikispaces.com (**www.wikispaces.com**)

Blogs

blogger.com (**www.blogger.com**)

Podcasts

BBC (**www.bbc.co.uk/podcasts**)

RSPB (**www.rspb.org.uk/podcasts/naturesvoice.aspx**)

Further Reading

Becta (2010, 15 January) *The 21st Century Teacher: Are you ready to meet the challenge?* Online at **publications.becta.org.uk/display.cfm?resID=41521&page=1835** (retrieved 25 October 2010).

Becta (2010, March) *The 21st Century Teacher: English; using technology to enhance English teaching.* Online at **schools.becta.org.uk/downloads/21stcentury_english.pdf** (retrieved 25 October 2010).

Richardson, W. (2009) *Blogs, Wikis, Podcasts and Other Powerful Web Tools for Classrooms.* London: Corwin Press.

The Learning Discovery Centre Team (2009) *Creative ICT in the Classroom; using new tools for learning.* Stafford: Network Continuum Education Publishers.

References

Becta (2003) *What the research says about ICT and motivation.* Online at **research.becta.org.uk/ upload-dir/downloads/page_documents/research/wtrs_motivation.pdf** (retrieved 21 October 2010).

Becta (2010) *Digital literacy: Teaching critical thinking for our digital world.* Online at **schools.becta.org.uk/uploaddir/downloads/digital_literacy_publication.pdf** (retrieved 12 April 2010).

Bennett, R., Hamill, A. and Pickford, T. (2007) *Progression in Primary ICT.* Abingdon, Oxford: David Fulton Publishers.

Carrington, V. and Robinson, M. (eds) (2009) *Digital Literacies; Social Learning and Classroom Practices.* London: UKLA/Sage Publications.

DCSF (2008) *Safer children in a Digital World: The Report of the Byron Review.* Nottingham: DCSF Publications. Online at: **www.dcsf.gov.uk/byronreview** (accessed 23 October 2010).

DfEE (1999) The National Curriculum handbook for primary teachers in England key stages 1 and 2. Online at **www.curriculum.qcda.gov.uk/key-stages-1-and 2/subjects/english/ keystage1/index.aspx** (retrieved 26 October 2010).

DfES (2005) *Harnessing Technology: Transforming Learning and Children's Services.* Nottingham: DfES Publications. Online at **publications.education.gov.uk/ eOrderingDownload/1296-2005PDF-EN-01.pdf** (accessed 26 October 2010).

Grant, L (2006, May) *Using Wikis in Schools: a Case Study.* Online at **www.futurelab.org.uk/ resources/documents/discussion_papers/Wikis_in_Schools.pdf** (accessed 20 October 2010).

Higgins, S. (2003) *Does ICT improve learning and teaching in schools?* Professional User Review of UK research undertaken for the British Educational Research Association. Online at: **www.bera.ac.uk/files/reviews/ict-pur-mb-r-f-p-1aug03.pdf** (retrieved 28 October 2010).

John, P. and Wheeler, S. (2008) *The Digital Classroom*. Abingdon, Oxford: Routledge.

Owen, M., Grant, L., Sayers, S. and Facer, K. (2006) *Social Software and Learning*. Online at **www.futurelab.org.uk/resources/documents/opening_education/Social_Software_report.pdf** (retrieved 20 October 2010).

Richardson, W. (2009) *Blogs, Wikis, Podcasts and Other Powerful Web Tools for Classrooms*. London: Corwin Press.

Rose, J. (2009) *Independent Review of the Primary Curriculum*. Online at **www.webarchive.nationalarchives.gov.uk/tna/+www.dcsf.gov.uk/primarycurriculumreview** (retrieved 20 October 2010).

Sutherland, R., Robertson, S. and John, P. (2009) *Improving Classroom Learning with ICT*. Abingdon, Oxford: Routledge.

The Technology Enhanced Learning phase of the Teaching and Learning Research Programme (2008) *Education 2.0? Designing the web for teaching and learning*. Online at **www.tlrp.org/tel/publications/files/2008/11/tel_comm_final.pdf** (retrieved 21 October 2010).

5. Refining and improving work
Eamonn Pugh and Ed Tyson

Learning Outcomes

By the end of this chapter you should:
- be able to identify opportunities across a range of curriculum subjects to use ICT to refine and improve work;
- understand how features of ICT, particularly its provisionality, can help children to refine and improve their work;
- recognise how ICT can personalise the 'refining and improving' process for children;
- have explored ICT tools that can raise the standard of children's work by enabling formative assessment, particularly self- and peer assessment.

Professional standards for QTS

Q8 Have a creative and constructively critical approach towards innovation, being prepared to adapt their practice where benefits and improvement are identified;

Q12 Know a range of approaches to assessment, including the importance of formative assessment;

Q23 Design opportunities for learners to develop their literacy, numeracy and ICT skills;

Q25 (b) Teach lessons and sequences of lessons ... in which they build on prior knowledge, develop concepts and processes, enable learners to apply new knowledge, understanding and skills and meet learning objectives;

Q28 Support and guide learners to reflect on their learning, identify the progress they have made and identify their emerging learning needs.

Introduction

The focus of this chapter is on using ICT to raise standards of work produced by children. In contrast to Chapter 4, this learning process is viewed principally as a personal, individual response by the child to her/his work so far, albeit enabled by the features of the technology used, giving feedback directly to the child or serving as a bridge to give feedback from others.

Firstly you will read and explore how ICT can be used in this way to improve work across all curriculum subjects. Next you will have opportunities to consider valuable characteristics of ICT, particularly 'provisionality', which contribute in this way. Moving on, you will reflect on the part ICT can play alongside personalised learning in helping each child achieve these improvements, before finally addressing the ICT role in supporting formative assessment practice (particularly self- and peer assessment) which seeks an outcome of refined and improved work.

The factors underpinning effective ICT use in this area and the way that they have been harnessed by teachers will be explored through case studies. You will then consider which technology tools are fit for which classroom purpose, through activities encouraging you to explore possibilities within your own school setting.

As successive generations of teachers will testify, changes in education seem almost as quick as the development of digital technologies themselves. So this chapter will also flag relevant policy and ICT pedagogy frameworks that influence the way teachers can see ICT's role in refining and improving children's work.

Being able to identify opportunities across a range of curriculum subjects to use ICT to refine and improve work

Whatever curriculum structure government policy dictates, subjects are powerful groupings of knowledge whose status will remain. There will therefore continue to be a place for digital tools across all subjects of the primary curriculum, even though most schools and teachers seek coherence between subjects in recognition that a heavily prescriptive subject curriculum is not always effective.

In this section you will reflect on, and exercise choices over, technologies which meet the requirements of a balanced curriculum through which children are 'refining and improving work'.

Your first thoughts might lead you to children's writing and the use of word processing software to capture fleeting thoughts and edit and improve poor prose at all levels. Indeed, particularly for children at the early stages of writing, this provisionality can instil confidence, because it takes away any feeling that they have to get it right first time (NAACE, 2007). However, the benefits of using technology to support the processes of improving work extend across the whole curriculum.

Case Study: Video sparks personal bests

Karen was a newly qualified teacher planning a unit of work in athletics for her Year 4 class. Her focus was on improving the children's running technique. In the first lesson, the children recorded each other's 60m sprinting times. The second lesson began in class by watching video clips of athletes running in the Olympics (**www.bbc.co.uk/schools/gcsebitesize/pe/video/athletics/sprintsrev1.shtml**). Karen discussed the athletes' running techniques with the class, particularly starting technique, use of arms and head position.

→

The children then used the tips gained from the video clips to go out and practise their own running technique. The lesson culminated in the children using a small camcorder *(Flip)* to video record each other's running. Back in class, the children had the opportunity to watch the video clip of their own performance and evaluate it for themselves. They then had further opportunities to go out and practise their technique again.

A group of children also engaged in video editing the clips using *MovieMaker* software *(Microsoft)*, producing an instructional video with text and animations added. This was shown to the younger children in the school in readiness for school sports day. The ICT was a significant factor in the children's motivation, facilitating the process through which the children selected the techniques that they wanted to use. By contributing to the refinement and improvement of the children's running technique, the use of ICT had contributed to, rather than distracted from, the PE objective as many of the children improved enough to secure new personal best performances.

The use of ICT to improve work in PE may not spring to mind with most teachers. However, a review of the National Curriculum Key Stage 1/2 Programme of Study for PE reveals the improvement processes that Karen had in mind for her class. Such opportunities to apply ICT exist in abundance in all of the primary curriculum areas.

Activity

- Visit the National Curriculum website home page (**curriculum.qcda.gov.uk**). Navigate via the *Primary Curriculum Key Stage 1 and Key Stage 2* tab via *Assessment* to the *NC in Action*. Use the dropdown menus to find examples for Year 2 Music (Egyptian Melody), Year 4 Art (Repeated Patterns) and Year 6 RE (Festivals). Read the commentaries and identify the improvement processes built into the activities.
- Visit the same homepage and follow this navigation route: Primary Curriculum Key Stage 1 and 2 → learning across the curriculum → ICT in subject teaching. Select each subject in turn from the left-hand menu, each time opening the *ICT opportunities* tab.
- Note the uses of ICT which support the refining or improving processes.
- Add additional notes to two activities which could be adapted to your placement class.

Links to National Curriculum

The English National Curriculum for ICT at Key Stages 1 and 2 (DfEE, 1999) requires children to have opportunities categorised under four strands, namely to:

- find things out;

- develop ideas and make things happen;
- exchange and share information;
- review, modify and evaluate work as it progresses.

Becta recommended that primary school children should be able to *refine and improve their work, making full use of the nature and pliability of digital information to explore options and improve outcomes.* (Becta, 2009, page 29). In doing so, they acknowledged the power of digital technology to help children, from a first attempt, to rethink all sorts of ideas and then rework the ideas into more thoughtful and consolidated notions. As such, the computer is a very valuable tool in extending thinking.

Arguably, the more recently coined concept of 'reviewing and modifying their work' permeates all four of the National Curriculum ICT strands. In 'Finding Things Out', older primary children are likely to check the content of their work for accuracy and relevance (for example, information from the internet) and check presentation (such as grammar and spellings) using word-processing software. ICT tools also give children who are 'developing their ideas' a means to easily amend and refine their work. The potential for using ICT to improve work through not just personal reflection but also collaboration has been addressed in more detail in Chapter 4. Suffice to say here that the 'exchange and sharing of information' with others can often take the form of feedback to which the child responds with refined and improved work. The link between the use of ICT to 'review, modify and evaluate their work as it progresses' and improved quality of work is perhaps more self-apparent.

Refining and improving work: making use of the features of ICT

Educationalists have presented for over a decade the idea that ICT has several definable 'characteristics' that can make a contribution to teaching and learning. As part of the Excellence and Enjoyment programme, an original list of four was expanded to nine such ICT features:

- *replication;*
- *multi-modality;*
- *non-linearity;*
- *interactivity;*
- *provisionality;*
- *communicability;*
- *automation;*
- *capacity;*
- *speed.*

(DfES, 2004, page 73)

As a framework, this allows you to reflect on the use of ICT by considering which characteristics are actually contributing to teaching or learning. It lets you explore how necessary the use of ICT is. For example, if a computer was being used to 'type up a story in best', you may conclude that none of the characteristics was being exploited and therefore there is no justification for the use of ICT.

We would argue that provisionality of ICT is likely to be the core benefit in terms of this chapter. Provisionality is the the non-permanent nature of ICT, the potential to change work easily. Writing text with a word processor is a classic example of provisionality. Children working with word processing software quickly learn the value of the 'undo' button and can learn to be systematic users of the 'synonym' tool.

There will be other characteristics that can be usefully employed too. The interactive and automatic features of a computer clearly help with the development of work. The response that ICT tools can give children can be an extremely valuable prompt for refining their work. When work is read back by software with a speech engine – *Textease* (Softease) or *Clicker* (Crick) come to mind – interaction can be of a very high level, especially if the child benefits from reading support to identify where improvements can be made. The automation of predictive software that corrects common spelling mistakes, even before a child notices, certainly improves the work. However, you may as a teacher be more concerned with the learning process than the outcome. If so, you should think carefully about when and when not to make these features available to the child. Software such as the titles named above have a high level of flexibility or pliability, enabling a knowledgeable teacher to turn on or off speech engine text reading or spellchecking functions.

Activity

- A Teachers' TV programme *Fun for free* (**www.teachers.tv/videos/ict-fun-for-free**) showcases a primary school making extensive use of software that children can use at school and, if they have domestic internet access, at home as well. This is because the software is all open access (downloadable free). The programs featured are *Audacity, BlockCad, Scratch, MonkeyJam, Gabcast* and *Phun* (**www.phunland.com**).
- Explore these programs (all are easily accessible via a search engine) and consider which have potential for supporting the refinement and improvement of models, writing, solutions, or any other activity that could be broadly termed 'work'.
- If you have Teachers' TV access, also watch the video. Note instances when the children have used the provisionality characteristic of the software, i.e. refined, modified or in some other way changed their work. For example, a Year 5 child talks of remodelling her work (occurring when the timer is on 4.48). What do you think are the factors motivating the children you see in the video?

Supporting personalising and learning with ICT

In the previous section, the importance of knowing the features of particular ICT applications was raised. Settings to switch on or off a speech engine or spellchecker are usually within a 'teacher only' area of the software. This puts you in a position of considerable power and responsibility. You could make a decision based on the main ability band within the class or group or according to each child's needs or somewhere in between. You may choose to control the settings or, alternatively, devolve that choice to the child.

In this section, you will read of teachers for whom technology is used to deliver more personalised experiences for their children. These are teachers who give the children greater ownership of the ICT and their learning, yielding higher quality work than would otherwise be achieved.

First though, let us look at the support of children's learning with a focus on your decisions as a teacher, rather than the qualities of the ICT itself. The National Association for Advisors for Computers in Education (NAACE), in partnership with Becta, considered the excellent teachers they had observed in their work and found five common learning features associated with this effective ICT practice. These features were *autonomy, capability, creativity, quality and scope* (NAACE/Becta, 2001, page 1). Two of the features have particular relevance to children 'refining and improving work'.

The first, *autonomy,* is typified by allowing your children to take charge of their learning through the ICT. Working alone or with other children, excellent teachers employ the technology at the most appropriate level and explain why they are using particular ICT tools for the task in hand. The children learn by doing, by making connections and making decisions. When this concept is examined more closely, it shows itself to be firmly aligned to both the idea of *personalisation* and of *refinement and improvement of work.*

Pupils make decisions or show initiative about which application or hardware is best suited to a task.
Pupils develop their own ways of thinking about the task and develop their own strategies for overcoming problems. They seem confident, prepared to take risks and learn from their mistakes.
Pupils use teacher intervention effectively to move them on to the next stage in their thinking.
Pupils use peer intervention effectively to develop their thinking. They recognise the potential of feedback from others to improve their work.
Pupils participate actively in formative assessment of their work. They know and understand how their work will be assessed and use these criteria to improve their work.
Pupils are inspired to learn with ICT. They transfer knowledge to other contexts, for example, when using ICT at home. They recognise and value how knowledge gained outside the classroom contributes to their schoolwork.
Pupils access independent, student-centred resources and use them to effect.

Table 5.1 Characteristics of autonomy (NAACE/Becta, 2001, page 2)

Case Study: Brendan, Part 1: starting from *Scratch*

Brendan was a trainee teacher on his first placement with a Year 2 class. In their last literacy lesson the children had lots of fun telling 'knock-knock' jokes. Building on this enthusiasm, Brendan introduced them to *Scratch,* software with which they were to create their own interactive compositions, i.e. knock-knock jokes. He modelled in front of the whole class the essential ICT skills needed to use the programming language, such as using scripts, blocks and sprites.

Brendan was guided by advice in National Curriculum for Key Stage 1 English that *teaching should ensure that work in 'speaking and listening', 'reading' and 'writing' is integrated* (DfEE, 1999, page 19). So the children first worked in pairs, composing and trying out the jokes on each other. When they were ready, they used the computers, controlling their created 'sprite' characters' use of word balloons, with many of the children also adding their own voice recordings activated on each speaker's turn.

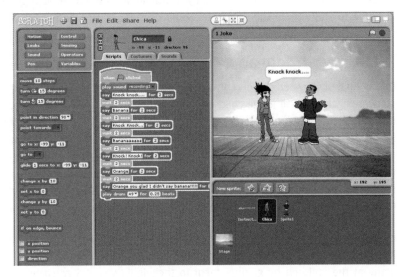

*Figure 5.1 Scratch program screen (***www.scratch.mit.edu***)*

Scratch is developed by the Lifelong Kindergarten Group at the MIT Media Lab. See **http://scratch.mit.edu**

Brendan also aligned his planning to the knowledge, skills and understanding of writing specified in the National Curriculum programme of study for Key Stage 1 English (page 20). He drew from the list of descriptors those emboldened below.

Composition
   1. *Pupils should be taught to:*
       a) *use adventurous and wide-ranging vocabulary;*
       b) *sequence events and recount them in appropriate detail;*

$\rightarrow$

c) *put their ideas into sentences;*
d) **use a clear structure to organise their writing;**
e) **vary their writing to suit the purpose and reader;**
f) *use the texts they read as models for their own writing.*

Planning and drafting

2. *Working with the teacher and with others, in order to develop their writing, pupils should be taught to:*
   a) *write familiar words and attempt unfamiliar ones;*
   b) **assemble and develop ideas on paper and on screen;**
   c) **plan and review their writing, discussing the quality of what is written;**
   d) *write extended texts, with support [for example, using the teacher as writer].*

Brendan's written lesson evaluation recorded an unexpected benefit; many children had impressed their parents by downloading the free Scratch programme at home to show them their projects. Some of them started additional ones with family members at home.

Brendan, Part 2: formative assessment with *Scratch*

On his final eight-week placement with a Year 5 class, Brendan went on to use the software again. This time the children applied their existing ICT skills to compose a mix of stories, animations, games, music and art. Brendan reasoned that this class would quickly pick up the core features of *Scratch* because, his placement mentor told him, the class had controlled screen turtles when they were in Year 4, using the control language *LOGO*, which has a similar programming structure. He was reassured about this learning link when he found reference to *Scratch* on the *LOGO* Foundation website (**http://el.media.mit.edu/logo-foundation/new/index.html**).

Brendan reasoned that a wider choice of themes and ICT tools personalised the learning experience that the activity offered each child. He also gave autonomy to many of the children by guiding them to the highly visual *Scratch* help screens, rather than solving their problems for them. In another strategy to encourage autonomous learning, he modelled a plan/do/review cycle for the children to follow; planning the initial challenge, doing the programming and reviewing through testing and modifying of the game. To help the children review their work, Brendan planned for the children to look at each other's work and give feedback as 'two stars and a wish'. This was built into the lessons and he also showed the class how they could each share their programme online with each other, thus enabling many of them to give peer assessment from home.

In his evaluations of these lessons, Brendan wrote of the need to build on the ICT skills the children had and the realisation that work of such depth and quality takes time. He was delighted at how well the children had participated in formative

$\rightarrow$

assessment of their work and attributed this largely to the positive yet critical feedback they had given each other to help improve their work. His overriding reflection, though, was of children autonomously seeking perfection and highest quality of composition; learners who were so engrossed that they didn't notice how much they were learning using this ICT tool.

Quality, the second of the features identified by NAACE, is demonstrated by children's ideas emerging and evolving, improving the quality of their work. They use ICT to enhance this learning and sometimes use it to enhance the presentation of their work. There is a sense of purpose, with redrafting and improvement in evidence.

Pupils use ICT to present and communicate their ideas to a high standard, redrafting as necessary to produce better quality outcomes.
Pupils have clear ideas of how they use ICT to improve the quality of their work.
Pupils readily engage in thinking about the task in hand. They explain what they have done and why. They justify their use of ICT in terms of the quality of the outcomes.
Pupils display evident pride and satisfaction. They value the outcomes of their endeavours. They develop a personal commitment to good-quality work and aspire to the highest standards.
Pupils have high expectations and demonstrate concentration, persistence and determination to develop work of a high standard.
Pupils are engaged in high-quality thinking and analysis through decision-making, predicting, hypothesising and testing.

Table 5.2 Characteristics of quality (NAACE/Becta, 2001, page 2)

For children to show the characteristics above and make this commitment to quality, they need to be interested in what they are doing. That is easily said, but it is a substantial challenge for a teacher when the class has so many individuals with diverse interests and abilities. Personalisation describes a system in which education is tailored to fit each child (DCSF, 2008). The embedding of the term in the English education system brought an overt challenge to teachers to enable both individual excellence for all their children and equality for all.

So how can ICT help you to personalise the 'refining and improving' process for each and every child in your class? Of course, we have to be realistic. The expectation that every teacher can respond to the individual needs of every child is just fantasy when you think what that would require of a typical primary teacher with a class of 30 (Laurillard, 2008). Nevertheless, ICT does offer opportunities to maximise impact on the personalised learning agenda, but teachers need to adopt flexible teaching methods and strategies, including mixed technologies in various environments. Teaching capability in the twenty-first century includes having the secure ICT knowledge and skills to make the right judgement calls on how and when to use technology (Stein, 2005).

To make the right calls, you need to know the technology under consideration. Chapter 1 introduced *Photostory 3* (Microsoft) to you in Case Study: Moving from skills to capability. Teachers have seen opportunities for children to use it independently in lower Key Stage 2 and successfully given younger children a supported introduction to the program. Next you will be invited to explore and evaluate this software yourself. This will enable you to make informed choices about when and how *Photostory 3* could give children a personalised experience, one which motivates them to work autonomously to improve the quality of the presentation.

Activity

Your task is to use *Photostory 3* to create a multimedia presentation. Centred on photographs of yourself arranged in sequence, it will include text, sound and image effects chosen to convey to the viewer a mood or message that the photographs evoke in you. So you will be inserting photographs or images, adding titles to them, selecting zoom in/out effects and recording voice-over narrations. In preparation you will need:

- *The Photostory 3 program*, if it is not already installed on your computer. It is downloadable from **www.microsoft.com/windowsxp/using/digitalphotography/photostory/default.mspx**
- *5–10 digital photographs* that include yourself.
- *A desktop microphone*, if there isn't one built into your computer or laptop. This is to add a narrative voice-over.
- *Suitable music*. The software includes a small library of music and an option to create your own. Alternatively, you can import music files to the presentation.

You can find tutorial video guides by searching for 'Photostory 3 tutorial video' via your web browser box, e.g. **www.teachertube.com/viewVideo.php?video_id=75267** Having completed your presentation, find a suitable audience to give you feedback. Your audience should tell you how effectively the message or mood was conveyed. Friends, family, teacher trainee peers or children would all be ideal.

Then evaluate the software in response to the questions below.

1. Case Study: Moving from skills to capability in Chapter 1 highlighted the need for a meaningful context. So how meaningful and motivating was the activity for you?
2. How autonomously were you able to work with the software? What functions would your children need support with?
3. How effective would *Photostory 3* be as a tool for refining and improving work in your class?
4. In which ways can this ICT tool support personalised learning for primary children?
5. Referring to the lists above, which characteristics of autonomy and quality could effective use of this software result in?

Research Focus

The chapter so far has associated effective ICT use with personalised learning and the outcome of refined and improved children's work.

A Becta-funded research project used a child empowerment perspective to study the influence children had over their teacher's ICT decisions. Conducted by researchers, teacher educators and teachers, it was entitled *Personalising learning: the learner perspective and their influence on demand* (Robinson et al., 2008) and reached important conclusions for teachers seeking autonomous learning from children with aspirations to always do better.

The research showed that children's involvement in decision-making ranged from minor to major decisions, even within the same school. In one school, some talked about being able to change the font colour, add a background to *PowerPoint* presentations and project some pictures onto the school plasma screen, while other children had the opportunity to choose which technologies best suited the researching, recording and presentation of their work. At one primary school history investigation, Year 5/6 children could decide what work to cover and how to present it. One child interviewed a local resident who was a World War II evacuee and recorded the interview as a podcast, others presented work as a *PowerPoint* (Microsoft) presentation and some chose to video their work, editing it in *MovieMaker* (Microsoft).

Most significantly, teachers who were keen to experiment with different technologies themselves were less prescriptive about the ICT children used to complete, amend and present work, and had confidence to devolve some control to them. This, of course, mirrored the approach Brendan used with his Year 5 class in Case Study: Brendan, Part 1: starting from *Scratch*. However it should be remembered that he first gained confidence in the technology (and his own developing teaching practice) by using *Scratch* in a more channelled way on his earlier placement. The name 'Scratch' derives from DJ mixing and, when his class used the program with a more multimedia approach on a later placement, the children became engaged in another type of refinement and improvement activity – the Web 2.0 notion of mixing and remixing work.

It will probably be of no surprise to read that when staff thought they had ownership of a particular digital technology, it was used more frequently to support the personalised learning of children. The obvious message is that the more ICT tools that you have experience of using, the better the match of learning objective, learner needs and supporting technology.

The use of ICT to support personalising of learning was more often initiated by staff and further developed by learners. Hence *learner-influenced* was a more accurate

→

description than *learner-led* (Robinson *et al.*, 2008, page 57). As a teacher, your responsibility includes the planning of structured and purposeful learning experiences for your class, so it is hardly surprising that you will often decide the technology to be used, or even, of course, if technology is to be used. Nevertheless, it may be the norm for you to listen to your children's ideas for using an ICT tool in a particular way and perhaps there are occasions when you are indeed *learner-led* and the children show their ICT capability by choosing the technology.

Formative assessment and ICT: a powerful combination to prompt improved work

In the previous section, you have considered choices of technology that enable children to have autonomous and high-quality learning experiences. So next you could look at the characteristics of ICT (speed or capacity, for example) and look for curriculum applications for them. First, though, there is another perspective with which you may view the use of ICT, which contrasts with the concept of ICT tools having characteristics, as described above. This is the idea of *affordances*, which moves a teacher on from asking *what does ICT have that we can make use of?* to asking *what can we use ICT for?* (Fisher et al., 2006). This may appear a subtle distinction, but is actually a very different way of thinking about teaching and learning with ICT. Earlier in this chapter we cited the National Curriculum ICT strands, which were drawn up as categories of what ICT has got, and we talked of ICT characteristics, a list based on inbuilt properties that we can use ICT for. For example, we referred to word processing programs that have high levels of interactivity and multimedia presentational software that has great provisionality.

As digital technology advances at such a pace, ICT tools become more mobile, powerful, multimedia and versatile. Teachers are constantly realising new potential for these technologies in the classroom; perhaps you have favourite ICT tools that you are still finding new uses for. So maybe the relevant challenge is now to see what *we can use ICT for*. This shifts the focus towards ICT as a resource. Important though it is, it's not about the ICT; it's about the intended teaching and learning. *It may be that it is the pedagogy of ICT that has to be reframed with much greater clarity on the specific affordances ICTs can provide in relation to subject pedagogies* (Prosser, 2006, page 8).

A subject pedagogy will include key understandings about how to teach and learn. One such concept is that personalised learning should underpin those choices. Another - which is integral to personalisation – is assessment, including an expectation that teachers will *support pupils in assessing and evaluating their learning through peer and self-assessment* (DCSF, 2008, page 24). Such formative assessment, together with teacher feedback, is crucial to the refinement and improvement of children's work. Perhaps there are ICT tools that can be useful. So let's rephrase the earlier proposal. You will next explore self-assessment and peer assessment opportunities to improve children's work in chosen subjects. To those ends, you will be introduced to some ICT tools that you might find useful.

A child can be supported in self-assessment by a rich range of established software that provides automated feedback. Common programs such as *Word*, *Excel* or *PowerPoint* (Microsoft) and software designed for primary school use, such as *Textease* (Softease), *Clicker* (Crick) and the *Black Cat* suite of programs (Granada) encourage a reflection on improvements through overt features such as spellcheckers or corrective spreadsheet functions. These are probably familiar to you and need no further elucidation here.

It is the growth of Web 2.0 technologies that we will explore a little further because these websites, designed for safe, creative and collaborative activity by children, open up innovative peer assessment opportunities. Typically they are online multimedia publishing tools through which users can process text, pictures, shapes, animations, sound, video, add links and embedded objects. You will have read more about their wider educational potential in Chapter 4.

The flexibility of websites such as j2e (**www.j2e.com**) and Wikispaces (**www.wikispaces.com**) goes beyond the personal to the social. With sharing tools built in, children with internet access can receive feedback from others. One such resource is the *PrimaryPad* website (**www.primarypad.com**) which opens collaborative possibilities for small group editing of text. Multimedia work is saved as web pages, each with a unique web address (URL) which can be accessed from anywhere, any time, any place, by a private or public audience.

PrimaryPad has the added benefit of an authorship colour coding system, which shows teacher and children who has done what and when. Identifying a child's contributions to a collaborative piece of work adds an assessment opportunity that couldn't be achieved without the ICT. The refinements and improvements can be tracked to allow self-assessment by the child and feedback by other children and the teacher. This, of course, should lead to further refinements and improvements. You can see a streaming video demonstration by searching for *PrimaryPad* on YouTube (**www.youtube.com**).

Case Study: *PrimaryPad* and peer assessment

Pamela's second placement was with a mixed Year 5/6 class of 24 pupils about to study the impact of the Second World War on the lives of men, women and children. Because the school was on the edge of a city that had been bombed during the war, this was also part of a local study of change over time. Though the core subject of the topic was history, Pamela was adopting a cross-curricular approach. This case study focuses on the combination of history with English composition, drafting and language structure. Pamela's decision to include ICT in this part of the topic was informed partly by her own pedagogic beliefs about assessment for learning (AfL). To clarify her intentions, she began by drawing appropriate content from national framework documents. This is summarised as Table 5.3.

→

National Curriculum History Key Stage 2*
Knowledge and understanding of...attitudes/experiences of men, women, children in the past (2a). Historical interpretation ... Pupils should be taught to recognise that the past is represented and interpreted in different ways, and to give reasons for this (3). Communicate knowledge and understanding of history in various ways [e.g. by using ICT] (5). Local study ... investigating how an aspect in the local area has changed ... over time ... (7). Britain since 1930 ... study of impact of WWII ... on lives of men, women and children ... (11b).

National Curriculum English Key Stage 2 (En3: Writing)*
Composition ... children should be taught to: • broaden their vocabulary and use it in inventive ways (1b); • use language and style that are appropriate to the reader (1c); • use and adapt the features of a form of writing, drawing on their reading (1d). Planning and drafting ... to develop writing on paper and on screen, pupils should be taught to: • draft - develop ideas from the plan into structured written text (2b); • revise - change and improve the draft (2c); • present - prepare a neat, correct and clear final copy (2e); • discuss and evaluate their own and others' writing (2f).

Primary Literacy Framework Pupil Writing Targets: 9 Creating and shaping texts		
Year 5 – Level 4c	Year 6 – Level 4b	Year 6 – Level 4a
Use a range of adjectives, adverbs, powerful verbs and phrases selectively ... to amuse, entertain, persuade and inform. Evaluate writing against success criteria; make changes considering audience, purpose.	Establish and demonstrate a consistent viewpoint in different forms of writing.	Use precise vocabulary (including figurative language) and sentence variation to contribute to the effectiveness of the writing.

National Curriculum ICT Key Stage 2: Attainment targets (extracts) *
Level 3: Use ICT to generate, develop, organise and present their work. They share and exchange their ideas with others. Level 4: Add to, amend and combine different forms of information from various sources. Level 5: Use ICT to structure, refine and present information in different forms/styles for specific purposes/audiences. Exchange information and ideas with others in a variety of ways.

*This content relates to the 1999 Programmes of Study and Attainment Targets.

Table 5.3 Pamela's cross-curricular focus

Broadly speaking, the learning experience was to be an understanding of air raids and a verbal and written sharing of thoughts and feelings about them. Pamela saw group work as the best method to prompt discussion and spark ideas, so the class were to be organised into six small groups.

→

At this point, Pamela used a PrimaryPad tutorial (**www.youtube.com/watch?-v=S3kzdKPqpl8**) and explored the software herself. She realised that it featured automatic authorship colour coding, having the same effect as highlighting text in different colours in *Word* (Microsoft). She saw not only collaborative potential, but also that the software could support AfL, affording not just self-assessment, but peer assessment feedback from fellow group members.

After watching videos and photographs of air raids over England and Germany, the children had an ICT lesson in the school computer suite, during which Pamela modelled the use of *PrimaryPad*. She demonstrated the writing of an acrostic poem and then each group created their own (examples included BLITZ, AIR RAID, BOMBING and TERROR). This was deliberately a comfortable English task because the main purpose was to learn the ICT skills. Each group was then timetabled to redraft and complete the poem later that week on the four classroom computers. The class returned to the computer suite the next week for a more challenging English task. In the same groups, the children now used the webpage to write from the viewpoint of a child in a city during an air raid. This collaborative account was to include contracted verbs, powerful verbs and suitable adverbs and adjectives. To prompt descriptions and feelings Pamela had put a video clip and two photos of air raids scenes in Coventry and Dresden onto each group's *PrimaryPad* page, with different photos for each of six groups. The children were supportive of each other and enthusiastic to the point that many of them continued the work as optional 'homework'.

Midway through the week, Pamela shared the criteria in Table 5.3 adapted into childspeak, and with each child's contribution colour coded, each group member gave the others feedback comprising 'two stars and a wish'. This resulted in higher quality redrafts and, such was the quality of the finished writing, they were moved from the private area for the group and teacher to being published on the web.

Research Focus

Diana Laurillard (2008) reported on research into whether learners' experience of personalisation, flexibility and inclusion can be aided by technology. These studies, conducted by the London Knowledge Lab (LKL), began with a premise already proposed in this chapter – that the starting point is not what the technology has to offer, but what learners might need.

The findings supported the view that digital technologies have the means to support mainstream activities of primary school teachers and led onto further LKL enquiries. This research concluded that, while the focus of *computer-supported collaborative learning* had so far been on learners doing the collaboration, teachers need this experience too.

It advocated giving teachers the tools they need to be reflective practitioners (Schön, 1987) working in a community of practice (Wenger, 1999). One of the few research projects that had focused on this was the project by Paul Black and Dylan Wiliam on assessment for learning (Black and Wiliam, 2006), where they showed how teachers were able to share their knowledge within and across schools. LKL echoed this and Laurillard, their Chair of Learning with Digital Technologies, argued how valuable ICT could be for teachers' social motivation. After all, we all have an impulse to share our outputs with peers, argue our ideas and learn from our peers.

So, as you prepare to engage with another activity, this appropriately shifts the focus of the chapter from children refining and modifying their work to teachers modelling that collaborative process.

A growing number of Web 2.0 tools are ideal for collaborative redrafting and improving work. Box.net (**www.box.net.com**), for example, has some really easy-to-use features that are suitable for the primary classroom, especially at Key Stage 2. However, it is aimed at the professional adult market and is therefore extremely well suited to sharing working on a document by several teachers. The site allows users to download and make changes and then upload files. Changes can also be tracked and it also has a comments feature. As such, it is an effective way to share files and gives good levels of collaboration for individual users.

Another such collaborative resource is Google Docs (**www. docs.google.com**), but this has the added feature of asynchronous reworking of files. Indeed, it allows up to 50 people to edit a document or spreadsheet at the same time and ten to edit a presentation. The central concept is that, instead of editing by sending and creating multiple versions of documents as e-mail attachments, there is only one centrally stored version of the document, which all of the collaborators can update, often at the same time.

Activity

1. View the Google Docs in Plain English video to gain a secure understanding of how it works (**http://video.google.com/ videoplay?docid=5270543939540408357#**)
2. Open a free Google Docs account from the same website.
3. Familiarise yourself with the key features using the website tutorials.
4. Choose a professional activity which requires, or would benefit from, a collaborative redrafting approach. This could be:
   - a placement lesson plan seeking input from teacher and teaching assistant;
   - a peer group presentation assignment;
   - writing up notes from a group or staff meeting;
   - a list to which people sign up;
   - or any task where a shared approach can refine and improve a document.

5. Upload that document to Google Docs.
6. Share the settings for the document with your collaborators via their e-mail addresses.
7. Each make contributions to the document until you are happy that it is fit for purpose.

Learning Outcomes Review

In search of ICT applications to refine and improve work, we have identified some well-established software and explored the potential of some Web 2.0 tools. You have read about ICT applications with potential to improve children's work across the curriculum, exploring examples of practice in PE, history and English, as well as a medley of subject applications used by one primary school. Additionally, we have recognised the necessity of skill development through ICT as a subject itself.

ICT has been viewed from different teaching perspectives, principally those of ICT strands, characteristics and then affordances. Examples of ICT tools, particularly Web 2.0 technologies, have been shared to illustrate how they can support the personalised learning and formative assessment practice needed to help each child improve their work. In this regard, self- and peer assessment opportunities have been emphasised.

In concluding with an activity for yourself and colleagues, we have emphasised the need to explore these emerging technologies yourself. From those experiences will grow confidence to model their use for children and knowledge to make informed choices from a wealth of ICT applications. The outcomes for the children will be higher standards through refined and improved work.

You should now:
- be able to identify opportunities across a range of curriculum subjects to use ICT to refine and improve work;
- understand how features of ICT, particularly its provisionality, can help children to refine and improve their work;
- recognise how ICT can personalise the 'refining and improving' process for children;
- have explored ICT tools that can raise the standard of children's work by enabling formative assessment, particularly self- and peer assessment.

Self-assessment questions
1. For each subject in the English National Curriculum for Key Stages 1 and 2, make a short note of how an ICT application could enhance the process of refining and improving children's work.

2. Think of an occasion when you have seen children using ICT to successfully change and develop work. Why was that choice and use of ICT so effective?

3. List a top five of low-cost digital tools which have potential to personalise learning and motivate most or even all of the children in your class.

4. You are going to plan a lesson in which the children will be refining and improving work and you intend to use ICT. What issues should this lesson plan address?

Futher Reading

John, P. and Wheeler S. (2008) *The Digital Classroom: Harnessing Technology for the Future.* Abingdon: Routledge

Laurillard, D. (2008) *Digital technologies and their role in achieving our ambitions for education.* Institute of Education, University of London. Online at **http://www.lkl.ac.uk/cms/index.php?option=com_comprofiler&task=userProfile&user=127** (retrieved 2 November 2010).

Sutherland, R., Robertson, S. and John, P. (2009) *Improving Classroom Learning with ICT.* London: Routledge.

References

Becta (2009) contribution to the Rose Review. Online at **www.publications.becta.org.uk/download.cfm?resID=40240** (retrieved 2 November 2010).

Black, P. and Wiliam, D. (2006) *The Reliability of Assessments*, in Gardner, D. (ed.) *Assessment and Learning.* London, Sage.

DCSF (2008) *Personalised Learning – A Practical Guide.* London: The Stationery Office.

DfEE (1999) *The National Curriculum handbook for primary teachers in England Key Stages 1 and 2.* London: The Stationery Office.

DfEE (1999a) *The National Curriculum handbook for primary teachers in England Key Stages 1 and 2.* Online at **www.curriculum.qcda.gov.uk/key-stages-1-and 2/subjects/english/keystage1/index.aspx** (retrieved 26 October 2010).

DfES (2004) *Excellence and Enjoyment: learning and teaching in the primary years: Learning to learn: progression in key aspects of learning.* London: The Stationery Office.

Fisher, T., Higgins, C. and Loveless, A. (2006) *Teachers learning with digital technologies: a review of research and projects.* Futurelab series, report 14 (SI). Futurelab.

John, P. and Sutherland, R. (2005) Affordance, opportunity and the pedagogical implications of ICT. *Educational Review*, 57(4).

Laurillard, D. (2008) *Digital technologies and their role in achieving our ambitions for education.* Institute of Education, University of London. Online at **www.lkl.ac.uk/cms/ index.php?option=com_comprofiler&task=userProfile&user=127** (retrieved on 2 November 2010).

NAACE (2007) *Primary Review Position Paper.* Online at **www.naace.co.uk/217** (retrieved 23 October 2010).

NAACE/Becta (2001) *Key characteristics of good quality teaching and learning with ICT: a discussion document,* Online at **revolution.caret.cam.ac.uk/pdfs/bectaadvice.pdf** (retrieved 28 October 2010).

Prosser G. (2006) *Education Policy, Management and ICT: the case of Citizenship Education in English secondary schools.* Online at **www.citized.info/pdf/commarticles/Gary_Prosser.doc** (retrieved 2 November 2010).

Robinson, C. *et al.* (2008) *Personalising learning: the learner perspective and their influence on demand.* Becta. Online at **research.becta.org.uk/.../personalising_learning_learner_ perspective0408.doc** (retrieved 23 October 2010).

Rose, J. (2009) *Independent Review of the Primary Curriculum.* Online at **www.webarchive.nationalarchives.gov.uk/tna/+www.dcsf.gov.uk/primarycurriculumreview** (retrieved 20 October 2010).

Schön, D. (1987) *Educating the Reflective Practitioner.* San Francisco: Jossey-Bass.

Stein, G. (2005) *How does ICT support personalised and individualised learning?* Online at **www.canterbury.ac.uk/education/.../gs-individualised-learning.pdf** (retrieved 23 October 2010).

Wenger, E. (1999) *Communities of Practice: Learning, Meaning, and Identity.* Cambridge: Cambridge University Press.

PART 2
ICT SUPPORTING
PRIMARY EDUCATION

6. Learning online: the internet, social networking and e-safety
Jayne Metcalfe and Debbie Simpson

Learning Outcomes

....

By the end of this chapter you should:

- understand what is meant by the term 'social networking';
- be able to identify risks associated with children's use of new technologies;
- be aware of the range of ways that schools and teachers can contribute to children's safe use of new technologies both in and outside of educational settings;
- recognise ways in which social and learning networks can support children's learning across the curriculum.

Professional standards for QTS

Q2 Demonstrate the positive values, attitudes and behaviour they expect from children and young people;

Q5 Recognise and respect the contribution that colleagues, parents and carers can make to the development and well-being of children and young people, and to raising their levels of attainment;

Q8 Have a creative and constructively critical approach towards innovation, being prepared to adapt their practice where benefits and improvement are identified;

Q21a Be aware of the current legal requirements, national policies and guidance on the safeguarding and promotion of the well-being of children and young people;

Q21b Know how to identify and support children and young people whose progress, development or well-being is affected by changes or difficulties in their personal circumstances, and when to refer them to colleagues for specialist support;

Q23 Design opportunities for learners to develop their literacy, numeracy and ICT skills;

Q25a Use a range of teaching strategies and resources, including e-learning, taking practical account of diversity and promoting equality and inclusion;

Q30 Establish a purposeful and safe learning environment conducive to learning and identify opportunities for learners to learn in out-of-school contexts.

Introduction

In this chapter you will read about the appeal of networked technologies for children and consider the issues of e-safety that are raised by children's use of the internet. You will consider whether banning children from using online technologies is realistic, or whether it is better to educate children about potential dangers and help them to develop transferable skills that will help them to protect themselves both in and out of school. You will explore ways to identify and manage risk in social networking environments and on the internet more widely. You will consider how the safe use of networks can support learning across the curriculum, and examine case studies that show how some schools and teachers are already using networking tools to help children communicate and learn together.

Social networking

The term *online social networking* is used to describe the way people use interactive online tools (sometimes known as *Web 2.0* tools), to participate in communities based on friendship or shared interests. Some of the best known social networks include *Bebo* (**www.bebo.com**), *Facebook* (**www.facebook.com**), and *MySpace* (**www.myspace.com**). You may be a member of one of these networked communities yourself; or you may have shared photos and videos through websites such as *Flickr* (**www.flickr.com**), or *YouTube* (**www.youtube.com**). You might enjoy multiplayer networked games such as *Farmville* (**www.farmville.com**). If so you may well find that children in your class use the same or similar sites. According to research (Ofcom, 2010) some children are flouting minimum age requirements to join social networking sites intended for adults and older teenagers.

Social networks are not only about exchanging text messages. Sharing media such as photographs, video and music is popular with all ages, including children, and facilities such as *Skype* (**www.skype.com**) allow people to chat face to face in real time. The accessibility of *any time, anywhere* connection to the internet via mobile phones and hand-held computers has also contributed to the rise of social networking. Using a mobile phone you can snap a photo or video with your phone camera, add your comments and share it instantly with a network of friends and potentially with the world.

Like adults, children use social networks to:

- keep in touch with existing friends;
- make new friends;
- exchange and share photos, videos and music;
- join in multiplayer games;
- join groups of people who share their interests;
- explore different ways of presenting themselves.

It is relatively uncommon however to find primary schools using social networks, or addressing issues about their use outside school. Parents and teachers have understandable concerns about the risks associated with children's use of new technology generally, and specifically about the dangers of children using social networks. Adults worry that children will make harmful contacts online, be bullied (or bully others) or be exposed to harmful or inappropriate material or excessively commercial content. There may also be concern about the potential damage to children's social development if too much time is spent online and too many of their friends are *virtual*. In response to these concerns, many primary schools have adopted e-safety policies that specifically discourage children's use of social networking both in and outside school. Here is an extract from a typical primary school e-safety policy:

- *The school will block/filter access to social networking sites.*
- *Pupils and parents will be advised that the use of social network spaces outside school is inappropriate for primary aged pupils.*

Activity

Reflect on your own use of Web 2.0 (interactive) technologies. Are you a member of any social networking sites yourself? If you are, think about the following prints.

- How do you use the sites (keeping in touch with friends, sharing photos and videos, etc.)?
- Do you take any precautions to protect your own privacy online or can everyone access your personal details? Check the privacy information for your social networking site at **www.digizen.org.uk** (Social Networking Evaluation Chart).
- Have you ever shared any information or media on a social network that you have later regretted? What are the possible implications of inappropriate sharing for you, your friends and family or your career?

If you are not a member of a social networking site, talk to a friend who is and discuss the issues with them.

Research Focus: Children, the internet and e-safety

A recent study (Livingstone and Haddon, 2009) into the online habits of children across 25 European countries shows that the fastest growing group of internet users is among six- to 12-year-olds (Key Stage 2). By 2008, 87 per cent of UK six-to-ten-year-old children were online and by 2008, six-17-year-olds in all European countries were more likely to use the internet at home than in school. Additionally, according to research by media regulator Ofcom (2010), 25 per cent of eight- to 12-year-olds surveyed have a social networking profile. The minimum membership age for most social network sites is 13; however, the research shows that younger children are falsifying their ages in order to join.

Tanya Byron conducted one of the first independent reviews to assess the risks to children from exposure to potentially harmful or inappropriate material on the internet. The Byron Review (DCSF, 2008a) makes recommendations as to how digital safety can be improved, with an emphasis on empowering children to understand and manage risk. The review brings perspective to the issue through acknowledging the benefits, both educational and social, of technology as well as the risks.

Teachers and parents seek to keep children safe; however the Byron Report argues that taking risks, testing boundaries and evading adult scrutiny are a normal feature of childhood and of children's development.

> ... genuine and unacceptable risks (of internet use) should be addressed and where possible prevented, but on the other hand, children learn to cope with the world through testing their capacities and adjusting their actions in the light of lessons learned.
>
> (Livingstone and Haddon, 2009, page 23)

Prohibition or education?

Ten years ago it seemed feasible to insist that children accessed the internet only with adult supervision. Today this seems unrealistic. Furthermore, preventing children from using networked technologies openly may lead to resentment and the chance that children will participate in the sites secretly. In this situation children may be reluctant to admit to any worries about their internet activities; they may also be less willing to ask for help if they believe that they will be *told off* or that they will lose access to the internet. In some cases they may not yet have developed sufficient social and emotional maturity to understand when a situation is actually or potentially abusive.

The Byron Review (DCSF, 2008a) concluded that parents have a key role to play in managing children's access to the internet; however some parents may themselves lack confidence with technology. Byron also suggests that there is a *massive mismatch* between parents' opinions of what their children do online and what they really do, and this raises the question of where else children will receive informed advice.

Schools are able to reach almost all children, irrespective of socio-economic or other types of inequality. School provides a safe environment where children can discuss attitudes and concerns and learn to use the internet safely and responsibly. They can also play a role in helping to inform parents of strategies to help them keep their children safe. The next section of this chapter investigates the risks associated with children's use of the internet and social networking sites, and identifies opportunities within the curriculum for teachers to introduce e-safety issues.

Understanding risks for children using the internet

Table 6.1 below, developed by the EU Kids Online Project, is a useful way of thinking about the risks posed by online activities. Potential risks for children can be classified under three main areas; content, contact and conduct. These risks are often determined by the behaviour of users rather than the technologies themselves and the boundaries are sometimes blurred or overlap.

	Commercial	Aggressive	Sexual	Values
Content – *child as recipient*	Advertising, spam, sponsorship	Violent/hateful content	Pornographic or unwelcome sexual content	Racism, biased or misleading info/ advice (e.g. drugs)
Contact – *child as participant*	Tracking/harvesting personal info	Being bullied, stalked or harassed	Meeting strangers, being groomed	Self-harm, unwelcome persuasion
Conduct - *child as actor*	Gambling, hacking, illegal downloads	Bullying or harassing other users	Creating and uploading pornographic material	Providing advice (e.g. suicide/ pro-anorexic chat)

Source: EU Kids Online (Hasebrink et al., 2008)

Table 6.1: A classification of online risks to children

Content: quality, reliability and appropriateness of information

While the internet is a valuable source of information, content may be unreliable or unsuitable for children. Many children believe online content has as much authority as books and encyclopaedias, and this intersection of information and technology is acknowledged in the National Curriculum both for English and ICT.

Links to the National Curriculum

In the English National Curriculum children at Key Stages 1 and 2 are expected to become familiar with a range of print and ICT-based reference and information materials. At Key Stage 2 children begin to become discerning users of online information (EN2: 9), able to distinguish between fact and opinion (3f) and consider an argument critically (3g).

In the ICT curriculum at Key Stage 2, children are expected to use the internet both to find things out (1a) and to exchange and share information through publishing it online (3b), paying attention to the quality of the information, its presentation and its appropriateness for the intended audience.

The internet has enabled a rapid increase in the distribution of pornographic, racist or other offensive material. It has also provided opportunities for marginalised groups or those with niche interests to spread their ideas through, for example, pro-suicide, anorexia or racist sites. Consequently the risk of children's exposure to inappropriate content and ideas, accidentally or deliberately, has grown. According to the Byron Review (DCSF, 2008a) the effects of encountering such materials is not well researched; however, a small but growing body of evidence shows links between exposure to such materials and the development of negative behaviours and attitudes. There are opportunities within the citizenship curriculum to raise and explore some of these issues, for example when considering gender stereotyping or racism.

Links to the National Curriculum

In the non-statutory curriculum for citizenship, Key Stage 2 children are encouraged to develop good relationships and respect the differences between people. They are taught to consider the consequences of their actions, including the impact on others of negative behaviours (4a, 4d), and how and where to seek help (4g). They think about other people's lives, values and customs and learn to recognise and challenge stereotypes. (4b, 4e.)

Contact and conduct

The internet brings real benefits and opportunities in terms of interaction and communication, but children are also vulnerable to unwanted contact from adults, occasionally with tragic results. Other well-publicised dangers include online bullying, and the glorification of inappropriate behaviour or risky activities.

Online grooming

Children often behave differently in an online environment, saying and doing things they would never do in a face-to-face situation, and often mistakenly view publicly available sites, such as social networks, as private and personal places. They do not understand the risks involved in giving out too much personal information and sometimes publish detailed accounts of their daily lives as well as contact information such as their address and telephone numbers.

This naive posting of personal details and the anonymity that the internet offers creates opportunities for online grooming by those who wish to exploit children. The dangers of paedophiles posing as children in internet chat rooms are well known. Once these predators have gained the trust of children online they may attempt to expose them to inappropriate sexual imagery and content, or manipulate them into doing things that they would otherwise not do. They may also try to make physical contact with children. According to research, *stranger danger*, and in particular adults posing as young people, is one of the greatest worries of parents (Ofcom, 2008).

Cyberbullying

Social networking sites can provide a platform for facilitating online bullying, slander and humiliation of others. According to the Anti-Bullying Alliance, cyberbullying is a growing problem in primary schools.

> *Cyberbullying involves the use of information and communication technologies to support deliberate, repeated, and hostile behaviour by an individual or group that is intended to harm others.*

> (Belsey, no date, cited on **www.cyberbullying.org**)

Cyberbullying can have a much greater impact and can be potentially more upsetting and damaging than face-to-face bullying. Cyberbullying can take place 24 hours a day and can invade victims' privacy, making them feel vulnerable to attacks at any time, even in personal spaces such as their home, which they have previously regarded as safe. In addition cyberbullying can be carried out anonymously. This inability to 'get away' from the bullying, and the issue of not being able to identify the perpetrator, can be particularly hurtful and make the victim distrustful and suspicious of others. The anonymity that the internet provides means bullies cannot see the impact of their actions and so there is less chance for empathy with the victim. In addition the lack of visual or oral cues can result in messages being misinterpreted.

Research (cited by DCSF, 2008a) has shown that people are generally less inhibited online and behave in ways that they would not do offline. There is also some indication that children feel it is acceptable to behave differently in the virtual rather than the real world. This can be further complicated by the fact that many children are still in the process of developing their moral conscience. Children need to learn how to consider the possible impact of their online activities, as well as how to interpret and cope with the behaviour of others. Scope for helping children to develop these skills within the National Curriculum programme for Personal, Social and Health Education is shown in the box below.

Links to the National Curriculum

In the non-statutory curriculum for Personal, Social and Health Education (PSHE), Key Stage 2 children are taught about the consequences of bullying and antisocial behaviours (2c); about how to recognise risky situations (3e) and how to resist pressure from others to behave in an unacceptable or risky way (3f). Children are encouraged to consider the feelings and viewpoints of others (4a) and made aware of how they can find information and advice (for example through helplines) (5h).

Case Study: Emily's secret

Just after Christmas, Emily moved to a new school. She received a warm welcome and soon became a popular member of her Year 5 class and made lots of new friends. About a month later Emily's parents noticed that she had stopped contacting and meeting her friends and seemed to prefer staying at home. They became concerned and tried to talk to Emily. Reluctantly, she told them that she and her friends had had a disagreement and were not getting along at present. However, it turned out that things were a little more serious.

It all started one day when Emily walked into class and people, including her so-called friends, began to laugh at her and make strange remarks. Emily sat down calmly at her desk and decided not to mention this to anyone; she thought it would just go away. However, later that day at home, Emily decided to check her social networking account and found that some of her classmates had posted embarrassing pictures of her on their pages. Emily was deeply upset, as she thought everyone really liked her. She decided not to mention this to anyone.

As time went on other people started to add their own hurtful comments and captions to the photos. Emily felt too humiliated to tell anyone and was afraid of the consequences from the perpetrators if she did. Both Emily's parents and her teacher noticed that she was not her usual self; she seemed more withdrawn, she spent more and more time on her own and her school work was also beginning to suffer.

Activity

- What signs does Emily display that something is wrong?
- What do you think are the motives of the bully/bullies?
- What is your role as the teacher of this class?
- What could the school do to prevent this happening again?
- What should happen to the bully/bullies?
- What could Emily have done differently?

The internet and children's social development

Prolonged periods of time spent on social networking or gaming sites may have emotional and developmental implications for some children. In addition to concerns about children's lack of physical activity it is possible that the frequent use of networking sites may result in children replacing real relationships for online ones and missing out on the development of essential social and emotional skills. This can have a negative effect on children who are less confident and self-assured, as they can equate their happiness and success as individuals with how many online friends they have (NetMums Ltd, 2010). Conversely, social networks such as *PostPals* (**www.postpals.co.uk**) that cater for children who cannot easily communicate with others, for example because of serious illness, may offer a supportive environment and contact with the wider world.

Children (and some adults), however, often do not realise that content published on the internet, for example on a social networking site, can spread rapidly beyond the audience for whom it was intended. Once published online content may persist for many years and potentially could damage a young person's self-image or reputation.

Another concern is that while children may be excited and empowered by the *Web 2.0* philosophy of finding, personalising, mixing and sharing media, they need to be careful that they do not break laws on copyright by downloading and distributing materials that legally belong to someone else. File sharing sites such as *LimeWire* (**www.limewire.com**) are sometimes used by children to access resources such as music and games without paying for them; however, they are unlikely to equate this *sharing* with stealing.

At Key Stage 2 children are beginning to understand abstract concepts such as respect for others, the right to privacy and the ownership of information. They are able to debate behaviour and responsibility in an online environment and these discussions, if well managed by the teacher, have the potential to develop children's core values and may help them to protect themselves and others. Relating online concepts to their *real world* equivalents may be an appropriate way to introduce a debate about ethical issues; for example through comparing behaviour in a *chat room* with behaviour in a playground, or equating taking someone else's work from the internet without proper acknowledgement with *copying* in class.

E-safety: whole-school approaches

This section introduces you to aspects of a whole-school approach to e-safety. You will examine the Acceptable Use Policy for the school where you work or train in the light of government guidelines. You will consider the training and development needs of teachers and parents, and explore some online resources designed to meet these needs. Finally you will read about examples of schools using their learning platforms to deliver e-safety messages.

> *Children and young people need to be empowered to keep themselves safe – this isn't just about a top-down approach. Children will be children – pushing boundaries and*

taking risks. At a public swimming pool we have gates, put up signs, have lifeguards and shallow ends, but we also teach children how to swim.

(DCSF, 2008a, page 2)

Every Child Matters: Change for Children in Schools (DfES, 2004) identified teachers and educational settings as key players in supporting children's learning and well-being. The Staying Safe Action Plan (DCSF, 2008b) which followed made it compulsory for schools to have measures in place to prevent all forms of bullying, including cyberbullying. It recognised the new threats to children's safety from new technologies and the need for children to be taught how to keep safe.

In addition, the Byron Review (DCSF, 2008a) recommended that e-safety be delivered as part of the primary school curriculum and that schools should be accountable to Ofsted for their performance in this area. Ofsted (2010) identified that the most effective schools in terms of e-safety were those where there was a clear strategy for e-safety, where senior leaders, governors, staff and families work together and their vision is reflected in unambiguous guidelines for the use of technology and the internet, usually known as an *Acceptable Use Policy* (AUP). Regular training for all school staff is critical to ensure knowledge and expertise is secure. Byron also highlights the need for trainee teachers to be equipped with e-safety knowledge and skills so that they too are prepared for their role in school.

A shared responsibility for delivery of an age-appropriate curriculum, plus strong relationships with families, means that safety messages and good practice can be reinforced at home. Research has shown that parents who are well informed and are themselves online are less worried about risks, and more likely to be aware of potential educational advantages of the internet, than those who are not. Encouraging parents to share in their children's online experiences is therefore likely to reduce anxiety (Livingstone and Haddon, 2009).

Acceptable Use Policies

An Acceptable Use Policy (AUP) *details the way new and emerging technologies may and may not be used, and [includes] sanctions for misuse.* Becta (2009, page 5)

Becta (2009) outlines some general principles for developing effective AUPs.

Acceptable use policies should:

- provide a framework to establish and reinforce safe and responsible online behaviours for children, staff and parents;
- reinforce the safe and responsible use of *all* technologies (rather than listing specific ones) and promote the benefits of using such technologies;
- be relevant to the setting and the characteristics of the users;
- involve users as far as possible in the development and review of e-safety policies and procedures;

- set out clearly what users are and are not allowed to do when using these technologies, and the consequences of breaching such regulations;
- be written in a tone and style appropriate for its users (which may mean having different versions for different users);
- be linked to other school policies such as child protection, anti-bullying and behaviour policies, as appropriate;
- be regularly monitored, reviewed and updated and ensure that any changes are communicated to stakeholders.

AUPs are often introduced as part of home–school agreements, and parents and children may be asked to sign to show they have understood and are in agreement with the content.

Activity

When you are next on school placement, ask if you can look at the school's Acceptable Use Policy. If you are not in school you can see some examples by entering the phrase *acceptable use policy primary school* into a search engine.

Does the AUP adhere to the general principles set out by Becta above? Consider whether the school policy:

- is clear and concise and written in an appropriate tone and style and relevant to the setting;
- clearly outlines acceptable and unacceptable behaviours and specifies the sanctions for unacceptable use;
- promotes positive uses of new and emerging technologies;
- is monitored and reviewed on a regular basis. When was the policy last reviewed?

Visit the Becta safeguarding learners website for further advice and information: **www.nextgenerationlearning.org.uk/safeguarding-learners/Case-studies/ Acceptable-use-policies/**

Parents, teachers, children: online resources for e-safety

Both Ofsted and the Byron Report recommend that e-safety should be taught as part of a continuous, cross-curricular programme and should be the responsibility of all staff. Discrete lessons on e-safety delivered during ICT lessons are not enough. Circle time, assemblies and National Curriculum subjects such as English and Personal, Social and Health Education (PSHE) provide opportunities for helping children to understand the consequences of online behaviour, whether their own or that of others.

Home–school partnerships can be an important way of raising the awareness of the whole school community to issues of e-safety, and of developing parents' and teachers' knowledge and understanding of new technologies. Schools can provide access to resources or offer family learning sessions. Involving families in e-safety provision helps reinforce key messages and the importance of e-safety both at home, school and in the wider world.

The Next Generation learning site offers a wealth of resources for home–school partnerships: **www.nextgenerationlearning.org.uk/At-Home/Internet-safety/**

Activity

Table 6.2 contains details of resources available online for teachers and trainee teachers, children and parents. Explore at least one resource from each of the rows in the table and identify:

- Which areas of e-safety are covered?
- How might the resources support development of children's personal, emotional and social skills?
- Which other areas of the National Curriculum are supported?

Consider how the resources might help you as a teacher to:

- develop your own knowledge, skills and understanding of new technologies and e-safety issues;
- deliver e-safety messages in school with children;
- support parents in protecting their children online.

	Think u know **www.thinkuknow.co.uk**	*Kidsmart* **www.kidsmart.org.uk**	*Know it all* **www.childnet-int.org**
Teachers	Visit the *Teacher/Trainer* area to find out how your school can take part in Safer Internet Day	Choose the *teachers section* of the site (*I work with kids*) to explore lesson plans for promoting e-safety messages	Choose *Know IT All* and locate the section for *trainee teachers*. Watch the short video explaining why e-safety is so important as you enter the teaching profession
Children	Try out some of the activities for either Key Stage 1 (5–7) or Key Stage 2 (8–10) children	Check out the *Being SMART Rules!* and think about how you might introduce these in your classroom	Explore *Captain Kara and Winston's SMART Adventure*, which promotes the *SMART Rules*
Parents	Visit the *Parent/Carer* area to view the internet safety film and take the *parent test*	Download the *Top Tips* information sheet for parents (*I have kids* section). Is this suitable for use at a parents' evening or as a school information sheet?	Choose *Know IT All* and locate the section for *parents*. Scroll down the page to explore community language versions of e-safety resources

Table 6.2. Online resources activity

Safety guidelines and reporting abuse

Children can be helped to stay safe online through being taught clear and straightforward rules and how to access immediate help. Two recent campaigns have been designed to promote these messages: *Zip it, Block it, Flag it,* and *Click CEOP.*

Figure 6.1 Zip it, Block it, Flag it: **clickcleverclicksafe.direct.gov.uk/index.html**

The Child Exploitation and Online Protection Centre (CEOP) www.ceop.police.uk/) provides an online facility for reporting abuse, sexually inappropriate or potentially illegal online activity towards a child or young person. The CEOP report button can also be found on other e-safety sites linking children to this service.

Figure 6.2 The CEOP report button

In addition, the Childline charity (**www.childline.org.uk**) offers a free 24-hour confidential helpline for children in distress or danger.

E-safety and social networks

Children may learn e-safety lessons about the use of social networks better while they are actually using networking tools. Using a closed network, sometimes known as a *walled garden*, children can discuss and rehearse the techniques of safe networking in school before they are tempted to join other less secure, open networks.

Case Study: Learning platforms

One primary school used their learning platform as a walled garden. The network was open only to Key Stage 2 children and their teachers. The aim was for children to gain confidence and to have fun in creating and managing an online identity, while learning that people online may not be who or what they seem.

Children:

- created their own personal profile on the learning platform;

→

- used an online site to create an *avatar* to express their personality and protect their privacy;
- uploaded their own choice of photos, videos and music files;
- exchanged messages and media files with friends;
- created and joined discussion groups for shared interests: football, dinosaurs and pets.

Teachers introduced the *SMART* rules (**www.kidsmart.org.uk/**) and used these to explore e-safety issues. They discussed appropriate photography, dangers of sharing personal information, legal issues of copyright and how to decide who should be able to see their pages. The children then edited their pages to make them secure and shared them with only their trusted friends.

Activity

If there is a learning platform in your next placement school such as *Frog, Fronter, Kaleidos, Moodle* or *UniServity*, request an account and login, and explore how you might use some of its features in a similar way to the case study school. Tools and features will vary from one platform to another so investigate what is available on your platform.

Most learning platforms will allow users to:
- have a personal page or 'wall' on the learning platform;
- make decisions about who can view their page;
- publish and exchange messages, images and other media with chosen contacts;
- create and join interest groups and discussions.

Using your school's learning platform, create and personalise your own page. Create an avatar to represent you and add it to your profile. See the end of this chapter for a list of sites where you can create your own avatar. Discuss the learning platform with your ICT subject leader or class teacher and find out how they use the network to support teaching and learning.

As an alternative to using the school's learning platform to mimic the features of popular social networks such as *Facebook*, some schools are delivering e-safety lessons using some of the social networking sites specifically designed for children younger than 13. Many of these sites employ moderators who are responsible for monitoring and regulating children's activities and discussions. Examples of social networking sites designed for children include *Club Penguin, Poptropica, Habbo, Stardoll, Moshi Monsters* and *Free Realms*. Children are able to choose an avatar and explore a virtual world, meeting other users and playing games.

Case Study: Club Penguin

Sally used *Club Penguin* (**www.clubpenguin.com**) to explore internet safety with her Year 3 class. The children themselves introduced her to the social networking site and she found that 75 per cent of her class already had accounts. Sally contacted the children's parents to gain permission for the whole class to have accounts. The project took place over one week.

On the first day children logged on and explored the environment. They were asked to only chat to, and add as buddies, other children from their class. During circle time the next day the children discussed their reactions to the activity. They discussed *online identities* and thought about how someone might be able to hide behind an identity and mislead others into thinking they are someone they're not.

The second visit to *Club Penguin,* Sally focused on looking for instances of children following or breaking common sense safety guidelines. On the final day of the project the class used circle time to create a list of rules for safe behaviour in *Club Penguin.*

Activity

Consider the possible difficulties of managing a similar activity using a commercial social networking site.

- How would you respond if some parents refused permission for their child to participate?
- What rules did the teacher introduce to ensure the children's safety?

Initial participation with *Club Penguin* and similar sites is free. However, children will quickly realise that only by signing up for paid membership or through obtaining *virtual money* (purchased of course with real money) will they be able to access some areas or acquire the coolest accessories for their igloos.

- What are your views on encouraging children to access commercial websites during school time?

Educational networks

Some schools subscribe to social and learning networks catering for the education market. *Learning Landscape for Schools* (**www.ll4schools.co.uk/**) and *SuperClubsPLUS* (**www.superclubsplus.com/**) are two examples. These communities are protected; all users, whether children or members of staff, must be registered by the school and members' activities are tracked. Networks are continuously moderated and language filters are used to ensure that postings are appropriate. Some of the networks also close down before 10 p.m. on school nights. Within these networks schools can create their own home pages and groups and join international, collaborative projects. There are regular opportunities for children to question special guests, such as sports people or scientists, on the *hotseat*.

Research Focus

Educational networks can support children's transition from primary to secondary school. During their last term at primary school, children can have a chance to learn about life in secondary school through joining in secondary school forums and chatting to Key Stage 3 students. Pine (2006), in an evaluative study of the *SuperClubsPLUS* network, cites an online discussion between Jacob, a Key Stage 3 student, and a group of children who are about to transfer to secondary school. Pine notes evidence of children *developing a morality of cooperation and social exchange* through providing *remarkably thoughtful advice* (2006, page 36).

Online learning networks and the primary National Curriculum

Many children are confident but not competent users of technology. They need to develop the knowledge, skills and understanding to critically engage with technology and use it effectively and safely. Integrating the use of new technologies across the curriculum in ways that meet the interests and needs of the children can be seen as an essential preparation for participation in an increasingly technology-based society. When planning online activities it is important that consideration is paid to potentially vulnerable children, for example learners with special educational needs (SEN), and to children who have no access to online technologies outside school.

Independent studies have shown that providing children with opportunities to communicate and work collaboratively on projects can support learning. You will recognise it as a very common strategy in primary classrooms; children talk, play and work together all the time. Online networking can extend your classroom almost indefinitely and give children opportunities to communicate and collaborate online with peers who have similar or very different backgrounds to themselves. This is illustrated in the following case study.

Case Study: Networked learning

Year 6 teacher Phil used open source (free) software to set up a learning network in his class. The network allowed children to create a personal profile and keep a journal or weblog which could be shared or remain private. Children could also post status updates and write on each other's 'walls'.

$\longrightarrow$

During the first year Phil explored with children ways they could use the network. They wrote about things that mattered to them, with the option of keeping it private or sharing their work. Phil found that the system worked best for most children when they were given a theme to write about, but he also found that some of the most interesting entries were from those who used the space to explore ideas of their own, or talk about experiences out of school.

The following year Phil teamed up with a teacher in another school to give children in both schools a chance to make new friends online and to write for a wider audience. As the children's confidence improved the teachers set up networked debates for teams to explore ideas and present a case. The use of media helped all children to contribute to the debate through expressing their ideas in writing, audio or video. The children responded eagerly to each other's postings. Children also wrote collaborative stories using the *wiki* facility of their learning platform.

Activity

- From the case study above consider which key skills from the English National Curriculum for Speaking and Listening (EN1) are practised through the networked activities undertaken by the children.
- Look at the range of purposes for writing in the English National Curriculum EN3: 9. Imagine you are teaching in a school that has an established collaborative network with a partner school. Can you identify a mini-project that would appeal to children and inspire collaborative and co-operative learning across the network?

Research Focus

The National Literacy Trust surveyed attitudes towards writing of 3001 children aged eight to 16, and examined the role of technology in developing literacy skills (Clark and Dugdale, 2009). The survey found that children who write on blogs or on a social networking site are more confident and prolific writers and demonstrate more positive attitudes to writing than those who do not. Rather than limiting their engagement with different types of writing, children who participate in online blogs or networks appeared significantly more likely to write in a range of formats (e.g. notes to other people, short stories, letters, song lyrics and diaries/journals).

Web-based networks for schools

The school in Case Study: Networked learning used its learning platform to create a networked community for upper Key Stage 2 children. Phil and his colleague are now planning to expand their network to include more distant localities. The potential for opening up a learning network to a wider audience, while still remaining safe and secure, makes it an ideal environment for co-operative international projects. The following case study is an example taken from a collection of case studies hosted by the learning platform provider *UniServity*, online at **www.school-portal.co.uk/resource/2750425/11_12201052010604_61.pdf**

Case Study: Learning about Africa

Teachers of Key Stage 1 children used a learning environment to support a theme focusing on learning about life in Africa from authentic sources. This is linked to the English National Curriculum Geography requirement for children to study a locality that contrasts with that of their school (6b). As part of the British Council's Connecting Classrooms project (**www.britishcouncil.org/learning-connecting-classrooms.htm**) the school was introduced to three schools from two contrasting localities in Africa. An area of the learning platform was designed with an African theme, and included links to sources of information and videos about the countries, along with maps of the area at different scales.

Children used forums to ask questions about the localities and their questions were answered by teachers and children at the partner schools. The online resources were combined with more immediate experiences, such as visits to the school by special guests who originated from the countries studied. A number of events were arranged for pupils to try different foods and look at different objects from Africa. Photographs and videos of these activities were added to the Learning Platform for the children to talk about later at home.

You can read more about global linking using ICT, including a detailed discussion of ethical and practical considerations, in Chapter 9.

Links to the National Curriculum

Within the geography curriculum there is an expectation that children will, by the end of their primary education, have been given opportunities to study a range of places and environments in different parts of the world. Through this study children begin to understand how physical and human processes can change places, and how these changes affect the lives and activities of people living in those places (Geography AT4). The religious education curriculum suggests that through the use of ICT, children's awareness of religions and beliefs globally may be enhanced (RE 3s).

Learning Outcomes Review

In this chapter you have explored what is meant by the term *social networking* and identified networks you may use yourself. Statistics show that primary age children are joining social networks and you considered whether prevention or education was the better strategy for keeping children safe. Through case studies you read about examples of schools using secure social and learning networks to provide a safe environment to nurture learning across the curriculum. You have seen how managed networks can promote cross-cultural and transnational projects that appeal to children's natural curiosity about the world and help them to explore issues of diversity of language, attitudes, lifestyles and faith.

The chapter identified risks associated with children's use of new technologies and you examined a range of resources for schools that support e-safety education for children, parents and teachers, both in and outside of educational settings.

> *The fundamental pattern of learning and innovation using social tools – find – remix – share – seems ideally suited to the way most young people like to discover and make sense of the world around them, which is reason enough for an optimistic view of their likely impact.*

(Bryant, 2007, page 18)

Self-assessment questions

1. What type of activities and resources do you associate with the term 'social networking'?
2. How would you categorise the risks associated with children's use of new technologies?
3. What are some of the ways in which schools and teachers can contribute to children's safe use of new technologies, both in and outside of educational settings?
4. Identify three examples of the ways in which social and learning networks can support children's learning across the curriculum.

Further information

E-safety

Becta (2007) Signposts to safety: Teaching e-safety at Key Stages 1 and 2. Available at **publications.becta.org.uk/display.cfm?resID=32422** (retrieved 15 July 2010).

CBBC, Stay Safe Internet Safety for children (**www.bbc.co.uk/cbbc/help/web/staysafe**).

CEOP, Child Exploitation and Online Protection Centre (**www.ceop.police.uk**).

Childline, a counselling service for children and young people (**www.childline.org.uk**).

Click Clever, Click Safe, internet safety campaign, includes the 'Zip it, Block it, Flag it' code. (**clickcleverclicksafe.direct.gov.uk/index.html**).

Cybermentors, experienced mentors available to discuss problems encountered online or during social networking (**cybermentors.org.uk/**).

Digizen, how to use the internet safely, creatively and responsibly (**www.digizen.org/**).

Hector's World, children aged two to nine can learn about topics like online privacy and safety (**www.hectorsworld.com**).

Kidsmart, Staying SMART online, e-safety resources for children, parents and teachers (**www.kidsmart.org.uk/**)

Safer Internet Day (**www.saferinternet.org/web/guest/safer-internet-day**).

Teachernet, positive uses of technology and links to e-safety resources (**www.teachernet.gov.uk/**).

Thinkuknow, resources for schools and parents from the Child Exploitation and Online Protection Centre (CEOP) (**www.thinkuknow.co.uk/**).

Learning networks

Avatar creators: **www.buildyourwildself.com/**; **www.reasonablyclever.com/mini/**; **www.stortroopers.com**

British Council Connecting Classrooms Project. Site offers collaborative projects for learners and teachers to help build lasting partnerships between schools in the UK and others around the world (**www.britishcouncil.org/learning-connecting-classrooms.htm**).

Club Penguin Social Network for Children is a virtual world where children interact and play games using penguin avatars (**www.clubpenguin.com/**).

Learning Landscapes for Schools is a social learning platform for schools, providing an environment for communication and sharing between users drawn from a wide range of schools (**www.ll4schools.co.uk**).

SuperClubsPLUS is a protected online learning community for six- to 12-year-old children. (**www.superclubsplus.com**).

UniServity Innovative Teacher Network is a learning platform provider hosting a selection of case studies and examples of innovative projects for learning platforms (**www.school-portal.co.uk**).

References

Becta (2009) *AUPs in context: Establishing safe and responsible online behaviours.* Coventry: Becta. Online at **www.nextgenerationlearning.org.uk/safeguarding-learners/Case-studies/Acceptable-use-policies** (retrieved 12 April 2010).

Becta (2010) *Digital literacy: Teaching critical thinking for our digital world.* Online at **schools.becta.org.uk/uploaddir/downloads/digital_literacy_publication.pdf** (retrieved 12 April 2010).

Belsey, B. *Cyberbullying Website.* Online at **www.cyberbullying.org/** (retrieved 12 April 2010).

Clark, C. and Dugdale, G. (2009) *Young People's Writing: Attitudes, behaviour and the role of technology.* Online at **www.literacytrust.org.uk/research/** (retrieved 15 July 2010).

Bryant, L. (2007) Emerging trends in social software for education. Becta: *Emerging Trends in Technology 2.* Coventry: Becta.

DCSF (2008a) *Safer children in a Digital World: The Report of the Byron Review.* Nottingham: DCSF Publications. Online at **www.dcsf.gov.uk/byronreview** (accessed 12 April 2010).

DCSF (2008b) *Staying safe Action Plan.* Nottingham: DCSF Publications. Retrieved from **www.dcsf.gov.uk/everychildmatters/safeguardingandsocialcare/safeguardingchildren/stayingsafe/stayingsafe/** (retrieved 12 April 2010).

Department for Education and Employment (1999) *The National Curriculum handbook for primary teachers in England key stages 1 and 2.* London: The Stationery Office.

DfES (2004) *Every Child Matters: Change for Children in Schools.* London: DfES. Online at: **www.dcsf.gov.uk/everychildmatters/about/aims/outcomes/outcomescyp/** (retrieved 12 April 2010).

Green, H. and Hannon, C. (2007) *Their space: Education for a digital generation.* Online at **www.demos.co.uk/publications/** (retrieved 15 July 2010).

Harrison, A. (2009) Children social network in secret says Prof Byron, BBC News Online. Online at **news.bbc.co.uk/1/hi/education/8369111.stm** (retrieved 12 April 2010).

Hasebrink, U., Livingstone, S., Haddon, L. (2008) *Comparing children's online opportunities and risks across Europe: Cross-national comparisons for EU Kids Online.* London: EU Kids Online.

Livingstone, S., and Haddon, L. (2009) *EU Kids Online: Final Report.* LSE, London: EU Kids Online. Online at **www.eukidsonline.net** (retrieved 12 April 2010).

NetMums Ltd (2010) *Your children and the internet: Social Networking sites.* Online at **www.netmums.com/olderchild/Your_Children_and_the_internet_Social_Networking_Sites. 4198/** (retrieved 12 April 2010).

Ofcom (2008) *Social Networking: A quantitative and qualitative research report into attitudes, behaviours and use.* London: Ofcom. Online at **www.ofcom.org.uk/advice/media_literacy/ medlitpub/medlitpubrss/socialnetworking/report.pdf** (retrieved 12 April 2010).

Ofcom (2010) *UK children's media literacy.* Online at **www.ofcom.org.uk/advice/ media_literacy/medlitpub/medlitpubrss/ukchildrensml/ukchildrensml1.pdf** (retrieved 12 April 2010).

Ofsted (2010) *The safe use of new technologies,* London: Ofsted. Online at **www.ofsted.gov.uk/ Ofsted-home/Publications-and-research/** (retrieved 12 April 2010).

Pine, K. (2006) *An Evaluation of the Educational and Social Benefits of SuperClubsPLUS for Children.* Online at **www.intuitivemedia.com/nn.html** (retrieved 12 April 2010).

Underwood, J. (2009) *The Impact of Digital Technology.* Coventry: Becta.

UniServity, *cLc Learning Platform Best Practice 316.* UniServity Innovative Teacher Network. Online at **www.school-portal.co.uk/resource/2750425/11_12201052010604_61.pdf** (retrieved 15 July 2010).

7. ICT in the classroom
Ian Todd and Mike Toyn

> ### Learning Outcomes
>
> By the end of this chapter you should:
> - understand how ICT tools can support learning across a range of subjects;
> - be able to identify suitable alternatives to common ICT tools;
> - be able to identify classroom management issues related to the effective use of ICT;
> - understand how ICT can enrich and enhance learning across the curriculum.
>
> **Professional standards for QTS**
>
> Q8 Have a creative and constructively critical approach towards innovation, being prepared to adapt their practice where benefits and improvement are identified;
>
> Q23 Design opportunities for learners to develop their literacy, numeracy and ICT skills;
>
> Q25a Use a range of teaching strategies and resources, including e-learning, taking practical account of diversity and promoting equality and inclusion;
>
> Q30 Establish a purposeful and safe learning environment conducive to learning and identify opportunities for learners to learn in out-of-school contexts.

Introduction

So far in this book you have looked at ways of developing children's ICT capability in a range of areas. Many of these will have clear and obvious links to other areas of the curriculum. In this chapter you will continue to look at ways in which you can plan to use ICT to support learning in other areas of the curriculum.

Clearly there is an enormous range of ICT tools that can be used and it is beyond the scope of any book to cover all of these. This chapter will use a case study approach to present a selection of ICT tools and how they relate to different areas of the curriculum. The use of a case study approach will help you to develop your ability to assess the value of other ICT tools in other situations. Case studies are presented which relate to a range of year groups across the primary phase.

As well as providing a demonstration of the use of specific ICT resources being used to support specific lessons with specific year groups, each case study is followed by a discussion which considers how ICT enhanced or enriched the activity, and what prior learning it built upon. The discussions will also consider elements such as assessment of the activity, management of the resources, alternative ICT tools which could be used and how the ICT might be used to support other curriculum areas.

The first case study looks at using video and e-mail within a writing activity. While reading it, consider how ICT enhances motivation and begin to identify further opportunities for the use of these technologies.

Case Study: Year 1 using video and e-mail

As part of a unit of work on *Superheroes*, Rob and Emma, the Year 1 class teachers, decide to use video technology and e-mail to enhance story writing. At the start of the unit, the teachers show the children a short film on the interactive whiteboard that had been made especially for the lesson, based on the film *The Incredibles*. In it, *Mr Incredible* (in reality, a trainee teacher in costume) presents the children with a problem and asks for their help. Some jewels have been stolen and there is only one week in which to find them and return them to their owners. During the recording, *Mr Incredible* addresses the children directly, as though he is having a conversation with them.

Throughout the week, the children then work in groups to brainstorm possible solutions to the above dilemma. These ideas feed into whole-class shared, and group-guided, writing sessions, helping the children to structure the plot of a story by focusing on two major factors: introducing a dilemma and presenting a solution.

At the end of each day, the Year 1 children compose group e-mails to send to *Mr Incredible*, with their ideas for how the mystery can be solved. Using this information, he sends them video updates the following morning, responding to their ideas and informing them of progress on the case.

As well as the e-mails, the shared writing sessions produce a complete story by the end of the week, with involvement from the whole class. Some of the more able children begin to compose similar *superhero* stories in their independent work, with less able children retelling the story as it unfolds.

The children are grouped according to ability for the writing activities and for the group e-mail sessions. In terms of organisation, each writing session has two focus groups; one led by the class teacher, the other by an experienced teaching assistant. One independent group works directly on a writing activity and another independent group works on another task, such as role-play, related to superheroes. Lots of group and paired discussion precedes any written activity.

Differentiation, then, is partly by outcome and partly by task, with the adults providing more structure and scaffolding for less confident writers. Questions are also adapted to the needs and ability of the groups.

$\rightarrow$

Below is a transcript of part of the initial recording by *Mr Incredible*:

> *Hi, kids, Mr* Incredible *here, coming to you from downtown Municiberg! Your teachers, Mr Steward and Miss Dawson, have told me how good you are at listening, finding clues, then working together to figure things out; which is a good job, because we've got ourselves a real problem down here.*
>
> *Mr and Mrs Denville, two very rich and very important visitors, have come to stay in Municiberg and they are planning to give lots of money to build a new park for kids to play in. The only problem is some evil villain has stolen Mrs Denville's favourite jewels, worth thousands and thousands of dollars! The Denvilles are leaving Municiberg at the end of this week and, if the jewels are not recovered, they will be so cross they will take their money home with them. No jewels, no park!*
>
> *So you see our problem? Do you think you can help us? Here is what we know so far, ...*

Links to the National Curriculum

This activity has links to a number of subjects such as Art (1a, 2a, b, c, 4b and 5a), PE (1a, b, 2a, 3a, 6a, b, c and d) and Design Technology (1a, c, d and e). However, its most significant contribution is to English, particularly Speaking and Listening, as the children will need to work in groups (*Speaking and Listening 3a, b and c*) and to share their ideas (*Speaking and Listening 1c and f*) and listen to the views of others (*Speaking and Listening 2b, c, d and e*). As they move from generating and discussing their ideas to recording them in written format they will be working on their composing (*Writing 1b ,c, d and e*). Through the sharing of ideas via e-mail the children will have the opportunity to develop their capability in ICT by Exchanging and Sharing their ideas (*3 a and b*).

ICT plays two main roles in this activity. Firstly, it provides the stimulus for the story writing, by creating a dilemma to which a solution has to be found. It also provides a *real* context and audience for the children's writing. *Real* is a relative term here: some of the more mature children will have known that this was not really *Mr Incredible*; although many believed it was. Even so, young children will often happily suspend their disbelief and 'play along' so long as they find the context credible; in this case, because it related to something with which they were very familiar. Linked to this, the stimulus provided a sense of urgency, with a daily deadline to complete the group e-mails and, of course, high levels of motivation, especially for the boys in each class. Secondly, it provided opportunities for discussion and interaction: interaction with each other, with adults, with the technology (by viewing the videos and composing the e-mails) and, of course, with the main character, *Mr Incredible*.

Several assessment opportunities present themselves through these activities. In terms of speaking and listening, careful questioning at the whole-class stage should ensure that children are contributing at their own level, and observation of group discussions would allow the adult to consider not only the level of contribution of the participants, but also the extent to which they were able to produce ideas for possible solutions.

The independent written work provided documentary evidence of the children's writing ability. All work was annotated with either an 'I' (independent) or a 'G', (indicating that an adult had given some guidance and therefore it was not all the child's own work), in line with school policy.

The group e-mail sessions were the hardest to assess in terms of product, as the e-mail was a joint effort, and it was appropriate to discount the end product in terms of evidence here, and concentrate instead on the process involved, i.e. observing the discussions that led up to the final e-mail.

Could this activity have been achieved without the use of ICT? Yes, you could argue that traditional stories could have set up the dilemma and conceivably an actor could have played the part 'in the flesh'. It is less likely however that the same credibility, sense of immediacy or sense that the children were actually shaping events could have been achieved without the videos and e-mails. Both teachers noted a significant increase in levels of motivation, and in quantity and quality of output from the children.

Research Focus: ICT – more than just a motivational tool

The above case study clearly demonstrates how ICT can be used to create a context in which children will be motivated to learn and will be eager to carry out associated activities. However, ICT can be more than just a way of generating enthusiasm for other subject areas.

Ofsted (2009, page 11) confirmed the motivating qualities of ICT, stating that *pupils showed great enthusiasm for learning using ICT* and the Becta (2008, page 3) study on gender and technology outlined that, *[t]he use of ICT in education improves the motivation of both girls and boys, though increases are more marked with boys.* Beyond this, however, Ofsted (2009, page 8) found that technology allowed children *to be creative and work collaboratively* and *enabled pupils to develop ... independence ... and improve their thinking skills.* It noted that ICT had *raised standards, particularly in English* (Ofsted, 2009, page 9). Furthermore, Becta (2009, page 2) cited a *strong body of evidence linking the use of technology to improvements in learning and outcomes for learners* and stated that *schools' use of technology across the curriculum in a variety of ways was a key factor in learning gains.*

→

However, Andrews *et al.* (2007) were inconclusive on the subject. Their article on the effectiveness of ICT on the teaching of written English suggested that further research was required to establish a causal relationship between the use of ICT and raised standards in English. Similarly, while Becta's (2010, page 2) literature review on the impact of technology on children's attainment in English pointed to several specific instances of how ICT benefits areas such as spelling and reading, it recommended *larger scale UK randomised control trials examining the educational impact of using technology to enhance English learning across age groups.*

There is then a strong case for suggesting that ICT can enhance learning skills in general. Specific links to English, while undoubtedly evidenced in isolated studies and examples, have yet to be comprehensively researched.

Not all ICT has to involve desktop computers in a computer suite. The next case study is based on the use of programmable floor robots in a mathematical context. Although this case study describes a Year 2 class, floor robots can be used effectively across both Key Stage 1 and 2.

It would be a valuable activity to think about their use in other year groups. Consider also which other ICT resources are available in schools, aside from desktop computers.

Case Study: Year 2 using a *Roamer*

Siobhan is a Year 2 teacher and has planned a sequence of lessons focusing on problem-solving and developing mathematical talk.

One lesson in this sequence involved using *Roamer* programmable floor robots (Valiant) in conjunction with some floor mats. *Roamers* can be given commands that make them move and turn; these instructions can be given one at a time or as an extended sequence. (They are capable of much more than this, but this is the feature that Siobhan is making use of in her activity.) Her class have previously been introduced to the *Roamer* and are able to make it move using single commands and short sequences of commands. Case Study: *Big Barn Farm* in Chapter 3 where a floor robot is used with a Reception/Year 1 class would be appropriate prior learning for this activity.

Prior to the lesson Siobhan set out some floor mats in the hall; an example is shown in Figure 7.1. The floor mats are the same dimensions as the *Roamer* so that each unit the Roamer moves forward or backwards corresponds to one mat.

Siobhan has placed the children into groups of five, and each group has a *Roamer* and a set of mats. Each group has also been provided with a set of cards which show a sequence of *Roamer* instructions. These can be seen in Figure 7.2. The groups are asked to discuss which sequence of instructions will send the *Roamer*

→

to the star, cross and circle respectively. When they think they have worked this out, they are told that they can enter the sequences into the *Roamer* and see if they are correct. The following is an extract of one group's discussion:

Helen: *I think that Card 1 is the circle because it is nearest the start.*

Tahir: *That isn't right because Card 1 doesn't have any turns on it and you need to do a turn to get to the circle.*

Luke: *That must mean that Card 1 is for the star because it doesn't need any turns.*

Harmony: *Shall we try it and see?*

Luke: *No, let's wait until we have worked them all out and then see.*

Nikki: *The other cards both have turns in the instructions. I can't work out which is which.*

Helen: *Is Card 3 for the cross?*

Luke: *Why?*

Helen: *Because the cross is further away and there are more instructions on Card 3.*

Luke: *Maybe ...*

Tahir: *No! We need to go through each list and think what the* Roamer *will do.*

Nikki: *OK, let's start with Card 2. It begins with 'Forward 3'. That will move the* Roamer *to the crossroads.*

Helen: *That doesn't help because you have to get to the crossroads for the cross and the circle.*

Nikki: *The next instruction is left 90.*

Tahir *(who is sitting by the star, opposite the start mat): If it turns left it will be heading towards the circle. Card 2 must be for the circle.*

The children enter the commands from Card 1 and find their prediction is proved correct: the *Roamer* goes to the star. They then enter the commands from Card 2 and are surprised to find that it goes to the cross.

Helen: *Why didn't it go to the circle?*

→

Luke: *We must have made a mistake. What went wrong?*

Tahir: *Well, it wasn't me because it is definitely left from the crossroads to the circle!*

Nikki *(who is sitting by the start mat): Isn't it right?*

Tahir: *No, I know my left and right!*

Nikki: *So do I.*

Tahir *(stands up and walks round to Nikki to show her): Oh! Now it is the right.*

Luke: *It depends where you are standing. You have to imagine that you are the* Roamer *and which way it is facing.*

The children enter the commands for Card 3 and confirm that it goes to the circle.

Although this lesson could easily be replicated by a number of non-ICT-based approaches (e.g. using children as a 'robot' or similar to follow directions), the ICT played a crucial role in the success of the children's mathematical thinking because it provided immediate non-judgemental feedback to the children. The group have been provided with a problem which has stimulated some high-quality mathematical discussion and thinking. However, without the *Roamer*, they have no way of knowing if their thoughts and decisions are correct. The *Roamer* carried out the sequence of instructions accurately and without fault, thus providing children with instant, independent feedback as to the accuracy of their decisions. Additionally, using ICT provided a motivation and a focus for the children during the activity.

Clearly, children need to be able to understand how to program the *Roamer* in order to successfully support their learning. More importantly, they need to know that programmable devices will respond to instructions that are given clearly, in a common language, using standard units. This kind of experience can be built up from the Foundation Stage using remote control toys and developed in Year 1 using resources such as *Pixies* (Swallow) or *Beebots* (Beebot.org). There are few alternative resources to *Roamers* despite the fact that they have been used in education for many years.

Roamers have established a long-standing link with mathematics but their use can go beyond this. Examples include writing instructions as a form of non-fiction text (English 3.9 and English 3.12). Alternatively, they might be used in geographic activities to develop mapping skills and awareness of direction (Geography 2a and 2c).

When you are planning for small groups of children working on similar activities at the same time, you will need to consider the following issues if the lesson is to be effective. Firstly, you should consider how you will assess the activity and secondly how you will manage the groups and children's access to resources. You may have grouped children to work together before and therefore have practised strategies for assessing these situations; if not then it is something that needs planning for before the activity. In this example of small group work there is a further complication as there will not be any written output to assess. While the children in the case study successfully identified the sets of instructions to match the correct destinations, it is not the case that all children contributed equally. In the case study transcript above it is clear that Helen had some potentially significant misconceptions about sequences and controlling technology. In her lesson plan Siobhan identified opportunities to observe each group in order to gather assessment information. She also planned for a question and answer session in the plenary to follow up her observations with targeted questions to children who had appeared to be struggling or excelling in the activity.

In the case study Siobhan was fortunate to have access to an adequate number of *Roamers* so that the whole class could take part in the activity in the school hall at the same time. However, this will not be the case in every school; many schools may have only one *Roamer*, but this should not prevent activities like this one from being planned. If there is only one *Roamer* then it may be possible to have a group working on an activity like the one in the case study under the direction of a teaching assistant, while the rest of the class work on different activities related to the same learning outcome in the classroom. A rota system would allow each group in the class an opportunity to take part in the *Roamer* activity. This might need to take place over a number of days in order to allow each group a chance to participate.

Siobhan had planned for other groups to be working on similar differentiated activities so that the whole class would be working on the same learning objective. An activity for a less able group had numbered mats in a linear arrangement and children predicted which number mat the *Roamer* would stop on. A more able group had a layout like the one in Figure 7.1; however, their instruction cards had some instructions missing. They needed to work out which card related to each shape and also which instructions were missing.

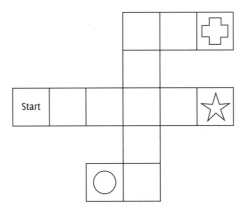

Figure 7.1 Roamer mat arrangement

Card 1	Card 2	Card 3
Forward 2	Forward 3	Forward 1
Forward 1	Left 90	Forward 2
Forward 2	Forward 2	Right 90
	Right 90	Forward 2
	Forward 2	Right 90
		Forward 1

Figure 7.2 Roamer instruction cards

Another example of a *non-computer* ICT resource is the digital camera. This is now a popular primary resource, as it is affordable, easy to use and has the capacity to store large quantities of high-quality images. Digital cameras provide excellent opportunities for teachers to capture images for assessment purposes. Their use by children is less common and this next case study provides an example of digital cameras used to support a geography activity. You should consider the way in which the cameras enhance the activity and think about other ways in which children could use cameras to capture images as an integral part of a learning activity.

Case Study: Year 4 using digital cameras to compare two localities

As part of a geography topic on *Comparing and contrasting two localities*, a Year 4 class was studying their home town of Thornton-Cleveleys, a small seaside resort, and comparing it with a small market town in Yorkshire, called Richmond. A number of activities were carried out in Thornton-Cleveleys, including studies of land use, traffic surveys, and interviews with locals recording their experiences and views of their home town. Aerial photographs were studied and maps and plans were made of commercial and residential areas. Digital cameras were used to photograph areas of interest and provide evidence.

This was followed up by a residential visit to Richmond in which very similar activities were carried out, in addition to which digital camcorders were used to capture the 'flavour' of the contrasting town.

The children were divided into small groups, each with a camcorder, and given a morning to take as much footage as possible of various aspects of Richmond, covering the same areas (traffic, land use, interviews, etc.) as in their home town.

On their return to the classroom, children remained in the groups they had been assigned to in Richmond. The groups then spent most of their Literacy sessions and each afternoon for two weeks collating all the information they had collected. Children were made aware at this stage that all information was to be shared with parents and friends at a special evening session, ten days hence, thus creating a sense of urgency as well as a real audience for their efforts.

→

144

Information was to be presented in three ways.

- *Fact files* were made, using Microsoft *Word*, which incorporated photos of both towns, use of various fonts and captions, as well as transcripts of interviews, in order to provide a contrast between the two towns. The fact files formed part of a static display that the parents would come and view.
- Information on both towns was put into a basic presentation created with *PowerPoint* (Microsoft), that included text and photographs, but not video (given the age and ability of the class). The children prepared a talk to accompany the presentation, to be delivered during the open evening.
- Finally, some basic editing was carried out on the video footage and this too was presented to the audience during the evening.

The evening itself was a great success, with a combination of ICT, children's personal presentation skills and the ready-made display providing both variety and a showcase for the children's talents.

In terms of classroom organisation, timetabling, differentiation and assessment, several issues presented themselves in the case study above. The teacher chose to use mixed-ability groups, partly because the variety of activities and skills made it difficult to identify ability groupings (the combination of geography, mathematics, ICT and English meant that, for example, while some children were very able mathematicians they were less confident with regard to speaking and listening). Also, it was useful to produce presentations that were of a similar standard for the external audience to enjoy. Within the groups, specific tasks were allocated to ensure that everybody was productively engaged and also to use the skills that each child excelled in. Further differentiation was achieved by adult support, particularly with regard to some of the more advanced features of *PowerPoint*. The teacher ran the topic over a two-week block which inevitably led to other foundation subjects not being taught in that time. However, as this accounted for a whole term's geography work, it was possible to recoup that time later in the term. It is important to note that this was not left to chance, however, and all the subjects were carefully mapped for coverage at the start of the term.

Assessment is less straightforward when children work in groups, especially if they are mixed ability. For the unit of work described in this case study, it was carried out almost entirely by observations recorded by the class teacher and support staff. This was seen to be more reliable than using a finished product which would have contained multiple contributions, making individual work hard to identify.

Links to the National Curriculum

ICT played a crucial role in this case study. Children developed a number of ICT skills: developing multimedia presentations (ICT 2a), sharing information in a variety of forms (ICT 3a) and for different audiences and purposes (ICT 3b). They discussed the impact and effectiveness of their work (ICT 4b) and explored a variety of technologies and ICT resources (ICT 5b).

Secondly, the ICT undoubtedly enhanced the children's understanding of both localities, by providing different vehicles for investigating them. It also helped to meet the needs of visual, auditory and kinaesthetic learners due to the various approaches to learning that were adopted throughout. By providing a format for both oral and written communication, it met several requirements of the National Curriculum for English and encouraged interaction between children and also between children and adults on many levels.

Finally, ICT framed the context of the whole activity. Since there was a very definite end product in sight, that of presenting findings to parents, ICT provided both motivation and a sense of purpose for the children.

Research Focus: Keeping up with an ever-changing world of ICT

The case studies in this chapter demonstrate how a range of different ICT tools can be used to support and enhance learning. Some of them show the use of relatively new technologies; however, it is a safe bet that within a fairly short space of time they will seem commonplace and that newer technologies will come along.

Compare these two statements:

The prospect of the information society is exciting and invigorating, offering potential solutions to many of the problems that confront us today.

We are moving to a knowledge-based economy where the ability to find, process, assess and analyse information will be key.

The first statement was written by Fothergill (1982, page 1) in 1982 and the second by Becta (2006, page 1) in 2006. They demonstrate that, despite the changes in technology, there are many issues regarding its use which remain the same. One of these is that of teacher confidence in using ICT.

Becta (2006, page 2) argues that *[t]echnology is not just about digitising existing learning, but about enabling new and better ways of learning.* This is a view which is supported by Gibson (2001, page 43) who suggests that there are two types of technology use: *type I,* which is characterised by technology being used to do things which have always been done, and *type II,* which is concerned with new opportunities and pedagogies.

$\rightarrow$

This poses the question of how teachers can maintain their confidence to use ICT in the face of new developments. Becta (2004, page 7) suggests that confidence is built through *frequent practice with more than one or two uses of ICT*. Higgins (2003) develops this idea further and draws together the issue of teacher confidence and changing technology. He suggests that developing familiarity alone is not enough, and effective adoption of new technologies takes time. Teachers need to continue to engage in continuing professional development activities to build their technological and pedagogical skills.

Becta (2006 page 3) has argued that ubiquitous access to technology, the so-called *anywhere any time connectivity*, is an emerging trend that will have a significant impact on teaching and learning through the way it allows computing power to be used when and where it is needed. This next case study describes use of a school's wireless network to enhance a science activity.

Case Study: Year 5 working with branching databases

Malcolm is a final year trainee teacher on placement in a school which is well equipped with ICT resources. He has planned to integrate ICT into a science-based activity about plants and animals in the local environment. The children have previously considered adaptation and how plants and animals are suited to their environment. They used branching databases in Year 4, and have been given a brief reminder of how to use them by Malcolm. (Branching databases are covered in more detail in Chapter 2.)

For this activity, Malcolm has booked the suite of wireless laptops for his class to use, and has tested that the school's wireless network extends into the school grounds. Most of the grounds are covered, although some areas behind trees and shrubs are outside the range of the network. The children are used to working in small groups for science activities and Malcolm has decided to stick with these groups for this activity. He has prepared a partially completed computer-based branching database which contains a selection of plants and animals that can be found in the grounds. See Figure 7.3 for details.

The groups take their laptops into the grounds to each find five different plants or animals that they will either identify using the database or add to the database if it does not already contain them.

Claudia: *Let's do this one, it will be easy. I know it is a dandelion.*

Anothai: *OK. Odile, bring the laptop here.*

Odile: *The first question is, Is it a plant? Yes.*

Jamie: *What is next? Can I answer it?*

→

Odile: *Does it have a yellow flower?*

Jamie: *Yes! What does it say?*

Odile: *Is it a buttercup?*

Jamie: *That must be it. I'll take a picture with the camera and we can add it later.*

Claudia: *No, that isn't right. I know that that is a dandelion. It isn't a buttercup!*

Anothai: *Which is right? I'm getting confused now.*

The children go to find Malcolm who explains that the database *asked* them if the plant was a buttercup (rather than telling them it was). They also had a brief discussion about checking information and about using websites (identified beforehand by Malcolm) to search for photos and information about common garden plants and animals to help them with their task.

Claudia: *Odile, can you look up 'dandelion' on the internet?*

Odile: *OK ... wait ... here it is.*

Anothai (looking closely at the screen and the flower): *OK, that is definitely the one we have here.*

Jamie: *Right, that means we need to add it to the database. Click on No when it asks, Is it a buttercup?*

Odile: *I've done that. It wants a question that will sort out a dandelion from a buttercup.*

Claudia: *Dandelions are bigger. Why don't we ask which is biggest?*

Anothai: *But bigger than what?*

Jamie: *The petals are totally different. Can we ask something about that?*

Claudia: *That's a good idea. How about, Does it have lots of thin petals?*

Anothai: *Yes, that would work.*

Odile: *OK, I'll add it in.*

The children then test the database to see if their new question correctly identifies the plant. They then go on to add other plants and animals that they find.

Branching databases are not new technology and their use in science activities such as this one has long been a common use of ICT. It has endured because of the way in which it enriches the activity. By encouraging children to create their own branching database (which is effectively an identification key) they are required to employ key scientific skills such as observation and classification. It would not be possible to complete the activity without thinking about the ways in which the plants were similar and different. The ICT provides a tool to structure children's learning and ideas. Formal scientific plant identification keys are generally more structured and need planning from the outset. By using an ICT-based branching database, children can extend and develop it in an *ad hoc* manner. The activity encourages the development of more sophisticated information handling skills.

The ICT helps to keep the children's ideas structured and prevents them from forgetting where they are and losing track of which plants and animals they have already added. Wireless internet access allows children to search for images and information to confirm their identification before adding the item to their own database. They were planning to enrich their database through the inclusion of digital images taken of their findings in order to support future users of the database.

The children in the Case Study: Year 5 working with branching databases had been introduced to branching databases in their previous school year and familiarity with the branching database program to be used is a prerequisite for this lesson. However, at a more fundamental level, children would need to understand the concept of how the data in the database was organised. Playing games such as *20 Questions* and *Guess Who* (Hasbro) will allow children to develop this understanding. This activity has strong links with the development of ICT capability in finding and selecting information aspect of the curriculum.

Malcolm utilised the school's existing branching database software for this activity. There are several such packages that are available to use; however, if no such resources are available it would be possible to create a template using *PowerPoint* (Microsoft) with hyperlinks set up for the yes/no options, although this kind of arrangement would lack some of the functionality of a purpose-made branching database package.

The use of branching databases develops children's ability to recognise similarities and differences. This is a key scientific process and there would be many other opportunities within science activities to employ the use of branching databases. An example would be sorting and classifying different materials. The ability to recognise similarities and differences is integral to recognising patterns and sequences within mathematics. Thus, there would be many opportunities to employ branching databases within mathematics activities, such as sorting numbers (factors, primes, whole numbers, etc.) or identifying 2D and 3D shapes.

In this case study the children work to create a finished product, but it is important to remember that it is the thinking behind the product which is likely to be more revealing than the product itself. Building opportunities into lessons to observe and question children should reveal valuable assessment information. Asking questions such as, *Which questions were hardest to think of and why?* or, alternatively, *Could you have asked a different question here?* will be useful prompts to get children to talk about their design choices.

The management of this activity relies on children having had previous experience of using laptops or other portable devices. It would have been highly unlikely to be successful if this was the children's first experience of using these devices, as the novelty of the technology would have got in the way of meaningful learning. As the children are using the ICT resources outdoors, then establishing an acceptable use agreement with the class will clarify expectations and ensure that the resources are treated with care. In terms of managing the group dynamics, it would be helpful to allocate roles within the groups such as *database controller, plant and animal observer, internet researcher, digital photographer,* etc. This will avoid the problem of all the children wanting to use the laptop at once. The size of the group will need to be established in advance: too small and there will be too many tasks for each child, too large and there will not be enough for each child to be engaged in the task.

Activities such as this can be differentiated by providing more or less information already in the database, or by restricting or extending the range of data to be added. For example a less able group might work with quite an extensive database already provided and only be asked to work with plants. A higher ability group might work with a pre-prepared database with fewer records already entered and be asked to add both plants and animals.

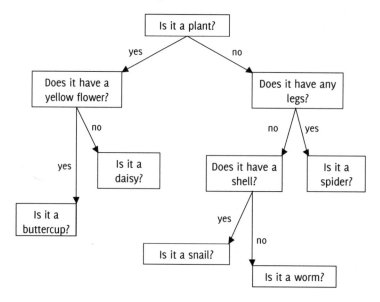

Figure 7.3 Adding to a branching database

The final case study shows how use of a Web 2.0 tool enhanced a history activity. (See Chapters 4 and 6 for more information about Web 2.0 technologies.) This is an interesting example because on one hand it simply uses ICT to digitise existing activities (e.g. children writing diaries), but on the other it makes use of ICT to offer new learning opportunities (e.g.

the ability to share and comment on each other's work in an interactive and collaborative way). You might like to reflect on your own use of ICT as your read it and think about how you have used it to digitise existing learning and ways in which you have created new learning opportunities.

Case Study: Year 6 creating a blog

Kirsty is a newly qualified teacher working in a Year 6 class. She has planned a topic of work based around life in Tudor England. This has involved some historical research, art work, food technology and PE activities. As part of the children's learning, Kirsty wants the class to try to imagine what it would have been like to have lived in Tudor times. In order to do this she has asked the class to imagine that *blogging* technology would have been available during that period. She has provided the children with details of Tudor people such as a farmer, child, mayor, farm worker, baker, etc. and asked them to maintain a diary for one of these characters using the blogging tool. The children are given a weekly opportunity to update their blog in relation to the learning that has taken place during that week. As part of the blogging activity, children are encouraged to read other children's blogs as a source of further inspiration and also to give feedback using the 'comments' facility.

Kelly's entry in the role of the daughter of a farm worker.
I am really tired. Dad got me up before the sun had risen today. He made me work all day and I hardly had a break. I don't normally have to work so hard but we had to get the barley harvested. At least it means we will have plenty to eat this winter. I am also glad because it is good to get to eat some fresh barley, I am fed up of eating stale oat cakes left over from last year.

Yusef's entry in the role of a clergyman.
Life has been hard since the King decided he wanted a divorce. I keep getting asked questions by my parishioners and I don't know how to answer them. I was taught that you cannot get a divorce but now everyone has heard about the King and wants to know all about it. It has been ages since my bishop has been to visit so I have not had any news about this and I am scared that I will say the wrong thing.

Sean's entry in the role of a baker.
I have hardly had time to write this I have been so busy. I have been baking loaves all day. My 'King's Special' bread has been a best seller and since the news of the divorce has got round, everyone wants to buy one. At least there is lots of fresh barley now that the crops are in.

Table 7.1 Children's blog entries as Tudor characters

The idea of asking children to keep a diary as a way of encouraging them to think about what life would have been like in different historical periods is not new. However, Kirsty's idea to ask the children to keep their diaries via a blog offers some distinct advantages. Children have to be clear that blogging technology is a recent development in order to avoid any historical misconceptions. The ease of publishing blogs and the ability to comment on the blogs of others have been instrumental in the way that ICT has enriched this activity. The children have easily been able to publish their work and they have been involved in reading each other's work. This would have been more difficult if the work had been written in paper format. The influence of this can be seen in Sean's entry where he has taken on board information regarding the harvest and the royal divorce from the two previous blogs to create his entry.

By receiving comments from other children, there is an opportunity to receive peer comments and feedback relating to points of historical accuracy or to suggest other content which may be covered.

This activity would draw on children's prior experience of using ICT for drafting and writing work. It draws upon learning done in relation to collaborating, communicating and sharing information as well as in refining and improving work. Some familiarity with blogging would be helpful and this could have been covered in prior lessons. While the use of an online blog is helpful, it would be possible to use a school website or learning platform to publish the work so that it could be shared. Publishing blogs to blogging sites, school websites or virtual learning environments is reasonably straightforward but it does require access to a computer for each child in the class. If the school has a computer suite then it could be done as a whole-class activity all at once; as writing and posting the blog should only be a quick activity, it could be done before or after any other activity taking place in the computer suite. If the school does not have a computer suite then it would be easy to organise access to computers on a rota basis; for example, children might complete their blog entry during registration each morning.

Blogs could be used in other curriculum areas where you wish children to consider things from the perspective of another person. Examples might be writing a blog from the point of view of a character in a book or of a child living in a different part of the world. However, blogs don't have to be used just to write from a different person's perspective. Children could just as easily write from their own point of view: for example on a residential trip, they might maintain a blog that could be read by parents to find out what the children had been doing while they were away.

Kirsty's activity involves children working individually on a task with an end product (the blog entry), and can be assessed as such. By using the ability to comment on individual blogs, she is able to provide formative feedback to each child. By making use of the comments facility there is also scope for the class to become involved in peer assessment of each other's work. Kirsty might ask the class to provide two types of comments: first in the role of their Tudor characters and secondly as themselves evaluating the quality of their blog.

Learning Outcomes Review

In this chapter you have been introduced to a range of case studies from across both key stages which employ a selection of ICT tools. The discussion which follows each key stage will allow you to begin to make your own decisions about the ways in which ICT can support learning in other subjects and the factors that influence these decisions. Each discussion considers alternative ICT resources which could have been used, which will support you in selecting appropriate ICT tools in schools, even if the resources are not ones you have come across before. The discussions make explicit the ways in which the use of ICT has enhanced and enriched the children's learning; this will support you in making effective use of ICT in your own practice.

Self assessment questions

1. What kinds of ICT resources might you expect to find in schools other than PCs or Macs?
2. What issues need to be considered when assessing children working in groups using ICT resources?
3. What are the ways in which ICT can enhance or enrich teaching and learning in the classroom?
4. How might you plan to incorporate ICT into a Year 3 PE topic on dance?

Further Reading

Learning Centre Discovery Team (2006) *Creative ICT in the classroom.*, Stafford: Network Continuum.

Potter, F. and Darbyshire, C. (2005) *Understanding and Teaching the ICT National Curriculum.* London: David Fulton.

Reid, M., Burn, A. and Parker, D. (2002) *Evaluation Report of the Becta Digital Video Pilot Project.* Coventry: Becta.

Rudd, A. and Tyldesley, A. (2006) *Literacy and ICT in the Primary School.* London: David Fulton.

Warwick, P., Wilson, E., Winterbottom, M. (2006) *Teaching and learning primary science with ICT.* Maidenhead: Open University Press.

Williams, J. and Easingwood, N. (2004) *ICT and primary mathematics.* London: RoutledgeFalmer.

References

Andrews R. *et al.* (2007) The effectiveness of information and communication technology on the learning of written English for 5 to 16 year olds. *British Journal of Educational Technology*, 38(2): 325–36.

Becta (2004) *An investigation of the research evidence relating to ICT pedagogy.* Available at **www.becta.org.uk**

Becta (2006) *Emerging Technologies.* Available at **www.becta.org.uk**

Becta (2008) *Gender and technology: How do boys and girls differ in their use of ICT?* Available at **www.becta.org.uk**

Becta (2009) *Evidence on the impact of technology on learning and educational outcomes.* Available at **www.becta.org.uk**

Beca (2010) *The Impact of Technology on Children's Attainment in English: A Review of the Literature.* Available at **www.becta.org.uk**

Higgins, S. (2003) *Does ICT improve learning and teaching in schools?* Southwell: British Educational Research Association.

Fothergill, R. (1982) The Information Society, reproduced in *Sharing Good Practice*, issue 101, available at **www.ictopus.org.uk** (accessed 18 February 2011).

Gibson, I. (2001) At the Intersection of Technology and Pedagogy: Considering styles of learning and teaching. *Journal of Information Technology for Teacher Education*, 10 (1 and 2): 37–61.

Ofsted (2009) *The Importance of ICT.* Available at **www.ofsted.gov.uk** (acccessed 18 February 2011.

8. Researching teaching and learning with ICT

Peter Cheung, Debbie Simpson and Mike Toyn

Learning Outcomes

By the end of this chapter you should:

- be aware of the importance of research-informed practice in teaching and learning with ICT;
- be able to find recent and relevant research on ICT in schools and know how to evaluate it;
- be aware of key messages from recent research;
- understand how ICT can be used to enhance practitioner research;
- be able to plan and carry out a simple practitioner research project.

Professional standards for QTS

Q7a Reflect on and improve their practice, and take responsibility for identifying and meeting their developing professional needs;

Q8 Have a creative and constructively critical approach towards innovation, being prepared to adapt their practice where benefits and improvements are identified;

Q10 Have a knowledge and understanding of a range of teaching, learning and behaviour management strategies and know how to use and adapt them, including how to personalise learning and provide opportunities for all learners to achieve their potential;

Q14 Have a secure knowledge and understanding of their subjects/curriculum areas and related pedagogy to enable them to teach effectively across the age and ability range for which they are trained;

Q17 Know how to use skills in literacy, numeracy and ICT to support their teaching and wider professional activities;

Q23 Design opportunities for learners to develop their literacy, numeracy and ICT skills;

Q25a Teach lessons and sequences of lessons across the age and ability range for which they are trained in which they use a range of teaching strategies and resources, including e-learning, taking practical account of diversity and promoting equality and inclusion.

Introduction

In this chapter you will consider the importance of research-informed practice; making decisions which are firmly based on evidence about how to use ICT most effectively. You will read about different types of research and develop your ability to evaluate research studies which may present conflicting conclusions. You will become more aware of a range of sources which present relatively easy access to recent research findings on teaching and learning with ICT and consider key messages arising from recent research. You will also explore ways in which you can plan and carry out a simple practitioner research project of your own in the classroom and consider the role that ICT can play in enabling and enhancing the research process.

The Importance of research-informed practice

Teaching is a complex and challenging activity, with or without ICT. A well-planned, successful lesson is the culmination of dozens of decisions. 'How do I decide what to do? Should I use ICT as part of the whole-class introduction to this lesson? Would it be better to pair children for this task on the computer?' Teaching that is informed by research is more likely to be effective. The following framework, developed by Peter Cheung, is designed to guide you in using research to develop your own teaching with ICT.

For some of us, decisions about how to use ICT in our classroom are based largely on three Ps:

- *Precedent* – What have I done previously? Repeating approaches which have been used in other lessons is something all teachers do. It is most likely to be useful when it is selective, based on reflecting on what worked or didn't work in the past.

- *Peer practice* – What does Teacher X do? Using ideas from colleagues is also common practice. Few, if any, teachers can claim their own teaching is not influenced by imitation of others.

- *Prescription* – Primary teachers in the UK have been subjected to wave after wave of centrally prescribed initiatives in the past two decades. Whether we like it or not this has had a significant impact on our practice.

Better teaching and learning (and professional development) happens when we mind not only the three Ps but also some Qs – quality and questioning.

- *Quality* – How can I improve the quality of learning experiences for these children?

- *Questioning* – An enquiring mind is one of the teacher's greatest assets. Querying accepted practice; questioning top-down initiatives. Is the best way to start a lesson by gathering the children in front of the interactive whiteboard (IWB); and how effective are IWBs in supporting or enhancing teaching and learning?

We can begin to find some answers to our questions through reflection, reasoning and by an awareness and understanding of key messages from research (stretching our alphabet game a little further).

- *Reflection* – It is no accident that trainee teachers are constantly required to evaluate their teaching and the children's learning. Reflective practice is the key to improving the quality of both. Reflection needs to go beyond recalling what happened and passing judgement on it. It's not enough to think *that was a disaster* or, *that went really well.* Why didn't the internet research activity work? Did the children need more support with search skills? Did they need to clarify the questions they asked? Would it have been better to group them differently? Why were the children so motivated in this science lesson? What difference did the digital video cameras make to the recording of the investigation?

- *Research* – The problem for teachers is that they only have their own experience to reflect on and that experience may be limited. For trainee teachers it certainly will be limited. A further problem is that it may be hard to narrow down the factors involved in the success or failure of a particular ICT approach. Classrooms are complicated places and teaching and learning with ICT is a complex business; if it were not then anyone could teach. Making use of research on ICT in classrooms gives us access to the experience of hundreds if not thousands of other teachers and other classrooms. Some of that research is likely to have been carried out in ways which seek to control at least some of the variables that make reflection on one's own experience so challenging.

- *Reasoning* – Applying the lessons from research to your own classroom involves careful reasoning. The messages from research are not always clear cut and the contexts in which some research was carried out may be very different from that in which you are working.

Having minded your Ps and Qs and paid attention to the three Rs you can reasonably expect to arrive at S.

- *Success* – Reflective practice and research-informed practice are the keys to success in teaching and learning with ICT. That is not to say that every lesson you teach is guaranteed to succeed, but there is a much greater probability of success if the decisions you have taken are underpinned by a good understanding of research and are grounded in a reflective approach to your teaching.

- *Satisfaction* – Teaching in this way is arguably more satisfying then relying on precedent or the practice of peers as a guide. It is certainly more satisfying than slavishly following every centrally led initiative without questioning the research that these are built on.

Traditionally, the world of research and the world of practice have been seen as separate. Research took place in an ordered academic context where researchers worked in systematic ways to develop theory and to make knowledge explicit; teachers and practitioners worked in 'the real world' where things didn't always fit into neat categories. They were seen to work in a more *ad hoc* manner with knowledge and practical wisdom that was often implicit rather than explicit.

Over the past 35 years or so, however, there has been a growing recognition of the value of research to teachers and of the need for practice to be underpinned or informed by research.

Research-informed practice in teaching is part of a wider movement of evidence-based practice across a number of disciplines and professions such as medicine and social care. Since the late 1990s the UK government has placed much greater emphasis on policy-making which is evidence based and The Research Informed Practice Site (TRIPS) (**www.standards.dfes.gov.uk/research**) is one example of the importance placed on this approach. However, despite the trend towards evidence-based policy, it is important to note that several educational initiatives emanating from central government in recent years have a questionable evidence base. For example, the evidence underpinning the use of synthetic phonics to teach early reading has been challenged (Wyse and Goswami, 2008).

Activity

Review some recent planning which you have carried out for placement. Identify strategies which you have used in the teaching of (or with) ICT. Which strategies do you know are supported by evidence? Which are not? Consider the balance – to what extent is your own practice informed by evidence?

Types of educational research

There are many different types of educational research and a variety of ways in which they may be classified. This is a complex area and only a brief overview of the subject is provided below. For further reading about this area, see the further reading section at the end of this chapter.

Quantitative and qualitative research

The most common classification differentiates between *quantitative* and *qualitative* research methodologies. Quantitative research emphasises objective analysis of those things that can be observed or measured. It involves the collection and analysis of quantitative (i.e. numerical) data. An example of such data would be figures for the growth in the number of interactive whiteboards in primary schools in the UK between 2007 and 2009. Qualitative research acknowledges the subjective nature of knowledge and involves the use of qualitative (non-numerical) data which is analysed and interpreted in order to explore or describe an educational issue or phenomenon. For example, a case study might focus on the adoption by a primary school of tablet computers. The study might collect data through observations, questionnaires and interviews with both teachers and children. The study would aim to explore the different perceptions of children and teachers to the new technology and contrast ways of using the tablets, perhaps by comparing Key Stage 1 and Key Stage 2 children's experiences.

Mixed methods research

A third type of research methodology is known as *mixed methods* research and this typically combines aspects of both quantitative and qualitative approaches. The final evaluation report of the ICT Test Bed project (Somekh *et al.*, 2007) is based on three strands: quantitative data – for example, performance on national tests against matched comparator schools and national averages; qualitative data – for example, site visits including classroom observations; and action research data - 90 or more teachers from the ICT Test Bed schools completed more than a hundred action research studies of their work with ICT.

One way of conceptualising different approaches to research is to use the analogy of looking at an old tapestry hanging on a wall. Quantitative research might count the number of threads in the tapestry, measure the intensity of the dyes used to colour the threads and analyse in percentage terms how much each dye had faded since the tapestry was made. On the other hand, qualitative research might explore the responses of different groups such as children, young adults or older people, to the tapestry.

Scale of research

Some research is large scale. This is analogous to creating a low-resolution picture of the entire tapestry. Large surveys fall into this category. For example, the Harnessing Technology School Survey (Becta, 2010a) provides an overview of technology provision and use across all schools in England.

Some research is small in scope but very focused and detailed. This is analogous to making a study of a small area of the tapestry, examining each thread in detail. Case studies are the most obvious example of this approach. For example, a case study of learning and teaching at Lickhill Lodge First School (Becta, 2006), explores how ICT has impacted upon learning through a semi-structured interview with the headteacher, observation of lessons and analysis of school documentation.

How to evaluate ICT research

Research is of variable quality and not all research seems to come up with the same conclusions. Where two or more research reports present conflicting evidence they cannot both be equally true. It is important therefore to be able to evaluate research.

When comparing quantitative studies a few simple indicators may be used as a guide in determining how much weight to give the conclusions of a study.

Sample size: the larger the sample size, the more likely it is that a study's results are reliable and able to be generalised. Where small sample sizes are evident there is a risk that, if a different sample was used, results would be different.

Control groups: if a group is compared in some way with another group, how were the groups chosen? The 'gold standard' is the randomised control trial (RCT) where participants are allocated on a random basis to either the intervention group or the control group. RCTs are becoming more common in educational research but are still comparatively rare.

The largest UK-based RCT to date was conducted with 155 pupils aged 11–12 in a school in northern England to evaluate the effectiveness of software designed to boost reading and spelling. (Brooks *et al.*, 2006) For spelling there was a small increase in post-test scores but this was not statistically significant; reading scores actually showed a significant decrease as a result of the intervention!

Much qualitative research takes a case study format. In evaluating this sort of research a key question to ask is the extent to which the conclusions are able to be generalised. The context of the study will be important. Are there any factors which make the study context unusual? How similar is the context to your own (a placement school, for example)?

Key sources of research

Original ICT research is published primarily in journals. The following list will provide a starting point when you are looking for relevant and recent research to support your teaching and studies.

Advancing Education Through ICT (formerly published as *Computer Education*);
British Educational Research Journal;
British Journal of Educational Technology;
Journal of Computer Assisted Learning;
Technology, Pedagogy and Education (formerly published as *Journal of Information Technology for Teacher Education*).

Much ICT research is also available online and the following websites provide access to a wide range of important material.

Becta Research
http://research.becta.org.uk/

British Educational Research Association (BERA)
www.bera.ac.uk/

Best Evidence Encyclopedia UK (BEE UK)
www.bestevidence.org.uk/index.html

The Evidence for Policy and Practice Information and Co-ordinating Centre (EPPI-Centre)
http://eppi.ioe.ac.uk/cms/Default.aspx

ICT Test Bed Project
www.evaluation.icttestbed.org.uk/

The Research Informed Practice Site (TRIPS)
www.standards.dfes.gov.uk/research/

Teaching and Learning Research Programme (TLRP)
www.tlrp.org/index.html

UK Educational Evidence Portal
www.eep.ac.uk/DNN2/

> **Activity**
>
> Search the UK Educational Evidence Portal (at **www.eep.ac.uk/DNN2/**) for research evidence about ICT in primary schools. Narrow down the search to look for studies relating to specific subjects such as mathematics.

What the research tells us

This section presents key messages arising from recent research. In selecting sources more weight has been given to large-scale studies and to systematic reviews. (Systematic review is a method of synthesising findings from multiple studies in a systematic way.)

Research Focus: ICT pedagogy

A report for Becta (Cox *et al.*, 2004) reviewed the research literature to establish what was known about ICT and pedagogy. Some key messages from their summary of the research included the following.

- Teachers own pedagogical beliefs and values help shape their use of ICT.
- An extensive knowledge of ICT is required for teachers to fit ICT to their own pedagogy or to extend pedagogical practices to incorporate ICT use.
- Pedagogical practices of teachers using ICT vary from the use of ICT to support or enhance existing approaches to more radical changes to pedagogy.
- ICT has limited effectiveness when teachers do not rethink pedagogy.
- Teachers need to understand how a range of appropriate ICT resources relate to subject needs.
- Teachers need to be able to select the most appropriate class organisation (whole-class, individual, paired or group) when using ICT.
- The most effective uses of ICT are those where the teacher and ICT combine to challenge children's thinking or understanding.

There has been relatively little research into teachers' roles in ICT-enabled learning environments but one study with children and trainee teachers in Israel is particularly illuminating. Klein *et al.* (2000) compared the effect of different types of adult interaction with five- to six-year-olds using computers. They found that simply responding to children's questions or providing technical assistance had no effect but that where the adult actively mediated (focusing, expanding, encouraging and regulating behaviour) there was a significant effect on children's cognitive performance.

$\rightarrow$

Sometimes research combines evidence from previous studies in ways that generate new insights. Meta-analysis is a quantitative method for synthesising results from a number of different studies. For example, Lou *et al.* (2001) extracted the results from 122 separate studies and combined these to show that social context matters when children learn using computer technology. On average, small group learning had significantly more positive effects than individual learning on both individual achievement and group task performance.

Case Study: Using research to help decide how to use ICT most effectively in the classroom

Su-yin is planning an ICT lesson for her Year 2 placement class. One group of children are going to be using a *Beebot* (a small, programmable floor robot) to navigate around a large-scale map of the school. The children in this class began using *Beebots* in the Early Years Foundation Stage and are relatively confident with them. This lesson also builds on work they have been doing over the past two weeks.

Intuition suggests that these children are likely to be confident in their use of the *Beebots* and are not likely to need a significant amount of teacher support. Consequently, Su-yin plans the activity to be carried out by a small group working independently following an initial input. A teaching assistant will be available to answer children's questions or to provide support if they get stuck. However, Su-yin then remembers a recent discussion in one of her ICT sessions at university about the role of the teacher in supporting children's learning with ICT.

Recalling the Klein *et al.* (2000) study referred to above, Su-yin reconsiders how to make the children's use of the *Beebot* more effective and changes her planning to allow the teaching assistant to work directly with this small group. She and the TA discuss how to support the children by helping them to focus on key aspects of the task and asking them to expand their ideas for a sequence of instructions.

Links to the National Curriculum

In the ICT curriculum at Key Stage 2 children are expected to talk about the information they need and how they can find and use it (1a) and to interpret information, to check it is relevant and reasonable and to think about what might happen if there were any errors or omissions. This is likely to be in the context of another curriculum area, for example geography, where children should collect, record and analyse evidence and draw conclusions (1b, c). Children might compare two localities and collect data on types of buildings (homes, shops, etc.) which they then enter into a spreadsheet and produce comparison graphs.

In deciding what data to collect and interpreting the graphs the active involvement of a teacher is vital to encourage and mediate children's talk and to probe and extend understanding.

Research Focus: ICT and attainment

The evidence in this area is complex and does not easily lend itself to simplistic headlines of the sort that newspapers and other media tend to like, such as, *computers transform children's attainment*; or alternatively, *computers have no impact on attainment*. The evidence linking the use of ICT in teaching and learning with measurable outcomes has been ambiguous. Large-scale studies and meta-analyses tend to show smaller effects than small-scale studies which look at more specific and targeted uses of ICT.

For example, Moseley *et al.* (1999) found only a weak link between attainment and higher levels of computer use and a Becta study in 2000 also found only a very weak link between computer resourcing and attainment (reading and mathematics) at Key Stage 2 and none at all in Key Stage 1 (Becta, 2000). However, Moseley *et al.* also reported the impact on attainment of a number of development projects in primary schools, and here the evidence was of a more dramatic improvement in outcomes. For each month of the project, children made 2.8 months progress in numeracy and 5.1 months' progress in literacy.

One point to note here is that computer use in itself is only weakly linked to higher attainment. What is more important is *how* ICT is used. Higgins (2003) suggests the evidence shows that *more substantial gains in pupil attainment are achievable where the use of ICT is planned, structured and integrated effectively* (page 6). In both the Moseley *et al.* research and Becta's 2000 report to the DfEE, the focus was simply on ICT use rather than how it was used, whereas in the development projects, the way in which ICT was used was carefully planned and structured. Teachers (including trainee teachers) sometimes feel under pressure to use ICT in their lessons, but the research shows that it is only when ICT use is *carefully planned* that there is likely to be any significant benefit.

The picture which emerges from research is changing over time and studies which are only a few years old may well have been superseded by more recent findings.

A literature review carried out for Becta in 2004 found that there was evidence of a positive effect on children's concepts and skills in both mathematics and science but that in English evidence was inconsistent (Cox and Abbott, 2004) In 2006, the *Evidence for Policy and Practice Information and Co-ordinating Centre* (EPPI-Centre) carried out a systematic review on the effectiveness of different information and communication technologies (ICTs) in the teaching and learning of English, and concluded that there was insufficient research of high quality to answer the

$\rightarrow$

question (Andrews *et al.*, 2006) Part of the problem is that much of the research available is small scale or lacks the rigour that is needed to generalise findings.

However, in the UK there have been several significant reports by Becta and others since the EPPI review and, although some caution is required, in general it can be said that the evidence suggesting that ICT use can lead to improved academic attainment for children is growing stronger, including in English. Becta's Impact2 study (Harrison *et al.*, 2002) looked at the impact of the use of ICT on learning across the curriculum and reported a significant positive impact in English, where the average gain from ICT use in Key Stage 2 was 0.16 of a National Curriculum level (deemed to be the same as an extra term's progress). A recent update (Becta, 2010b) to Becta's 2004 literature review suggests evidence of benefits of multimedia e-books, some (but importantly not all) literacy activity software and software that provides text-to-speech feedback.

There may be a number of reasons for the apparent change in the message emerging from research in relation to ICT and attainment. One factor which is likely to be involved is teachers' growing competence and confidence with ICT and their developing understanding of how to use it most effectively. More schools and teachers are embedding ICT in their practice rather than using it in patchy or *ad hoc* ways. Becta coined the term *e-maturity* to denote the school-wide strategic and effective use of ICT to improve learning outcomes. It is also the case that, increasingly, researchers are asking more sophisticated questions; moving beyond the simplistic approach which groups all ICT use together regardless of how, or in what context, it is used.

An important study, the ICT Test Bed, was a DfES-funded project that ran for four years from 2002 to 2006. Three clusters of schools in socially disadvantaged areas were helped to embed ICT in their teaching and learning processes and to build e-maturity. The evaluation of the project (Becta, 2007) showed that outcomes at Key Stage 2 improved more quickly than both comparator schools (selected for similarity in size and socio-economic factors) and the national average over the four years of the project.

Activity

Reflect on the following key points from the research focus above.

- The evidence linking ICT to increased attainment is ambiguous.
- Several studies show weak links between ICT use and increased attainment.
- The message from the research may be changing as schools and teachers gain confidence both technically and pedagogically with ICT.

What are the implications of this for the decisions you make when planning whether or not to use ICT in a lesson? Should you be more cautious about using ICT as the benefits may be uncertain? Or should you be working to develop your understanding of ICT so that you are more likely to use it effectively?

How ICT can support practitioner research

Research is not the preserve only of academics and professional researchers. Much valuable ICT research is carried out by busy teachers working in their own classrooms and schools and by trainee teachers working in placement schools and other settings. Many teacher education courses require trainees to undertake a small-scale research project. One of the best ways to understand research is actually to do it.

This section provides a brief overview of the areas to be considered in planning and carrying out a small-scale ICT research project in the classroom. It also examines ways in which ICT tools can be of use to the researcher at different stages of the research process.

The National Foundation for Educational Research (NFER) maintains a very useful online resource for researchers called *Practical Research for Education-Online*. Their free series of *Toolkit* articles is helpful and the first of these, *Planning Your Research Project* is available, at **www.pre-online.co.uk/feature_pdfs/34_f.pdf**

Although the intricacies of carrying out practitioner research are beyond the scope of this chapter, the process can be summarised as in Figure 8.1. Phase 1 is characterised by the work which is done before data collection commences, Phase 2 by the collection and analysis of data and Phase 3 by the sharing and presentation of the outcomes in an academic style. This section will consider the ways in which ICT tools can support you in each of these stages.

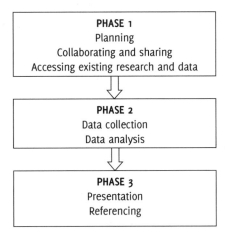

Figure 8.1 The process of carrying out practitioner research

Phase of research project	Potential of ICT to support
Planning Collaborating and sharing Accessing existing research and data	Internet searches for funding sources Mind-mapping tools Web/video conferencing Online collaboration/storage tools Social networking Online bookmarks sharing e-books Electronic copies of journals Article database searches
Data collection Data analysis	Online questionnaire tools (e.g. SurveyMonkey) Audio and video recording of observational data Electronic voting systems (e.g. ActiVote) Spreadsheet analysis and graphing of quantitative data
Presentation Referencing	Word-processed research report Online dissemination via podcasts or blogs ICT-based multimedia research presentations Video Bibliographic management software

Table 8.1 Stages in the research process

Research Phase 1: Planning, collaboration and accessing existing data

Planning

Time spent in planning your research project is essential if it is be successful. You need to think carefully about what you are trying to find out and why.

Perhaps *inclusion* is a topic that interests you, and you have some experience on placement in using ICT to support children with special educational needs. You decide you would like to evaluate the effectiveness of ICT in supporting SEN. As a broad area to investigate this is certainly worth exploring, but it is not realistic to expect that, given the resources available to you, any definitive answers could be found to such a wide-ranging topic. You need to define a more precise focus; and one way of doing this is to examine key words carefully.

Initial research query: *How effective is ICT in supporting children with SEN?*

- *Effective:* what is meant by this in the context of this study?
- *ICT:* which specific resources or applications of ICT?
- *Supporting:* what constitutes support; how might it be observed or measured?
- *Children:* which children?
- *SEN:* which aspect of special educational needs?

After some consideration the question might be refined to:

Does the use of speech support in talking word processors improve the writing of Year 5 boys with dyslexia?

Identifying an area of interest which you want to research and defining a focus can be made easier through the use of ICT-based mind-mapping tools such as *Freemind* (**freemind. sourceforge.net/wiki/index.php/Main_Page**), *Exploratree* (**www.exploratree.org.uk/**) or *Bubbl.us* (**bubbl.us/edit.php**). These examples are either free to download or to use online; however, commercial titles are also available. One feature that they all have in common is the ability to represent ideas visually and dynamically. Sometimes, seeing ideas in a visual way can help to clarify them or help find solutions to problems.

Many practitioner research projects will be small-scale and might well take place in your own classroom. Consequently they may not need huge funds or budgets to make them successful. This does not mean that they will not incur any costs, rather that the necessary funding to support them might be modest. Funds might be needed to purchase a resource or piece of equipment to use in the research, to enable transcripts to be typed from taped conversations or to provide supply cover. ICT can help you identify sources of funding and support to enable your research ideas to come to fruition. Sources of funding and support can frequently be time-limited or in relation to specific areas of research, which makes it hard to provide specific links; however, some useful search terms might be: *funding, practitioner, research, best practice* and *scholarship,* as well as terms from the area you wish to research.

Creative partnerships (**www.creative-partnerships.com**) have provided funding for projects looking into creative practice in schools. The currency of ICT offers advantages over using paper-based directories of sources of funding and support, as these can quickly become out of date. Locating relevant information and applying for funding online is much quicker than using postal/telephone enquiries.

Collaborating and sharing

ICT can support collaboration and sharing during the process of practitioner research. When working alone it can be hard to motivate yourself, particularly if you are also teaching a full timetable; it can be easy to let deadlines slip and you can find yourself facing a mental block about how to proceed. Working with a colleague with whom you can share ideas, developments, data, etc. can be invaluable and ICT can support you in a number of ways.

There are many online forums for teachers where you might locate a research partner, or you could join a professionally oriented network such as *LinkedIn* (**www.linkedin.com**). If you find that you share a research interest with colleagues who are not in your school or maybe not even in your county or country, you may decide to set up a social and professional network for your group using Ning (**ning.com**) or Wiggio (**http://wiggio.com**). These work in a similar way to Facebook to allow you to share ideas and keep up to date with colleagues. You can add the facilities of web or video conferencing (**www.elluminate.com** or **www.skype.com**) for face-to-face chats with your colleagues. You might also create online spaces that allow the group to work together simultaneously, such as *dabbleboard* or *PrimaryPad* (**www.dabbleboard.com;**

www.primarypad.com) or *OneNote 2010* (Microsoft), discussed below. You may wish to store and update collaborative documents online using *box.net* (**box.net**) or *Google.docs* (**docs.google.com**). The advantages of these tools mean that there is less scope for confusion among different versions of documents, or risk of filling up your inbox space e-mailing documents to and fro.

As you begin to develop a bank of online resources, create bookmarks or favourites to record them. You can then share these with other collaborators using tools such as *delicious* (**delicious.com**). The advantage of *delicious* is that it allows you to link to other users who share your favourites. For example, if you have a specialist educational website as a favourite, *delicious* will allow you to see and access sites that appear on the favourites lists of everyone else who also lists that site.

Accessing existing research and data

If you are studying at university then you will have access to library resources, as well as hard copies of books. There is an increasing number of e-books available to view online as well as electronic copies of journals. Most universities have access to databases of journals, which are searchable, making it easy to identify sources of existing research and data to support your study. If you are studying independently then the *Directory of Open Access Journals* (**www.doaj.org**) or *Searchpigeon* (**www.searchpigeon.org/**) will be worth a visit, or consider signing up for a free trial to a service such as *Highbeam* (**www.highbeam.com**) to investigate their range of educational academic literature.

As well as university-based sources of literature and data, you can search the contents of the world's libraries (for example, the British Library (**bl.uk**)) as well as using tools like Google Scholar (**scholar.google.co.uk**) to find specific research articles related to your area of study.

Depending on the nature of your practitioner research, you may wish to draw upon statistical information such as **www.statistics.gov.uk** which has a wealth of information from data on class sizes to expenditure on education. It might also be relevant for you to draw upon historical archives or census data (**www.ons.gov.uk/census/index.html**). The advantage that ICT brings to all of these activities is the availability of such a wide range of resources, far greater than would be accessible via a single library. The speed with which these resources can be searched and accessed is also far greater than with hard copies in libraries.

Case Study: A collaborative research activity

Michael and Jayne studied at university together before starting their teaching careers in different parts of the country. They continued to keep in touch via e-mail and Facebook and as they have a shared interest in the potential of podcasting to support speaking and listening activities they decided to carry out some collaborative practitioner research.

→

Michael represented their ideas as a mind map and shared them with Jayne to confirm he had captured everything. In the meantime, Jayne had been busy sourcing a small pot of funding by searching the internet to cover the purchase of resources and consumables to allow the project to go ahead. They made use of blogs and social bookmark tools to share relevant resources and through these located new resources and contacted other practitioners interested in the same area. They set up a social network site where they could share ideas, thoughts and current research. Michael stated that *without these ICT tools at my disposal I don't think I would ever have done anything about my interest in podcasting. By making full use of them, I am really excited about starting on my research.*

Research Phase 2: Data collection and analysis

Data collection involves uncovering evidence related to your research question and recording it systematically. *Data analysis* consists of looking for patterns and trends in your collected data. *Data interpretation* involves considering and finding possible explanations for your findings. ICT can help you with the collection and analysis of data but interpretation is more subjective; you will need to think carefully about your findings by comparing them with the ideas you have identified in your literature review, for example, before reaching any conclusions. ICT can't interpret data for you. However, to avoid making unsupported inferences and assumptions you can use ICT to organise, store and analyse your data systematically so that you can return to your data time and time again and model it in different ways in order to test and develop your ideas.

The main methods for data collection in the social sciences are surveys, interviews and observation; and the role of ICT to support these activities is considered below.

Surveys and questionnaires

One traditional tool of the researcher is the questionnaire. Large numbers of respondents can be surveyed relatively easily and the possibility of anonymous response may increase engagement. Data gathered from well-designed questionnaires is in a standard format and is therefore comparatively easy to analyse. Using online questionnaires such as *Surveymonkey*, (**www.surveymonkey.com**) or *Kwiksurveys* (**www.kwiksurveys.com**) can have several advantages over the traditional paper-based version.

- Large amounts of data can be collected at lower costs than with paper-based methods which may incur postage costs (Couper *et al.*, 2007).

- Data can be collected more quickly (Harris, 1997).

- Survey data can be downloaded into your word-processing or spreadsheet software for analysis.

- Some online survey services offer integral analysis tools.

It should be noted that online questionnaires can have disadvantages. Perhaps the most widely cited of these is sample bias. Some types of respondent are more likely to use a computer than others and the sample may therefore be biased. This is an issue which ICT researchers should pay close attention to since respondents to online surveys about ICT are more likely to be ICT confident and competent (Carini *et al.*, 2003).

For large-scale paper-based surveys, researchers sometimes use optical mark reading (OMR) scanners and software. You may have filled in OMR forms yourself for surveys or tests; you certainly have if you have ever purchased a national lottery ticket, but this equipment is expensive and only worthwhile if you intend to carry out a very large paper-based study.

Interviews

Whether you are using structured or unstructured interview methods with one individual or a focus group, you will need to record participants' responses. Traditionally, researchers have used paper and pen methods, but portable tablet PCs, and electronic note-taking pens such as *Livescribe* (**www.livescribe.com**) are changing this, offering digitisation of handwritten notes without time-consuming transcription. Alternatively, you may decide to use ICT to record audio or video records of your interviews.

Interviews can be recorded using mp3 recorder/players and transcribed with the help of software that allows you to control the speed of playback while you type. *Express scribe* (NCH software) is an example (**www.nch.com.au/scribe/index.html**). It would be great if technology could automatically transcribe audio recordings directly from your portable mp3 recorder, but unfortunately this is still a little way off. Speech-to-text convertors do exist, but these demand perfect clarity of playback and minimum background noise, and they struggle with accents. As all human voices have accents (even yours) the more reliable speech recognition programs such as *Dragon NaturallySpeaking* (Nuance), require a period of *training* to accustom the software to recognise your voice. If you have hours of audio recordings to transcribe, and you don't want to pay for professional transcription, then it may be worthwhile listening to the audio playback through headphones and repeating it into a speech recognition program. Although transcription is a time-consuming process, it can be much slower in the long run to constantly refer back to audio files.

Web-conferencing tools such as *Skype* were introduced earlier in this chapter, but the facility of ICT to overcome geographic boundaries can also allow you to interview participants at a distance. By using video web-conferencing tools in conjunction with a conference recorder such as *Vodburner* (**www.vodburner.com**) you can save your interview data for later analysis.

When carrying out interviews and observations, the use of digital audio or video recording overcomes several problems.

- In a busy classroom environment it can be difficult to capture all relevant events or behaviour. A key ICT characteristic is *replication*: digital recording technologies allow a videoed teaching episode to be replayed over and over to enable comprehensive analysis.

- Digital video recording enables the researcher to recall, revisit and reflect on key events and critical incidents (Sparrman, 2005). This process can be supported using video editing and annotation tools such as *VideoAnt* (**http://ant.umn.edu/**) or *Viddler* (**www.viddler.com**), to insert timed comments and notes into your video file.

Additional methods of data collection

Your research may involve collecting data about children's ideas, opinions and understanding. Young children can find it difficult to explain their ideas in words, or write them down, so you may decide to use alternative data collection methods such as the ones listed below.

Voting systems

Electronic voting systems such as *TurningPoint* (ShowMode) or *ActiVote* and *Activexpression* (Promethean) are becoming more common in schools and these have potential for collecting data during educational research.

Concept mapping

Using concept- or mind-mapping software was discussed earlier in this chapter in relation to developing your research plans, but this software can also be used to elicit children's ideas. For example, Pearson and Somekh (2003) explored children's perceptions of computers using concept-mapping techniques. *2Connect* (2simple) or *IdeasMap* (Textease), are examples of concept-mapping software for children.

Screen recording

If you need to collect data about children's direct interaction with ICT, for example to examine how they explore unfamiliar software, or edit writing with a word processor, then screen-recording software can capture a screen video of the user's actions. *Screentoaster* (**www.screentoaster.com**) and *Camstudio* (**sourceforge.net**) are examples of free screen-recording software.

Managing your data

ICT can help you to keep your data organised. Professional research management and analysis software such as *Nvivo* (QSR) allows you to import a range of media files for organising and annotation. *Nvivo* also supports text analysis, for example by searching for the frequency of key terms. Office software such as *Project* or *OneNote* (both Microsoft) offer some of the same features and support collaborative editing. *OneNote* can automatically link your notes with your original source data whether it is a document, video, audio recording, spreadsheet or website. One particularly interesting feature of *OneNote* is the ability to take a screenshot of any document, web page or program and make the text on the screenshot searchable.

If you are familiar with relational database software such as *Access* (Microsoft) you will know that it is useful for handling and storing large volumes of information. Setting up a database forces you to think carefully about data structure and to consider possible relationships between data elements, which is in itself a good thing. Storing data in a database will also ensure that you will have a useful archive after your project has finished.

Data analysis

The ICT characteristics of speed and automatic functions that offer teaching and learning benefits for children also offer researchers the same advantages when analysing data. Spreadsheets are ideal for manipulating and analysing quantitative data and databases are useful for categorising qualitative data. The graphing functions of spreadsheets help display results in ways which make patterns or trends in the data explicit. *Excel* (Microsoft) includes some built-in statistical functions such as calculating mean, median and mode or standard deviation. However, a professional data analysis tool such as *Statistical Package for the Social Sciences* (SPSS) offers more advanced tools for statistical analysis. Although superficially SPSS looks like a spreadsheet it does not work in the same way. For a clear, interactive guide to SPSS see an introductory SPSS textbook or an interactive online guide such as **openlearn.open.ac.uk/ course/view.php?id=3791**.

Research Phase 3: Presenting your research

The traditional method of presenting the outcomes of your research is the written research report or paper. It goes without saying that this will be a word-processed document benefiting from automatic tools for layout and formatting, but ICT offers other ways of sharing your findings with others, including:

- online dissemination via a podcast or blog. Although these are unlikely to be primary methods for presenting your research, they could be a good way of communicating key findings to a wider audience;

- multimedia presentations. These can be effective for communicating key messages, especially if you are able to illustrate essential points using still or video images or audio recordings from your data. The online multimedia tool Prezi (**www.prezi.com**) allows you to represent relationships between your ideas visually, and Glogster (**www.glogster.com**) or Wix (**www.wix.com**) support creation of media-rich poster presentations and webpages.

Visualising data

Statistical tools such as spreadsheets and SPSS will present data in tables, charts and graphs which can then be exported (or copied and pasted) into a word processor. If you would like to explore other ways of presenting your data graphically you should try Web 2.0 *infographics* tools such as *Many Eyes* (IBM) (**www-958.ibm.com/software/data/cognos/manyeyes/**) which can help you to construct charts and diagrams in dozens of different ways. The key consideration, of course, is to represent your data as clearly as possible.

Referencing and citation management

Bibliographic and citation management systems such as *RefWorks* (**www.refworks.com**) or *Mendeley* (**www.mendeley.com**) link to your word processor to ensure that citations and references are correctly formatted. If you are studying at university, and your institution has subscribed to an online referencing management system, then the software will also link automatically to electronic journals.

Plagiarism checker

Finally, although you will be certain that your research paper is fully original and meticulously referenced, you may consider using a plagiarism checker. This can help to highlight any instances of missed citations and references. If you are at university then you may already use a plagiarism monitor such as *Turnitin* (**www.turnitin.com**), but free online services are available such as *Dustball* (**www.dustball.com/cs/plagiarism.checker**) and *Viper* (**www.scanmyessay.com**). Note that both *Turnitin* and *Dustball* keep a copy of all submitted papers but that these are not accessible by other services.

Ethical considerations

The sections above have highlighted a wide range of ICT tools that can be used to support your research project. It goes without saying that before you begin to collect and analyse data and disseminate your research findings you must ensure that you fully comply with relevant legal and ethical frameworks. It is outside the scope of this chapter to explore the implications of data protection legislation and issues of informed consent of research participants. You should seek advice from your research supervisor, mentor in school, or head teacher about the type and extent of permissions you require, and the safeguards you will need to apply to ensure that data is collected, stored and handled legally and responsibly.

Activity

Which areas of ICT particularly interest you? Would any of these be suited to investigation through a small-scale research project? Reflect on your recent experience on placement in school. Are there any aspects of ICT use in the classroom which you consider might inspire a small-scale investigation?

Once you have established a broad area of interest, try to narrow this down to identify a specific question which could be answered through research.

Which ICT tools might help you carry out this research? If any of the online tools mentioned above are unfamiliar, spend some time evaluating their potential.

Learning Outcomes Review

In this chapter you have considered the importance of research-informed practice in teaching and learning with ICT. You have examined different types of research, and seen how to locate recent and relevant research on ICT in schools. You have considered how you might evaluate research when findings conflict. Key messages from recent research have been presented for two areas: ICT and pedagogy and ICT and attainment. Ways in which you might use ICT to support and enhance a small-scale practitioner research project have been explored.

Self assessment questions

1. Which 3Rs can help teachers move beyond precedent, peer practice and prescription to improve the quality of ICT learning experiences for children?
2. What does the research tell us about the role of the teacher in ICT learning experiences?
3. If you ensure that you make use of ICT in your lesson, can you be certain that children's learning will be enhanced?
4. How might you use ICT to support the collection of data as part of a small-scale ICT research project?

Further Information

Books

The following books provide valuable support for teachers and trainees undertaking educational research for the first time.

Bell, J. (2005) *Doing your research project: a guide for first-time researchers in education, health and social science* (4th edn.) Maidenhead: Open University Press.

Hopkins, D. (2002) *A Teacher's Guide to Classroom Research*. Buckingham: Open University Press.

These books provide guidance on using ICT tools to support your research.

Coombes, H. (2001) *Research using IT*. Basingstoke: Palgrave.

O Dochartaigh, N. (2002) *The Internet research handbook: a practical guide for students and researchers in the social sciences*. London: Sage.

Websites

Becta Research. All ICT research commissioned by or carried out by Becta is available here (**http://research.becta.org.uk**).

The British Educational Research Association (BERA) is a key organisation for anyone interested in educational research. Their website provides access to BERA academic reviews and professional user reviews, both of which summarise research in particular areas. The site also provides guidance on good practice in educational research writing and research ethics. (**www.bera.ac.uk**).

The National Foundation for Educational Research (NFER) provides much helpful advice for researchers on their site, Practical Research for Education-Online. (**www.pre-online.co.uk**).

The Evidence for Policy and Practice Information and Co-ordinating Centre (EPPI-Centre) carries out systematic reviews of research evidence in education and other areas such as health. (**http://eppi.ioe.ac.uk/cms/Default.aspx**).

The Research Informed Practice Site (TRIPS) offers access to essential research findings for teachers and trainees. (**www.standards.dfes.gov.uk/research**). See particularly Appendix 'Ethics for classroom research'.

References

Andrews, R., Dan, H., Freeman, A., McGuinn, N., Robinson, A. and Zhu, D. (2006) The effectiveness of different ICTs in the teaching and learning of English (written composition), 5–16, in *Research Evidence in Education Library*. London: EPPI-Centre, Social Science Research Unit, Institute of Education, University of London.

Becta (2000) *A preliminary report for the DfEE on the relationship between ICT and primary school standards*. Available at **http://research.becta.org.uk/upload-dir/downloads/page_documents/ research/ictresources.pdf** (retrieved 12 September, 2010).

Becta (2010a) *Harnessing Technology School Survey*. Available a: **http://partners.becta.org.uk/ upload-dir/downloads/page_documents/research/official_statistics/becta_htss_ict_lead_ teacher_ revised.pdf** (retrieved 21 September, 2010).

Becta (2010b) *The impact of technology on children's attainment in English: A review of the literature*. Available at **http://research.becta.org.uk/index.php?section=rh&catcode= _re_rp_be_ 03&rid=18005** (retrieved 20 November 2010).

Brooks, G., Miles, J.N.V., Torgerson, C.J. and Torgerson, D.J (2006) Is an intervention using computer software effective in literacy learning? A randomised controlled trial, *Educational Studies*, 32(2) (June): 133–43.

Carini, R. M., Hayek, J. C., Kuh, G. D., Kennedy, J. M. and Ouimet, J. A. (2003) College students responses to web and paper based surveys: Does mode matter? *Research in Higher Education*, 44(1): 1–19.

Couper, M. P., Kapteyn, A., Schonlau, M. and Winter, J. (2007) Noncoverage and nonresponse in an Internet survey. *Social Science Research*, 36: 131–48.

Cox, M.J. and Abbott, C. (2004) *ICT and attainment: a review of the research literature.* Available at **http://partners.becta.org.uk/upload-dir/downloads/page_documents/research/ict_attainment_summary.pdf** (retrieved 28 August 2010).

Cox, M., Webb, M., Abbott, C., Blakeley, B., Beauchamp, T. and Rhodes V. (2004) *ICT and pedagogy: a review of the research literature.* Available at **http://publications.becta.org.uk/download.cfm?resID=25813** (retrieved 12 September 2010).

Harris, C. (1997) *Developing online market research methods and tools.* Paper presented to ESOMAR Worldwide Internet Seminar, Lisbon, July.

Harrison, C., Comber, C., Fisher, T., Haw, K., Lewin, C., Linzer, E., McFarlane, A., Mavers, D., Scrimshaw, P., Somekh, B. and Watling, R. (2002) *Impact2: The Impact of Information and Communication Technologies on Pupil Learning and Attainment.* Coventry: Becta.

Higgins, S. (2003) *Does ICT Improve Learning and Teaching in Schools?* BERA Professional User Review. Macclesfield: BERA.

Klein, P.S., Nir-gal, O. and Darom, E. (2000) The use of computers in kindergarten, with and without adult mediation; effects on children's cognitive performance and behaviour. *Computers in Human Behaviour,* 16: 591–608.

Lou, Y., Abrami, P.C. and d'Apollonia, S. (2001) Small group and individual learning with technology: A meta-analysis. *Review of Educational Research,* 71(3): 449–521.

Moseley, D., Higgins, S., Bramald, R., Hardman, F., Miller, J., Mroz, M., Tse, H., Newton, D., Thompson, I., Williamson, J., Halligan, J., Bramald, S., Newton, L., Tymms, P., Henderson, B. and Stout, J. (1999) *Ways forward with ICT: Effective pedagogy using Information and Communications Technology for Literacy and Numeracy in Primary Schools.* Newcastle: University of Newcastle.

Pearson, M. and Somekh, B. (2003) Concept-mapping as a research tool: a study of primary children's representations of information and communication technologies (ICT). *Education and Information Technologies,* 8: 5–22.

Somekh, B., Underwood. J., Convery, A., Dillon, G., Jarvis, J., Lewin, C., Mavers, D., Saxon, D., Sing, S., Steadman, S., Twining, P. and Woodrow, D. (2007) *ICT Test Bed Evaluation Final Report: Overview.* Coventry: Becta. Available at **http://www.evaluation.icttestbed.org.uk/files/test_bed_evaluation_report_2006.pdf** (retrieved 10 September, 2010).

Sparrman A. (2005) Video recording as interaction: participant observation of children's everyday life. *Qualitative Research in Psychology,* 2: 241–55.

Wyse, D. and Goswami, U. (2008) Synthetic Phonics and the Teaching of Reading. *British Educational Research Journal,* 34(6) (December): 691–710.

9. ICT linking our world
Donna Hurford and Eleanor Knowles

Learning Outcomes

....

By the end of this chapter you should:
- be aware of ways in which schools can develop ICT links with a range of educational and cultural settings;
- be able to evaluate how potential ICT links may contribute to children's learning;
- be familiar with ways to integrate ICT linking into children's learning;
- be aware of the ethical issues associated with developing a link with a school in a less economically developed country (LEDC) and know how to engage with these issues appropriately.

Professional standards for QTS

Q2 Demonstrate the positive values, attitudes and behaviour they expect from children and young people;

Q5 Recognise and respect the contribution that colleagues, parents and carers can make to the development and well-being of children and young people, and to raising their levels of attainment;

Q6 Have a commitment to collaboration and co-operative learning;

Q7(a) Reflect on and improve their practice, and take responsibility for identifying and meeting their developing professional needs;

Q8 Have a creative and constructively critical approach towards innovation, being prepared to adapt their practice where benefits and improvement are identified;

Q10 Have a knowledge and understanding of a range of teaching, learning and behaviour management strategies and know how to use and adapt them, including how to personalise learning and provide opportunities for all learners to achieve their potential;

Q14 Have a secure knowledge and understanding of their [subject]/curriculum areas and related pedagogy to enable them to teach effectively across the age and ability range for which they are trained;

Q15 Know and understand the relevant statutory and non-statutory curricula and frameworks, including those provided through the National Strategies, for their [subject]/curriculum areas, and other relevant initiatives applicable to the age and ability for which they are trained;

Q18 Know how children and young people develop and that the progress and well-being of learners are being affected by a range of developmental, social, religious, ethnic, cultural and linguistic differences;

> Q23 Design opportunities for learners to develop their literacy, numeracy and ICT skills.
>
> Q25a Use a range of teaching strategies and resources, including e-learning, taking practical account of diversity and promoting equality and inclusion.
>
> Q29 Evaluate the impact of their teaching on the progress of all learners, and modify their planning and classroom practice where necessary.
>
> Q30 Establish a purposeful and safe learning environment conducive to learning and identify opportunities for learners to learn in out-of-school contexts

Introduction

In this chapter you will be invited to review ways in which schools can use ICT to develop links with a range of educational and cultural settings. You will be given the opportunity to develop your awareness of national and international school linking projects; to review how schools can link with cultural settings like museums and galleries, and other opportunities to extend learning beyond the classroom. You will be invited to review examples of how to embed linking within cross-curricular or subject-specific areas of learning providing you with practical ways to embed linking into your teaching and children's learning. The chapter includes school linking case studies and you will be encouraged to evaluate the potential and actual contribution these links may make to children's learning. As school linking is currently recommended and facilitated by the British Council as a way for schools to engage with the global dimension we will take the opportunity to review ethical issues associated with school linking projects and consider how to develop meaningful partnerships.

Defining terms

To define terms in this chapter we are using 'cultural setting' to mean a place like a museum, gallery, archive, or library. By 'linking' we mean a range of ICT-enabled ways to access and engage with resources, for example through online interactive activities; to communicate and to interact using e-mail, video or web conferencing and learning platforms.

Schools linking with cultural settings

Although schools and different cultural settings have a history of working together, such as borrowing books and resources from museums and libraries and organising educational visits to local libraries, museums and galleries, there is a growing awareness of the significance of these partnerships for children's learning. In July 2009 a cultural guidance (Partnerships for Schools, 2009) document was published identifying how educational and cultural settings will work more closely together to provide all children with opportunities to benefit from cultural learning experiences. These cultural settings are also committed to developing their digital technologies to improve and facilitate access to their collections and to further develop interactive learning and communication.

When would I start thinking about linking with a cultural setting?

When you are doing your medium-term planning (MTP) would be a good time to think about what is available both locally, nationally and internationally to support your teaching and children's learning. Being able to actually visit a library, a museum, an archive or a gallery can provide exciting and diverse opportunities for children to experience different environments, meet colleagues with special expertise and get involved with hands-on workshops and tours. However, not all our schools are in walking distance to even local cultural settings so you would need to arrange transport, adult helpers and think carefully about how to fund the visit as parents and carers often have to contribute to the costs. Transport costs are a significant issue for schools as many parents and carers are not in a position to make regular or even one-off contributions, so the visits you can arrange may be limited. Furthermore, the nearest museum with a relevant collection may be prohibitively far away and without some form of ICT-enabled access your children would miss out on what could be valuable and stimulating learning experiences.

How do I know what's out there?

There are a variety of organisations and gateway websites that can help you locate cultural settings relevant to your subject or topic area. The Museums, Libraries and Archives (MLA) service has a programme called Renaissance which is seeking to work with all regional museums and you can access an online list of regional Renaissance teams and hubs (www.mla.gov.uk/what/programmes/renaissance). Alternatively you can go to your county council or local authority's webpage and look for links to local libraries, archives, museums and galleries. The Learning Outside the Classroom (LOTC) (**www.lotc.org.uk**) website provides links to organisations like Engage which offers lists of national galleries. You can also do your own internet search: a quick search using a search engine for *Cumbria museums* led to a very useful tourism site with a thorough listing of places to visit in the region; a search for *toys museums education* led to a wide range of links to national and international museums.

What can cultural settings offer?

Once you have identified museums with relevant collections take a look at what they can offer online. For example, The Museum of London, in collaboration with local partners including the fire brigade, provides a variety of online resources focusing on the Fire of London (**www.fireoflondon.org.uk/resources**). Children can interact with objects from the museum's collection, guided by the avatar Molly who reads and rereads questions to stimulate historical enquiry, and an interactive game is also available. The museum recognises that teachers are time-pressed and in response to this they have designed e-inset for teachers, with an introduction to museum services, guidance on how to support children's learning with museum objects and notes to support lesson planning.

Activity

Choose a Key Stage 1 or 2 subject-based topic (e.g. the Vikings; rivers; portrait painting) or a cross-curricular theme (e.g. water; people who look after us; exploring) for a medium-term plan.

- Try using the Renaissance, LOTC and county council or local authority webpages to identify some local and national cultural settings offering online and interactive access to their resources.
- Use a search engine such as **www.google.co.uk** to carry out a more specific search.
- Find another way to locate a relevant cultural setting.
- Note what online resources these settings can offer that would be relevant to your focus area.
- Review the process and make a note to remind you what to do when you are next planning.

How could the link be more interactive with opportunities for video-conferencing?

Thanks to innovative teachers, head teachers and museum practitioners, opportunities for interaction and video-conferencing (VC) are much more available and developed than just a few years ago. In fact there is now so much demand for interaction that the most popular museums like the Museum of London and the Victoria and Albert Museum offer a range of non-synchronous interactions or scheduled VC sessions. Less well-known cultural settings may still be able to provide more individual opportunities for interactions; it would be worth checking this out with the setting's education officer.

Video-conferencing

Some museums like the National Coal Mining Museum (**www.ncm.org.uk**) offer schools free access to scheduled VC sessions including *A Bevin boy remembers* and *Meet a real miner*. For pupils who are too far away to visit the museum, or for teachers wishing to consolidate learning following a visit, a video-conference workshop is an exciting and interactive way for pupils to access the museum's resources and learn about coal mining (**www.ncm.org.uk**).

Ask your school's ICT co-ordinator about local ICT networks, such as Cumbria and Lancashire Education Online (**www.cleo.net.uk**) in the north-west, which provides a list of museums offering VC with schools. When you review a museum's webpage (see **www.museumoflondon.org.uk**), you may find that your school needs to be a member of Global Leap to be able to book VC sessions. Global Leap (**www.global-leap.org**) is an organisation, funded by school subscriptions facilitating VC links between schools and between schools and other educational settings like museums. If subscribing to Global Leap is not an option you could try accessing settings that offer free VC links and, if children's learning benefits, you would have some evidence to persuade your school to subscribe to Global Leap in future.

Video- or web-conferencing equipment

If your school does not have VC equipment it can be a relatively cheap purchase, depending on the quality of the equipment. Local ICT organisations can be useful sources of information: the UK's organisation and research network, ja.net (**www.ja.net/services/video/vtas/index.html**), provides free support to schools and colleges using VC; and Wakefield Internet Learning Domain (**www.gowild.org.uk/CurriculumStandardsAndSupport/NationalStrategies/ VideoConferencing/Video.htm**) offers advice on reasonably priced and good-quality VC equipment. If you think it would be appropriate for small groups to access a web-conference link then a good-quality webcam would be sufficient; however, you would need a good-quality microphone either using the inbuilt computer microphone or an external one. Remember to check with the school's ICT co-ordinator whether the school has parental permission for children to engage with online communication.

Case Study: Medium-term plan for a Key Stage 1 focus on toys

Adam is in his second year of teaching and he is preparing a medium-term plan on toys for his Year 3 class. He wants to develop the cross-curricular potential with the Victorians (National Curriculum: (NC) 4a, b), Design and Technology (NC: 1–3), ICT (NC: 1, 3 and 4) and English (NC: 3 and NC: 4). This is the first time Adam has taught the Victorians through a cross-curricular approach and he wants to make it a rich and stimulating learning experience for all the children. He is particularly concerned about the reluctant readers and writers in the class and he is keen to find ways to motivate them. A Teaching Assistant mentioned that there is a local museum with a Victorian classroom and a display of toys from Victorian times to the present day. Adam hopes they will be able to arrange a visit but the transport costs may be a problem for the school and some parents. Ideally he would like to extend the engagement with the museum to something more interactive and he has heard that some offer video-conferencing but he does not know where to go from here.

Activity

What would you suggest Adam does first?

Which national museums could be appropriate? Try an internet search to identify possible national museums with online access and offering VC.

How do you think VC might contribute to the children's learning?

Research Focus

This research focus reviews how children's learning can be developed and enhanced by linking with cultural settings using ICT to enable and facilitate the link. If we ask you to think of a memorable event from your time in primary or secondary school you may well recall an outing, a school trip, time out of the classroom rather than a particular lesson in class. When we ask the same question of trainee teachers they often recall a visit to a farm, a trip to a museum, a day out at a zoo or the beach. So why do these times out of the classroom resonate so strongly for many of us? According to the Learning Outside the Classroom Manifesto opportunities to learn in places other than schools are

> often the most memorable learning experiences; [they] help us to make sense of the world around us by making links between feelings and learning. They stay with us into adulthood and affect our behaviour, lifestyle and work. They influence our values and the decisions we make.

> (DfES, 2006, page 1)

This idea of making sense of the world around us by physically experiencing it is known as experiential learning. As the word suggests, experiential is about experiencing something in order to understand it better. What we now understand about learning indicates the importance of *interaction between thinking and experience* (Pollard, 2008, page 175) and the need to provide children with social, physical, sensory and emotional learning experiences (Barnes, 2007). Think about learning to swim: most of us who have learned to swim have probably got wet doing it. Trying to learn how to co-ordinate your limbs, breathe in air rather than water, float and move forwards all at the same time is not too easy if we just study it in a book or even watch a video. We need to have a go, preferably with an encouraging and supportive adult swimmer, to help us make sense of it. As Barnes says, *personal, social and physical experiences are great teachers* (2007, page 172) so it could well be in children's interests to incorporate 'beyond the classroom' experiences into school life.

However, what is being recommended in this chapter is using ICT to enable virtual linking rather than real-life experiences. Having just offered an argument for experiential learning, what role do virtual experiences have to play? This is where *maximising the learning benefits of ICT thus requires responsive, reflective pedagogy which values pleasure and engagement as well as operational skill* (Teaching and Learning Research Programme, no date). This need for responsive and reflective pedagogy is echoed by Pollard who advises that ICT should only be used in a lesson *where it is the best way to promote learning* (2008, page 269). This requires some careful thinking by the teacher to choose when it is most appropriate to use ICT resources and when alternative resources may be more

→

effective. As children develop their awareness of the potential of ICT for accessing, processing and sharing information they will develop their ability to make informed and creative decisions about when and where to use ICT resources.

The virtual linking experiences highlighted in this chapter may not be appropriate for your class but they illustrate how learning through interactive webpages and video-conferencing can offer unique opportunities afforded by the internet to access otherwise inaccessible places and people. As Kennewell *et al*.'s (2000) research into the use of ICT in the primary classroom identified, accessing the inaccessible through the internet and e-mail can provide the motivational stimulus needed by a reluctant reader and writer. Arguably, online access to otherwise inaccessible cultural settings could engage children with forms of experiential learning that would not otherwise be possible, *allow[ing] us to transfer learning experienced outside to the classroom and vice versa* (DfES, 2006, page1).

Links to the National Curriculum

In the National Curriculum there is a section called *Learning across the Curriculum* which includes guidance on using ICT in subject teaching enabling children to develop their understanding of how ICT can be applied to all subjects. Children can easily access information that is relevant for all curriculum subjects using the internet and other ICT tools. In addition, using ICT can provide opportunities for children to learn and develop their investigative, organisational, editing and presentational skills.

In the ICT curriculum at Key Stages 1 and 2, children are expected to develop their awareness of how to use ICT to find things out and to check the validity and accuracy of ICT-sourced information (1a) and to do this effectively working with others (5b). They need to develop their ideas and use different ICT tools and programs to present their learning (2a). They need to know how they could improve and further develop their work (4c).

Schools linking with schools

Developing links between schools is not a new initiative; you may remember your own schools having links with other primary or secondary schools. However, more recently there has been increased government interest in school linking as a way to address certain agendas, and the Labour government of 1998–2009 actively encouraged international school linking as part of its international strategy for education (DfES, 2004a).

The global gateway website (**www.globalgateway.org.uk**) was established to facilitate global school linking and significant funding was made available to cover the costs of reciprocal visits and shared curricular projects by teachers from linked schools. Since 2006 all schools in England are legally required to comply with the community cohesion agenda and Ofsted has been instructed to report on school engagement (**www.teachernet**). Schools have shown significant interest in developing national school links, with support provided by the *School Linking Network*, as these can offer an effective way to develop partnerships and tackle prejudices. A report in *The Times Educational Supplement* (O'Malley, 10 June 2006) noted that in 2005 approximately 4,000 schools had expressed interest in developing links nationally or internationally. Setting up a link is relatively easy; however, sustaining a link so it develops as a meaningful partnership is a long-term commitment and requires a shared agreement between the partner schools on their expectations and commitment.

What might be some of the benefits of school linking?

Activity

- Make a list of the benefits you think school linking could offer.
- Consider the opportunities for curricular learning and skill development.
- How might a link with another school be a way to engage with PSHE and Citizenship?

Compare your list with this one developed by the *Cumbria Development Education Centre (CDEC)*.

Some of the benefits of school linking

- *Enjoyment,* because linking should be fun.
- *Improving personal skills* (confidence, self-esteem), for example gaining skills from project involvement and getting their work valued by a wider audience.
- *Improving interpersonal skills* (sociability, communication) through the wide range of communication opportunities that a collaborative linking project brings.
- *Knowledge of development issues* (citizenship, human rights, conflict resolution, social justice, fair trade, democracy, equality, environmental awareness and sustainable development locally and globally) if this is carefully planned into a programme of curriculum development within the link.
- *Respect for other cultures, values and beliefs* as a result of getting past stereotypes and building relationships, which can contribute to greater understanding of diversity at home.
- *Understanding interdependence* (how our actions impact on others), which can lead to making changes in our own lifestyles. Part of this is learning to see the world from another point of view and can improve skills of critical thinking and questioning.
- *Affecting the school ethos* through activities that involve children and staff across the whole school. A link can also involve and strengthen the wider community, if this is carefully planned into the programme of work.

How do your lists compare? Which points do you think you may need to think about some more? Why?

How can I set up a school link?

Before setting up a link it would be wise to check with your head teacher to see if there is an opportunity to involve the wider school, rather than just linking between two classes in different schools. There is so much we can learn from each other, you might decide to begin by linking with a neighbouring school. You may not think there will be many differences, as your schools will be in the same or similar localities, but schools are very individual places and each one has its own community, ethos and approaches to teaching and learning.

If you are looking for a link with a contrasting locality to support a geography topic, or with a contrasting cultural community to support your RE and Citizenship/PSHE curriculum, you could start by thinking about friends and colleagues who work in schools in different localities. Links built on personal relationships can be easier to sustain. If you do not know anyone who will be interested then, with your head teacher's agreement, you could register with the Schools Linking Network (**www.schoolslinkingnetwork.org.uk**) and see how they can help. Once you have developed and are maintaining a link with a school in the UK you may want to consider widening your range to other countries. But before you start searching for possible partners on Global Gateway (**www.globalgateway.org.uk**), spend some time with colleagues talking about your school's expectations of the link, what learning outcomes you hope to achieve for both staff and pupils, and what areas of the curriculum you are hoping to enrich.

It is exciting to imagine setting up links with schools in many different countries, but extra time spent in planning is time well spent. Think carefully about the practicalities of, for example, time zones, in case you could use synchronous interaction like video- or web-conferencing. And consider the issue of language, either seeking partners where English is a shared language, or having foreign languages as a curriculum focus. The crucial question, and easily overlooked, is: 'Why do we want this link?' When a school in the UK is planning to link with a school in a less economically developed country (LEDC) it is especially important that both partners are clear about their motivations and intentions for the partnership.

Schools might have a range of motivations for developing global links. Teachers at Shaw Wood Primary School, South Yorkshire decided they needed to broaden the children's horizons (QCA, 2007, page 18) and initially developed links with Spain to help children think of themselves as European citizens (QCA, 2007, page 18). From this starting point they linked with a school in Japan before feeling ready to explore the children's role as wider world citizens able to engage with some of the challenging issues facing an LEDC like Ghana. This incremental approach to developing school links indicates the teachers' awareness of the responsibilities and the school's readiness for these different types of partnerships.

How can ICT support school linking?

If you think back to Adam's story, shared through Case Study: Medium-term plan for a Key Stage 1 focus on toys, the reasons for school linking or for making links with cultural settings tend to be very similar. Generally, school links can offer more diverse and personalised learning opportunities and the chance to communicate meaningfully, sharing ideas and resources with one another, making decisions and developing relationships. ICT resources like e-mail, learning platforms and video- or web-conferencing can facilitate such communication. Learning platforms are increasingly being used by schools as safe ways to communicate and facilitate learning: the *Next Generation* site (**www.nextgenerationlearning.org.uk/At-School/ Technology/Learning-platforms-/**) provides further information on how they are being used by schools. You may wish to refer to Chapters 4 and 6 in this book for further information on learning platforms.

School access to the internet provides learners with a vast range of information and resources and, in order to learn how to use this resource effectively, learners need to practise the necessary skills like selecting appropriate information; copying and pasting; editing and reformatting information for sharing and reviewing. Collecting data for a collaborative curriculum project can offer children meaningful, contextualised opportunities to develop their skills and expertise using a wide range of ICT resources and programs including: internet search engines, digital cameras, videos, audio recorders, data-handling, data-logging, word processing, graphics and presentation design programs. As teachers we need to be aware of how ICT can enable learning through school linking and we need to teach children how to make their own informed and independent choices about using ICT resources.

Case Study: Ways in which ICT can facilitate effective school linking

Shabana is a Year 5 teacher in a two-form-entry city school and Rachel is the Year 5 teacher in a one-form-entry school in a rural town. The teachers set up the school link a year ago and, having seen the children's excitement and engagement with the shared projects, they are keen to develop it further. Now that the schools have web-conferencing facilities they are planning to provide the children with opportunities to collaborate on locality-based projects. In the autumn term they spent time developing relationships between the two classes with a strong focus on PSHE/Citizenship and community cohesion, by sharing information about their schools, how children spent their free time and what was important to them. The classes have never actually met; all the communication has been by class e-mail and web-conferencing.

The teachers set their classes a challenge to identify a common problem in both localities that they could research, share ideas and develop proposals for change to

→

be presented to the local communities and authorities. Shabana and Rachel identified some possible areas of the curriculum that could be addressed through the project including: comparing contrasting localities and recognising how the environment could be improved (Geography: 3a, f and 5a); recording from experience, evaluating their own work and collaborating on presentations (Art and Design: 1a–c; 4a; 5a, b); using ICT to find out about the locality; exchanging and sharing ideas and collaborating on presentations (ICT: 1–c; 2a, 3a, b; 4a, c); developing communication; presenting ideas; persuasive writing and collaboration (English: Speaking and Listening). After some e-mailing and web-conferencing discussions the two classes decided to find out more about opportunities for outdoor play and recreation in their localities to identify some suggestions for improving the provision for members of the local community.

Shabana's and Rachel's classes each have access to the following ICT resources: six digital cameras; two hand-held Flip video cameras (60 min. film capacity); one digital audio recorder; web-conferencing resources (small webcam, works best with groups up to six and six headsets); laptops (two hour-access a week); four class computers with internet access, storyboard program, *PowerPoint*; class e-mail.

As this is a cross-curricular project Shabana and Rachel estimate at least three half days a week for six weeks will be allocated to the learning, with local community meetings planned at the end of the half term to share the presentations. The two teachers see meaningful opportunities for the children to develop their peer assessment skills through the project and have paired groups of five/six children from each class to work together as co-researchers and reviewers of their group presentations.

Activity

Take a look at the start of the plan for ICT developed by the two teachers, shown in Table 9.1 (overleaf), and add what you think would be appropriate resources, noting the skills that the children would need to learn as the project develops.

How could the children's ICT skills be extended further? What other desired learning outcomes (DLOs) might you add to the plan?

Desired Learning Outcome (DLO)	Project Activity	ICT resource	ICT skills
I can collect and choose a selection of images of the locality.	Find aerial photos of localities; walk to local park(s) to collect data on current situation. Data needs to be of a high quality to support the presentation.	Google Earth; digital cameras; Flip videos.	Familiar with digital cameras and video cameras: change settings; save and select; download and save to computer.
I can share my ideas with my linking partner.	Record audio file summarising group's ideas on situation with local park/s to share with linking partner for their feedback. Email audio files and selected photos to linking partner. Download linking partner's audio files; discuss and evaluate; provide feedback by e-mail.	*Which resources would be appropriate?*	*Which skills will children need to learn and be taught?*
I can choose between different ICT presentation programs by applying appropriate criteria for our group's presentation.	Develop awareness of the features of two presentation programs like *PowerPoint* and Multimedia storyboard programs.	*Which resources would be appropriate?*	*What skills will children need to learn and be taught?*
I can co-present with my group members our draft presentation on suggestions for improving our local parks.	Trial draft version of presentation with linking partner one week before community presentation; respond and give appropriately constructive feedback.	*Which resources would be appropriate?*	

Table 9.1 Example of a cross-curricular planning grid

Case Study: Making links with schools in the wider global community (part one)

We have looked at some examples of schools developing links with schools in contrasting localities. Let us now consider how two schools in different countries, for example England and China, could set up, develop and sustain a school link using a range of resources including ICT.

Background to the school linking project between schools in Chengdu, China and Cumbria, England

The head teacher arranged to take part in an expedition to China and saw an opportunity to involve the schoolchildren through linking with a Chinese school. Her initial motivation was to excite the children about travel and adventure and to widen their horizons by challenging stereotypes and celebrating diversity.

> *Our children need to realise that the world is made up of many different people and beliefs, so that when they come across someone different they don't think there's something threatening about that.*

> *(Cumbria school's Head Teacher)*

Details of the project

All the children were involved in preparations for the head teacher's visit to China. For example the Head Teacher used assemblies to talk about what she should take with her, children used the internet to map the journey, see aerial views of the locality, collect data on the weather, research buying flight tickets and other travel preparations (ICT, 1a–c). The children waved her off on her journey and they received regular e-mails giving updates of the trip. A range of curriculum activities took place throughout the half-term before the trip so all children contributed to the materials that were taken to China.

The children were set the challenge of representing their village/locality/country in a set of objects. They were asked: *What objects could I take with me that represent our village?* Or *what images of our community could I share?* These activities supported children's engagement with PSHE and Citizenship (4b, e) and ICT (1a, b, 3a and b). The Head Teacher was aware that the school in China that she was going to visit needed English language books and children were asked to write some stories for the Chinese school. Some children used an outdoor trip to a local valley as the motivation for writing a story about a river adventure. This was a useful literacy exercise as the children had to explain their terms and contexts, thinking carefully about their audience, who wouldn't have knowledge of local places, history, names or dialect. In addition, Years 1 and 2 produced a paper book showing *A day at school* and children from Key Stage 2 took digital photographs that reflected a normal day in their lives. These activities supported children's

→

engagement with English (En3, writing) and ICT (2a and 3a, b). The Head Teacher asked the children what they wanted to know about the children in the Chinese school and many asked about the different foods they eat. The Head Teacher saw potential here to develop the school's focus on healthy eating. She collected data from both schools on diet which was analysed by the children developing their data-handling skills. Not only did this contribute to mathematics (Ma 4) and ICT (1b, 2b, 3a and b) but it also addressed the *Every Child Matters* aim for children to be healthy (DfES, 2004b) by sending a very strong healthy eating message as the Cumbrian children's chocolate consumption was far higher than that of their peers in Chengdu.

Following the visit, the Head Teacher used assembly time to share photos and video clips from the visit. These resources were made available on the school's learning platform, enabling children to explore the visit further in class and at home.

Activity

Before looking at part two of the Case Study on sustaining the school link, consider what ICT-enabled learning opportunities you would recommend. Bear in mind that there is a seven-hour time difference between England and China. Consider how the use of ICT resources could be developed further to facilitate and vary communication and sharing information between the classes.

Case Study: Making links with schools in the wider global community (part two)

Initially the focus was on developing personal relationships between the children and teachers in the different schools, similar to the focus adopted by Shabana and Rachel in the previous school linking case study. Both schools had e-mail access and the Chinese school could access the English school's learning platform. The English school used many of its PSHE sessions to compare and contrast ways of life and to explore stereotypes. Initially both schools were keen to develop penfriend relationships between children using e-mail but on reflection they decided to use class e-mail instead of individual email to sustain communication through ongoing curricular projects. Translation between the two first languages was sometimes necessary and the children enjoyed experimenting with online translation tools and learning some words and phrases from each other's languages. Photos and drawings of artefacts from different aspects of daily life, accompanied by audio or written explanations, were shared between Chinese and English classes. The schools began to explore the possibility of video-conferencing but the seven-hour time difference presented challenges for synchronous conferencing. Some of the teachers used web-conferencing to develop class projects and the Cumbrian school

$\rightarrow$

looked into holding video-conference sessions in an evening, English time, between the older classes.

The children were already familiar with aspects of the contrasting locality, having been involved with the preparations for the visit. They were now able to develop this comparative learning further by exploring the contrasting localities both geographically and culturally. Chinese and English classes were paired and each pair chose from a range of themes including: weather, seasons, land use, population, transport, work and homes to develop shared learning using e-mail and the learning platform to exchange questions and information.

The Head Teacher recognised that a link of this kind needs a lot more time to become established. The first phase had been a great success. The schools took advice from linking organisations and are developing a partnership agreement, agreeing on the aims and the shared responsibilities for the school link. The Cumbrian school is keen to integrate the global dimension into its curriculum and draw on guidance from the QCA (2007), DfID/DfES (2005) and Oxfam (2006) in developing more cross-curricular and globally aware opportunities for learning.

Ethical issues associated with school linking

Whenever we develop partnerships between organisations and individuals we need to know what this partnership means for all involved and to agree on roles and responsibilities. A working partnership agreement is as important for virtual partnerships (which rely on ICT for communication and sharing information), as it is for partnerships between local schools where children and staff can meet face to face. When the partnership relies on e-mail and short conversations through web-conferencing, teachers and children need to be particularly careful that communication and ideas are expressed in a way that is always sensitive to the other partner. If the partnership is between people from different cultural and geographical settings we need to be aware of possible misunderstandings and spend time finding out what each partner finds appropriate. For example, Islamic teaching does not always include art lessons, and expecting Moslem children to draw self-portraits may not be acceptable to the school's Islamic teaching. Developing shared understanding is a fundamental part of developing empathic relationships; we need to remember that although ICT may facilitate certain types of communication we need to be individually sensitive to cultural, social and religious norms.

Our perceptions of other places and people are influenced by a range of factors including media coverage and the reinforcement of stereotypes. Tanner warns how a *damaging school link is one which fuels negative stereotypes* (2007, page 159). Developing links with schools in LEDCs warrants very careful consideration, as evidenced in the Shaw Wood School's approach (QCA, 2007). An ICT-enabled school link will not necessarily encourage children to challenge stereotypes unless they are equipped with appropriate questioning and thinking skills.

Activity

Why do you think developing a link with a school in an LEDC warrants careful consideration?

Which of the following motives do you think are appropriate?

- We can develop children's awareness of what it means to be a member of the global community through shared curricular projects.
- We can show our children how lucky they are to be living in such a well-off country.
- We can fundraise for the link school and buy them things they need.
- We can help children understand the differences and similarities between different people and their ways of life.

You may have ticked all of the options and some would argue that is fine. However, it is important to be mindful of ways that we can give children opportunities to challenge stereotypes and not reinforce them. Which two motives do you think could most easily lead to reinforcing stereotypes?

Research Focus

The rationale for school linking includes opportunities for social interaction, personalised learning, meaningful learning activities and community cohesion. Research into learning by Vygotsky has inspired current thinking about social interaction and its significance for learning (Pollard, 2008). According to Pollard, the *influence of social constructivist ideas is implicit in much of the documentation of the National Curriculum* (2008, page 180): the focus on speaking and listening and exchanging ideas is evident across the various curricular subjects. Developing relationships with children from different communities and working on collaborative projects may offer those *meaningful and contextual* (Pollard, 2008, page 201) opportunities which are so vital for deep and sustained learning. Personalising learning (DCSF, 2008) is seen as a way to make these learning opportunities more diverse and inclusive, enabling learners to more effectively access the curriculum. Examples of effective personalised learning include active use of video-conferencing and learning platforms to support school linking projects (BECTA, 2008).

The community cohesion agenda is very much akin to the aims of Global Citizenship, which is a non-statutory curricular subject or approach to learning. Global Citizenship focuses on helping children know how to develop respectful relationships and to develop the *skills and values to participate as active citizens* (Oxfam, 2006, page 3). And, in addition to all these sound pedagogical and ethical reasons for developing effective links between schools, it is important to remember that some children are globally aware and are sustaining long-distance friendships

$\rightarrow$

and family relationships using e-mail; web-conferencing; online translation programs and social networks (Hurford, 2009). So there is an opportunity to capitalise on this global awareness and help children learn how to communicate in safe, appropriate and innovative ways.

Despite all these potential benefits to children's learning, ICT resources are most effective when they are appropriately selected by the teacher and the learners and make a unique contribution to learning. Teachers at Chopwell Primary School have developed a link with a school in Japan using the *structured learning network Japan UK LIVE!* (QCA, 2007, page 28). The schools share learning on curricular themes, including the environment, homes and houses and food and health by using the learning platform talkboards and uploading photos, films and letters. Teachers at both schools collaborate on ways to improve children's writing and they have noted marked improvements in the standard of independent writing. Apart from the academic impact of the link, teachers at Chopwell recognise how the children are more enthusiastic about coming to school and have improved self-esteem because someone in a distant country cares enough about them to send them a letter.

We need to understand the potential of these different information finding and sharing technologies so we can offer children meaningful learning opportunities. School linking has to be worked at so the partnership develops and is sustained. ICT offers unique ways to stay in touch and to share learning but these opportunities will only be maximised if we select appropriate technologies, learn and teach relevant ICT skills, and evaluate the learning. It is by looking for ways to develop those meaningful interactions that we show how we value children's *pleasure and engagement* (TLRP, no date) through learning as well as providing the opportunities to develop the necessary *operational skills* (TLRP, no date).

Links to the National Curriculum

In the ICT curriculum at Key Stages 1 and 2, children are expected to develop their awareness of how to use ICT to find things out and to check the validity and accuracy of ICT-sourced information (1a). As they go through the key stages they are expected to develop as more confident users of ICT, knowing how to exchange and share information. In addition they need to become more aware of others so that they take care when choosing what to share and how to share information with others, for example, using e-mail or the internet (3b). They need to develop their ability to review working with ICT and to evaluate alternative ways of working and how to improve their work (4a, b and c). Through their engagement with ICT they should be able to talk about ways in which ICT can be used in daily life (5c).

In the non-statutory curriculum for Citizenship, Key Stage 1 children are expected to learn how to share their opinions (1b), to take part in discussions and debates about issues relevant to them (2a and b), to recognise and respect people's diversity and differences. During Key Stage 2 children are encouraged to share their opinions on societal issues (1a); to appreciate the range of identities and cultural diversity in the UK (2i); to develop good relationships and respect the differences between people. They are taught to consider the consequences of their actions, including the impact on others of negative behaviours (4a and 4d). They think about other people's lives, values and customs and learn to recognise and challenge stereotypes (4b, 4e).

ICT offers schools opportunities to develop and sustain links with a variety of cultural and educational settings both nationally and internationally. The combination of online resources including the internet, e-mail, web- and video-conferencing and learning platforms provides unique ways to exchange ideas and information and to communicate. However, teachers need to make informed and considered decisions about selecting the most appropriate ICT resources to support and enhance children's learning. Furthermore, when developing partnerships with schools in the UK or overseas teachers must be particularly mindful of how these links are enabling children to challenge rather than reinforce stereotypes. While ICT provides the resources to facilitate linking with otherwise inaccessible partners, teachers and children need to reflect on the aims of the link and focus on developing equal partnerships.

Learning Outcomes Review

Through this chapter you have developed your awareness of how schools can develop ICT links with cultural and educational settings. You should now be able to identify how purposeful links can contribute to children's learning and have some awareness of how to look for and set up a variety of links. The examples and activities provided you with opportunities to consider how these links could be meaningfully integrated into your planning, teaching and children's learning. In addition you have had the opportunity to reflect on some of the ethical issues associated with school linking and particularly when considering linking with a school in an LEDC.

Self-assessment questions

1. Why might you consider integrating an ICT link with a cultural setting into an area of learning?
2. Why do schools link with other schools?
3. How can school links benefit from using ICT?
4. Why do I need to consider the ethical issues associated with school linking, especially if I am considering linking with a school in an LEDC?

Further Information

British Council Connecting Classrooms Project. This site offers collaborative projects for learners and teachers to help build lasting partnerships between schools in the UK and others around the world. (**www.britishcouncil.org/learning-connecting-classrooms.htm**).

Consortium of Development Education Centres. This site offers links to CPD and Inset opportunities for teachers run by Development Education Centres across England. Covers a range of global citizenship themes and approaches including 'Thinking of Linking; step-by-step to a School Link' offered by Cumbria Development Education Centre (**2ww.globalclassrooms.co.uk**).

Development Education Association (DEA). This site offers guidance on global citizenship for schools and communities including how to develop and sustain ethical school linking partnerships with schools in LEDCs (**www.dea.org.uk**).

Global Gateway, bringing an international dimension to education. This site offers guidance on developing links with schools beyond the UK and how to access funding to support partnerships including curricular projects with schools in LEDCs (**www.globalgateway.org.uk/**).

Schools Linking Network. This site offers information on setting up links with schools in the UK (**www.schoolslinkingnetwork.org.uk/**).

Teaching Outside the Classroom. This site offers information on accessing and setting up a placement as a trainee teacher or teacher in a wide range of cultural settings across the country (**www.teachingoutsidetheclassroom.com/**).

References

Barnes, J (2007) *Cross Curricular Learning 3–14*. London: Sage.

Becta (2008) *Next Generation Learning Right Now – Recognising ICT Excellence in Schools.* Online at: **www.becta.org.uk/excellenceawards**

Cumbria and Lancashire Education Online. Online at **www.cleo.net.uk** (accessed 18 February 2011).

DCSF (2008) *Personalised Learning a practical guide*. London: DCSF. Online at: **www.teachernet.gov.uk/publications** (accessed 18 February 2011).

DfES (2004a) *Putting the World into World-Class Education*. London: DfES. Online at **www.globalgateway.org/pdf/International-Strategy.pdf** (accessed 18 February 2011).

DfES (2004b) *Every Child Matters: Change for Children in Schools*. London: DfES. Online at **www.dcsf.gov.uk/everychildmatters/about/aims/outcomes/outcomescyp/**

DfES (2006) *Learning Outside the Classroom Manifesto*. Online at **www.lotc.org.uk/getdoc/f8891c8f-eec5-454c-b3d3-92f1aa36ae25/Manifesto** (accessed 18 February 2011).

DfID/DfES (2005) *Developing the global dimension in the school curriculum*. Online at: **www.globaldimension.org.uk/docs/dev_global_dim.pdf** (accessed 18 February 2011).

Global Leap. Online at **www.global-leap.org** (accessed 18 February 2011).

The Global Gateway. Online at **www.globalgateway.org.uk** (accessed 18 February 2011).

Great Britain. Department for Education and Employment (1999) *The National Curriculum handbook for primary teachers in England key stages 1 and 2.* London: The Stationery Office.

Hurford, D. (2009) Using dialogue to engage children with challenging ideas, in Rowley, C. and Cooper, H. (eds.) *Cross-curricular Approaches to Teaching and Learning.* London: SAGE.

Ja-net *JANET Video Technology Advisory Service (VTAS).* Online at **www.ja.net/services/video/vtas/index.html** (accessed 18 February 2011).

Kennewell, S., Parkinson, J. and Tanner, H. (2000) *Developing ICT in Primary Schools.* London: RoutledgeFalmer.

Museum of London *Fire of London Resources.* Online at **www.fireoflondon.org.uk/resources** (accessed 18 February 2011).

National Coal Mining Museum Online at **www.ncm.org.uk** (accessed 18 February 2011).

O'Malley, B. (10 June 2006) The World at your pupils' feet. *Times Educational Supplement.* Online at **www.tes.co.uk/article.aspx?storycode=2206573** (accessed 18 February 2011).

Oxfam (2006) *Education for Global Citizenship: A Guide for Schools.* Oxford: Oxfam. Online at **www.oxfam.org.uk/education/gc/files/education_for_global_citizenship_a_guide_for_schools.pdf** (accessed 18 February 2011).

Partnerships for Schools (July, 2009) *Culture Guidance Requirements and guidance on culture for local authorities entering the second half of the Building Schools for the Future programme.* Document Status: Issued.

Pollard, A. (2008) *Reflective Teaching* (3rd edn.). London: Continuum.

QCA (2007) *The global dimension in action. A curriculum planning guide for schools.* Online at **http://orderline.qcda.gov.uk/gempdf/1847216722.PDF** (accessed 18 February 2011).

Renaissance, Museum, Library and Archive Service. Online at **www.mla.gov.uk/what/programmes/renaissance** (accessed 18 February 2011).

Tanner, J. (2007) Global citizenship, in Hicks, D. and Holden, C. (eds.) *Teaching the Global Dimension – Key principles and effective practice.* London: Routledge.

Teaching and Learning Research Programme (no date) *Impact and Significance.* Online at **www.tlrp.org/pub/documents/ImpactLeaflet.pdf** (accessed 18 February 2011).

Wakefield Internet Learning Domain. Online at: **www.gowild.org.uk/CurriculumStandardsAnd Support/NationalStrategies/VideoConferencing/Video.htm** (accessed 18 February 2011).

Teachernet *Community Cohesion.* Online at **www.teachernet.gov.uk/wholeschool/Communitycohesion/** (accessed 18 February 2011).

Model answers

Chapter 1

1. Concepts, process skills and techniques and facts are the elements of ICT capability.

2. The development of new technologies can play an important role in shaping the way that ICT is used in school. Falling prices and increased funding allowed schools to move from low resources levels to ICT-rich settings. Mobile hand-held computing can be expected to play an important role in shaping future pedagogy, especially when combined with ubiquitous internet access. This will allow for ICT to be used as and when it is needed and will require teachers to plan for it as such rather than as a discrete activity.

3. Many children are confident users of technology; however, this does not automatically mean that they have a high level of ICT capability. Their understanding of techniques and facts might be quite high but it is important to develop their understanding of concepts and process skills. Don't assume that confidence with a mouse translates to a high level of ICT capability.

4. If ICT is unable to *enhance, enrich or enable* learning then you would be justified in questioning its use.

Chapter 2

1. 'Higher Order Information Handling' or 'Thinking Skills' encompass enquiry skills (e.g. asking questions, defining problems, planning what to do, predicting outcomes); reasoning skills (e.g. making judgements and decisions informed by reasons or evidence, drawing inferences and making deductions); information-processing skills (e.g. collecting relevant information, sorting, classifying, sequencing, comparing, contrasting, and analysing); creative thinking skills (e.g. extending ideas, suggesting hypotheses, applying imagination); evaluation skills (e.g. judging the value of what they read and do, developing criteria for judging the value of their own and others' work).

2. When planning activities for 'Finding Things Out', key issues to be aware of are:

   • the distinction between data, information and understanding, and that understanding is cognitively more demanding than knowing;

   • that in order to develop understanding children must apply 'Higher Order Information Handling' or 'Thinking Skills';

   • that using ICT does not guarantee the development of information handling or 'Thinking Skills';

- that teachers must plan for and children must be taught and given opportunities to develop 'Higher Order Information Handling' or 'Thinking Skills';
- that children must be taught to search, skim and scan, engage with and make use of the information available on the world wide web.

3. ICT applications typically associated with 'Finding Things Out' include graphing programs, branching databases, flatfile databases, CD-ROMs and the internet.

4. Children at Key Stage 1 might 'Find Things Out' through exploring CD-ROMs and previewed web pages; interacting with branching datafiles; and gathering information to construct graphs with graphing software.

5. Children at lower Key Stage 2 might 'Find Things Out' through raising queries which are addressed through simple searches of CD-ROMs, web pages and prepared datafiles. They might also answer queries through sorting, displaying selected fields and creating graphs in a database.

6. Children at upper Key Stage 2 might 'Find Things Out' through raising and accurately framing queries/hypotheses and conducting more complicated searches, for example, 'and', 'or' and 'not', via the world wide web and databases. Children might also be involved in designing datafiles for branching or flatfile datafiles.

7. Appropriate contexts for 'Finding Things Out' for children include any data sets that they have some familiarity with, for example via their everyday experiences or through cross-curricular school studies. Such contexts will be more meaningful to children and thus promote engagement and the ability to apply 'Thinking Skills' to the data. You might have identified contexts such as: Travelling to school, Ourselves, Victorian convicts, Favourite foods, Pets, Minibeasts, and Weather, etc.

Chapter 3

1.

a) Graphing programs and spreadsheets are ideal resources for the capture, organisation and investigation of data.

b) Spreadsheets can be used for financial modelling and an object-based graphics package for graphical modelling. Simulations and adventure games can also be used to try things out and explore the effects of different choices in a safe environment.

c) Data-logging equipment facilitates the collection of environmental data. Children's skills in control technology can be developed through use of floor turtles, LOGO, control boxes and associated software.

2.

a) Transport Theme ideas

Capture, organise and investigate data:

'Our High Street' traffic surveys; *for example, colour of car, type of vehicle, number of vehicles passing at certain times in the day...*

How we travel to school

Create and explore models and simulations

Create/explore a model for transporting containers from one location to another; which is the most cost-effective/speedy/environmentally friendly method?

Explore a traffic flow or car parking simulation (www.peugeot.co.uk/Resources/Content/1.0_Showrooms/107/107_game/parking_peugeot.swf);

Design your own custom car (www.abcya.com/create_and_build_car.htm); build a bridge (www.learn4good.com/games/simulation/build_bridge_across_canyon.htm); become a railway tycoon (railwayvalley.com/) or try and win the great balloon race (pbskids.org/dragonflytv/games/aerial_v4.swf).

Monitor environmental variables and control devices:

Use a light sensor to measure the speed of toy vehicles rolling down a ramp;

Design and control traffic lights; a pedestrian crossing; a car park barrier system

Design a 'driverless' vehicle that uses light or pressure sensors to detect and stay on its track.

b) Curriculum links are strongest with Mathematics, Science, Design and Technology and Geography.

3.

a) Refer to, and build on, children's previous learning of skills and concepts. Use cross-curricular subjects to provide opportunities for children to apply and consolidate their learning. Encourage children to make decisions about choosing and using ICT tools. Use scaffolding strategies; e.g. by developing children's ability to tackle a larger project though planning and linking together short focused tasks.

b) Modelling activities using spreadsheets, adventure games and simulations lend themselves to collaborative problem-solving. Encourage children to keep team diaries of their progress. Investigative work involving data handling, logging, and control and monitoring is an ideal context for you to assign team roles where children have responsibility for specific tasks and the opportunity to celebrate and share expertise in particular areas. A practical hands-on approach appeals to different learning styles. Limited resources for some aspects (e.g. data-logging or control) can be turned into an advantage by developing children's sharing skills.

c) Identify a small number of specific children for individual assessment in group activities (not always the same children). Use observation and questioning strategies and consider using digital video to record group processes. Avoid overreliance on product assessment as technology can mask children's achievements, e.g. calculations in spreadsheets.

Chapter 4

1. You could use a number of collaborative tools from wikis to blogs. It would also depend on whether you wanted the children to work in small groups, setting up their own blogs about a specific composer, or whether you wanted the class to contribute as a whole and by so doing generate an information database. This approach would suit a wiki approach as different pages could be set up on a number of composers. The advantage of using either a wiki or a blog is that the children could add in other media files, like digital images, sound or music files assuming you weren't breaching any copyright laws.

2. The potential benefits fall into many categories. Here is a list of some of the advantages you may have considered:

   • increased motivation and attitude towards learning;

   • collaborative allows a number of children to be involved;

   • easy of access both in school and at home;

   • extends the engagement of the child/children beyond the school gates;

   • allows for personalisation and creativity;

   • more effective and efficient means of communicating ideas includes ability to alter formats;

   • develops children's thinking skills along with their reading and writing capabilities;

   • provides feedback (from within the computer program and from peers);

   • provisional nature – the ability to change things easily;

   • multimodal – you can add a range of other digital items and tools;

   • non-linear (assuming it isn't a story): the use of hyperlink will allow for changes in direction to suit the reader.

3. The main characteristic that allows digital texts to be changed is its provisional nature. The format of the text is not fixed, nor is it fixed to a program, as you can cut and paste between most applications. An example would be a piece of work written as a story in *Textease* (Softease), utilising the *speech engine* within the program it can be copied and pasted into *PowerPoint* (*Microsoft*) to create a branching story using the action buttons within this program. Digital images can usually be copied between programs as well. The main thing to remember is the needs of the new audience. Simplifying a piece of work to make it suitable for younger children should address the learning needs of the new audience, hence you might need to make it more visual and also consider the possible need to include a program that has an inbuilt speech engine, such as *Textease* or *Clicker5* (Crick).

4. Your answer should recognise the need for one of two conditions. Supporting children's work both in school and at home means that similar programs must exist in both locations with files exchanged between them, or collaborative tools are used either on the internet or within a school-based learning platform. It is easier if you and the children are using a

system that allows file exchange and access to Web 2.0 tools, as this would ensure that work done in school could be continued at home and vice versa. Programs like *j2e* (**www.j2e.com**) and *PrimaryPad* (**www.primarypad.com**) offer the potential of developing this approach, but ensure that the safeguarding of children is also considered and fully addressed.

Chapter 5

1. Here are some examples of ICT applications that could enhance the process of refining and improving children's work. They relate to subjects of the National Curriculum (DFES, 1999) for which there are not already examples in this chapter. Your own may well be as good, if not better.

   - Mathematics: working in pairs using *BlockCad* to produce, through reasoning as well as trial and error, a Lego house of a given floor area using bricks with a maximum number of studs.

   - Science: children experimenting with missiles from a catapult use *Phun* software to model and amend their predictions of the missile trajectory.

   - Geography: a group of children with a floor map of the school building and grounds use a *Roamer* floor robot (Valiant) to work out distances and directions as the robot, with a postman's hat on, delivers the post to school.

   - Design and Technology: use *Scratch* to design, trial and improve a marble racer course to be negotiated as quickly as possible.

   - Art and Design: using *Paint* (Microsoft) to create a face in Picasso style. Each child can change one feature and then 'Save as...;' under a new filename.

   - Music: a group of children use *Photostory* (Microsoft) and create music with a mood and tempo to match the photos. Each version is saved for children to play back and decide upon near the end of the lesson.

   - Modern Foreign Language (non-statutory, but in most primary curriculums): the school council use Google Docs to rework a letter seeking support for a French Evening at school. Done collaboratively using the internet from home because it needs to be sent out the next day to parents.

   - Religious Education (again, non-statutory, but part of most primary curriculums): children create and film puppet plays telling the Muslim story of Imam Hussein and the beggar and the Christian story of Jesus and the paralysed man. The children edit the video footage to show similarities between the stories by watching clips, sequencing, choosing transitions, and adding titles, credits and sound.

2. Your choice should have been informed by the learning intentions for that lesson and particular aspects of that ICT use that were useful to help those children develop that work

in that situation. You will probably have referred to particular ICT strands, characteristics or affordances.

3. The important aspect here is to make justified choices; why *is* your first choice top of the list? The list is your own, but it may include some of the tools mentioned in this chapter.

4. The plan will need to include all of the ICT resources needed; for example PCs and internet access will be useless unless necessary software is downloaded first. You should have also included clear learning outcomes and success criteria to guide the children in refining and improving their work. For the same reason, planned assessment opportunities are crucial, for child and peer assessment as well as teacher assessment. Class management will also need to be clearly identified, especially if the children need to take turns and collaborate with limited ICT resources. Lesson planning includes other important features, but these are of particular importance when focusing on ICT use to refine and improve work.

Chapter 6

1. Social networking offers computer or mobile phone users opportunities to communicate and share files via the internet. Social networking sites allow users to create and customise online profiles, share photos, videos and other media, and exchange messages with an online network of contacts, or friends.

2. Children's use of new technologies has safety implications that are associated with their exposure to unsuitable or misleading *content*; the potential for *contact* with individuals or organisations intending to exploit young or naive users; and *conduct*, where children themselves may indulge in behaviour that is inappropriate, risky or hurtful to others.

3. Schools and teachers play a role in providing a safe environment where children can explore issues of risk and conduct associated with the use of new technology. Teachers can raise children's awareness of strategies to avoid risk, including helping them to identify appropriate sources of support when things go wrong. Through home–school partnerships parents and carers can be informed about the benefits and potential dangers of new technologies for their child's education and development.

4. You might have identified any of the following ways in which social and learning networks can support cross-curricular learning:

   • providing a 'walled garden' where teachers and children can explore issues of safety, self-presentation, ethics and responsibility;

   • enhancing teaching and learning in geographical and environmental education through global linking;

   • accessing 'experts', who may be local or geographically distant, for example Year 7 students in a local secondary school, or scientists working at NASA or the British Antarctic Survey;

   • presenting work in a range of media to a wide audience,

- learning about the daily lives, beliefs and cultures of others in local and distant places;
- learning and sharing language skills alongside native speakers in other countries and with children for whom English is an additional language;
- providing an additional or alternative means of communication and social interaction for children with special needs; for example, where children have difficulties making face-to-face contact with others for physical or emotional reasons.

Chapter 7

1. You might expect to find the following:

   (a) digital cameras;

   (b) digital video cameras;

   (c) scanners;

   (d) *Roamers*;

   (e) *Beebots* or *Pixies*.

In some schools you might find some of these ICT resources:

   (f) laptops;

   (g) tablet PCs;

   (h) iphones or ipads;

   (i) data-loggers;

   (j) digital microscopes;

   (k) control equipment;

   (l) *Lego Mindstorms*.

2. If children are working in groups using ICT then a number of issues are raised. Firstly, there is the question of who has done what? As you will not be able to recognise handwriting or other clues in computer-based work you will need to consider a way of assessing individual contributions. This might be compounded by one child being more dominant with the ICT resource than their partner(s). In this case the child who has 'been in control' of the computer might have had overall responsibility for the quality of the finished product but the 'silent partner(s)' might have had a better understanding or have contributed more ideas to the creation of the product.

   A further consideration is the fact that computers leave no trace of previous work; for example, there will be no rubbed out or crossed out work to indicate that revisions have taken place. Also, it will not be possible to tell by looking at the finished product whether a spellchecker was responsible for correct spelling or whether the children involved corrected spellings independently. A similar issue is that of text which has been copied and pasted from other sources; it can be very hard (or impossible) to tell when this has taken place.

This means that careful consideration of an assessment strategy at the planning stage will be needed if useful assessment data is to be obtained. This might include children saving drafts of their work, teacher observations and questioning, or asking children to complete a short evaluation of what they did and why they did it.

3. There are many ways in which ICT can enrich and enhance work, these include:

    (a) improving the quality of the presentation of the finished product;

    (b) providing a tool for developing thinking;

    (c) providing quick, automatic functions such as graphing tools which allow children to focus on the interpretation of results;

    (d) allowing children to try out different choices before deciding on a final product;

    (e) providing access to a wide range of information, for example, internet resources;

    (f) providing feedback and interaction which responds to children's actions and allows them to develop their understanding.

4. Some of the ways ICT could be incorporated in a PE topic on dance might include videos of dance performances viewed at the start of the topic to provide inspiration and to allow the children to see how expert performers use body shapes, speed and movement. This could be followed up by videoing the children performing so that they might evaluate their dance routines and decide how they might be improved. Children might use music composition software to create music to accompany their dance. Still images might be captured from the final performance and be used on a display as a way of capturing a transitory activity.

Chapter 8

1. Reflection, research and reasoning can help teachers move beyond precedent, peer practice and prescription to improve the quality of ICT learning experiences for children. The key to effective teaching is reflective practice and all good teachers reflect on their own teaching in order to improve it. An awareness of ICT research can provide a broader perspective beyond one's own classroom; and reasoning allows both the evaluation of research studies which may have conflicting findings and the identification of ways in which research may apply to your own context.

2. There is comparatively little research about the role of the teacher in ICT-enabled learning experiences. However, one study suggests that simply providing technical assistance has little impact, but actively mediating the learning by encouraging children to focus and to expand their thinking has a significant effect on cognitive performance.

3. Simply including ICT in your lesson provides no assurance that outcomes will be enhanced. The research does not show a strong correlation between the use of ICT *per se* and improved attainment. Rather it is how the ICT is used that is important. Schools and

classrooms that have embedded the use of ICT and are more 'e-mature' show greater benefits from the use of ICT.

4. There are several ways in which ICT might support the collection of data. Online questionnaire tools might be used to carry out surveys. Electronic voting systems might enable the simultaneous capture of answers to questions posed to a group of people. Digital audio and video recording might be used to capture observations of teachers and learners so that these can be analysed more thoroughly after the event.

Chapter 9

1. You might consider integrating a link with a cultural setting into an area of learning because it would offer children a unique opportunity to actively engage with an expert, a virtual approach to experiential learning or a resource that would otherwise be inaccessible. Through this link learners may be motivated to pursue learning through diverse, multimedia approaches.

2. Schools link with other schools for a variety of reasons including offering meaningful and deep learning experiences. Children can develop relationships with peers in different schools and be involved with curricular projects that expand their thinking beyond their school and local community. Purposeful school links can motivate reluctant learners and help boost self-esteem.

3. ICT offers opportunities for communication between schools through e-mail, web- and video-conferencing and learning platforms. Through this virtual access children can develop understanding of contrasting localities and ways of life and engage with a new group of peers. These relationships can develop enquiring minds and provide meaningful opportunities for new and more challenging learning.

4. ICT provides the resources to facilitate communication and information sharing; however, these are only tools. Links with schools overseas provide meaningful opportunities for teachers and learners to develop respectful and empathic relationships and to challenge stereotypes and assumptions. All partners in a school link need to be clear about the aims of the link and the shared responsibilities. Making a link sustainable is the most effective way to ensure ongoing learning but this does require the commitment and sensitivity of all partners.

Index